START-TO-FINISH
PATIOS

ORTHO®

Meredith® Books
Des Moines, Iowa

Ortho Start-to-Finish Patios
Writer: Martin Miller
Contributing Graphic Designer: Tim Abramowitz
Senior Associate Design Director: Tom Wegner
Assistant Editor: Harijs Priekulis
Copy Chief: Terri Fredrickson
Copy and Production Editor: Victoria Forlini
Editorial Operations Manager: Karen Schirm
Managers, Book Production: Pam Kvitne,
    Marjorie J. Schenkelberg, Rick von Holdt
Contributing Copy Editor: Sharon McHaney
Contributing Proofreaders: Sue Fetters,
    Steve Salato, Jim Stepp, Margaret Smith
Indexer: Donald Glassman
Editorial and Design Assistants: Renee E. McAtee,
    Karen McFadden

**Additional Editorial Contributions from
    Art Rep Services**
Director: Chip Nadeau
Designer: lk Design
Illustrator: Dave Brandon

Meredith® Books
Editor in Chief: Linda Raglan Cunningham
Design Director: Matt Strelecki
Executive Editor, Gardening and Home Improvement:
    Benjamin W. Allen
Executive Editor, Home Improvement: Larry Erickson

Publisher: James D. Blume
Executive Director, Marketing: Jeffrey Myers
Executive Director, New Business Development:
    Todd M. Davis
Executive Director, Sales: Ken Zagor
Director, Operations: George A. Susral
Director, Production: Douglas M. Johnston
Business Director: Jim Leonard

Vice President and General Manager: Douglas J. Guendel

Meredith Publishing Group
President, Publishing Group: Stephen M. Lacy
Vice President-Publishing Director: Bob Mate

Meredith Corporation
Chairman and Chief Executive Officer: William T. Kerr

In Memoriam: E.T. Meredith III (1933-2003)

Photographers
(Photographers credited may retain copyright ©
    to the listed photographs.)
L = Left, R = Right, C = Center, B = Bottom, T = Top
William D. Adams: 23TL; **Jim Allor:** 84TL; **Dennis
Anderson:** 53CR; **Laurie Black:** 35BR, 69B; **Bob
Braun/Burst:** 20B; **Bob Braun/Deehl:** 22TL, 25TR; **Ernest
Braun:** 21T; **Dick Canby/Positive Images:** 25B; **Concrete
Sawing and Drillin Association:** 86CL; **Grace Davies:**
105CL; **Todd Davis:** 31CR; **Richard Felber:** 57BR; **John
Glover:** 55TR; **David Goldberg:** 159BL; **Rick Hanson:**
77TR(A), 77TR(B), 92BL; **Jerry Harpur:** 6TL, 9TR, 11B,
28TL, 42TL; **Lynn Harrison:** 8TR; **Sue Hartley:** 7TL, 80T;
Shelly Hawes: 228TL, 228TR; **Margaret Hensel/Positive
Images:** 37CL; **Saxon Holt:** 30BL, 56TL; **Jerry Howard:**
7TR, 11T, 14TL, 19CR, 36TL, 39CR, 64T, 71T, 76T;
Instermatic WAGASC Stock: 47B; **Susan M. Lammers:**
34BL; **Michael Landis:** 19TR, 174C; **Lee
Lockwood/Positive Images:** 16C; **Craig Lovell:** 37TR;
Michael McKinley: 7CL, 23TR, 27CR, 40TR, 50BL,
85R(B), 85R(C); **Charles Mann:** 22TR, 24TR, 95T; **Bev
Murphy/Geoimagery:** 85R(D); **Jerry Pavia:** 17BL, 37BR,
62TL, 62TR; **Robert Perron:** 18BR, 35TL, 55BR; **Portland
Cement Co.:** 85R(A); **Ken Rice:** 5CR, 29BL, 38CL, 52TL,
60TR; **Richard Shiell:** 85R(E); **Studio Central:** 92T, 93TM,
93TR, 93CR, 93BR; **Dan Stultz:** 131CR, 143BL, 143BM,
143BR, 230CL, 230CM, 230CR, 230BM, 230BR, 231BR,
232TR; **Michael S. Thompson:** 26TL, 56TR, 226BL; **Cr.
Von dem Bussche:** 17CL; **Deidre Walpole:** 20CR. 24BL,
45BL, 69TR, 74BL, 75TR

All of us at Meredith® Books are dedicated to providing you
with the information and ideas you need to enhance your
home and garden. We welcome your comments and
suggestions about this book. Write to us at:
    Meredith Books
    1716 Locust St.
    Des Moines, IA 50309–3023

If you would like to purchase any of our home improvement,
gardening, cooking, crafts, or home decorating and design
books, check wherever quality books are sold. Or visit us at:
meredithbooks.com

If you would like more information on other Ortho
products, call 800/225-2883 or visit us at: www.ortho.com

Note to the Readers: Due to differing conditions, tools,
and individual skills, Meredith Corporation assumes no
responsibility for any damages, injuries suffered, or losses
incurred as a result of following the information published
in this book. Before beginning any project, review the
instructions carefully, and if any doubts or questions remain,
consult local experts or authorities. Because codes and
regulations vary greatly, you always should check with
authorities to ensure that your project complies with all
applicable local codes and regulations. Always read and
observe all of the safety precautions provided by
manufacturers of any tools, equipment, or supplies,
and follow all accepted safety procedures.

No matter how you use your patio, you'll want it to blend with its natural surroundings. The paving for this patio extends into the yard, unifying the entire site.

Here, all the elements work together to create a tranquil getaway for small gatherings of friends or family. Tall roses help soften the hard fence surface. An off-brown paint provides a muted complement to the red brick and the understated furnishings.

LIFESTYLE AND MATERIALS

As you plan your patio, consider the shapes, colors, textures, and patterns of patio materials to enhance style and comfort. Brick, concrete, flagstone, tile, wood, and gravel all express different styles, but some materials are better suited to certain purposes than others.

For example, you may like the rustic look of flagstone, but its rough surface may not fit the bill if you're planning a summer of dance parties. One solution in this case might be to extend the patio with a "dance floor" platform deck. Consider safety, too. Wood gets slippery when wet, so flagstone may prove safer for a tub or pool border.

A fresh-air living space, one that's as comfortable and inviting as this backyard patio, looks appealing and extends the interior family room beyond the walls of the house.

PLANNING TO SUIT YOUR STYLE

At first glance, building a patio might seem a simple enterprise. After all, how difficult can it be to construct a flat surface in the yard?

As you start planning, however, that patio becomes something more than a simple slab of paving. Numerous questions arise. Where exactly should you locate it? How big should it be? What special features should it have? How will the patio tie in with the overall landscape? What will it look like? Will it contain other structures? What materials should you use? And, finally, how do you build it?

Finding answers to all these questions will prove much easier if you create your patio with your lifestyle in mind. All patio plans start with the answer to one question: "How will you use your patio?"

Whether you plan to use your patio for family dining, entertainment, recreation, quiet contemplation—or all of these activities—

you'll enjoy it even more when you create it to meet specific needs. If you're not sure of those needs yet, don't start shopping for materials.

Consider how you want your patio to function, how you want it to look and feel, how it will complement your home and garden, and what kinds of weather and surface conditions will affect its comfort, appearance, accessibility, and durability.

Careful planning will save you from second-guessing and costly remodeling later.

Ask yourself this question: "What will make me want to spend time there?" Then build on that.

Style and practicality go hand in hand with these weatherproof furnishings. The umbrella shades the spot while adding to its sense of enclosure.

ADD VALUE TO YOUR HOME

A well-designed patio can increase the value of your home because you're actually adding to its livable area. The more work you do yourself, the more of your investment you'll recoup. A $3,500 patio built by a professional can return about 40 percent of its cost. By doing the work yourself, you can cut your costs to about $1,000 and add about $1,500 to the value of your home.

How much you get back can vary from 40 percent to more than 150 percent, depending on two factors:
- The area of the country in which you live.
- The average resale value of homes in your neighborhood.

One key consideration is how long you plan to stay in your home. If you're going to stay indefinitely, the return on your investment may not be important. But if you plan to sell your home in the near future, do a little research before building your patio. Ask a local real estate agent if potential buyers want patios and are willing to pay for them. Then add the cost of the patio to the average resale value of homes in your neighborhood.

As a general rule, total patio costs plus the current market value of your house should not exceed the value of any home in your neighborhood by more than 20 percent. Selling a house priced well above neighboring properties will be difficult.

HOW WILL YOU USE YOUR PATIO?

This patio provides a vacation-like escape and plenty of living space for an active family. It includes areas for relaxation, entertaining, and even exercise.

A special place to relax with your morning coffee; a shaded retreat for escaping with your favorite book; a spot to unwind after a hard day's work; an area for hosting festive parties, large and small. Your patio can serve any one—or all—of these purposes. How you design it will depend largely on how you want to use it.

A GETAWAY

If your needs are simple—adding an outdoor space for getting away from it all or simply getting outdoors to enjoy the weather—a small unused section of the lawn, like a narrow side yard, might be the perfect spot. You can keep it private with minimum investment; a few screening plants will do the trick. Add paving that fits the style of the surroundings and some built-in or moveable seating and you will transform an area you used to mow into a low-maintenance private room.

Wherever you place your getaway, remember that even small areas require comfortable seating. And if the area will double as a spot for family gatherings, you'll want enough seating and table space to accommodate everyone. If dining is on the agenda, you'll need room for a grill, too.

ENTERTAINING

Patio space for parties is like guacamole dip—there never seems to be enough of it. So if you entertain—even infrequently—that narrow side yard just won't do.

Consider guests in your plans, both those for planned gatherings and those who drop by. Patios are a great way to relieve a cramped kitchen and can quickly turn a crowded gathering into a festive occasion.

Small groups may not require much more space or furnishings than your family would need. But for large gatherings, increase the size of your patio seating, cooking, and dining areas. Remember teenagers, too—a patio can offer them privacy and at the same time reward you with some peace and solitude inside.

PLAY AREA FOR CHILDREN

Patios can be perfect for children's play, but your plans need to account for their ages

SHAPING SPACES

Most patios serve multiple purposes. They function as private retreats, family gathering spots, and centers of entertainment. Defining spaces will enhance your enjoyment of them. Use walls, fences, planters, and even container plants arranged along the edges of specific areas to give each space its separate identity.

PLANNING CHECKLIST

Good planning means taking a thorough look at both your lifestyle and your landscape. Here are some of the things you should keep in mind.

■ **Traffic Flow.** If your patio will lay between the house and other destinations in the yard—a utility shed, for example—add 3-foot walkways to your plans.

■ **Views.** Orient the patio to make the most of pleasing views. Set furnishings so you and your guests face the landscape.

■ **Sun, Shade, and Wind.** Use lightweight, moveable furniture to take advantage of shade patterns, or create your own shade with an overhead structure. Attractive windbreaks will thwart prevailing winds. A lattice fence or a tall hedge will help buffer the wind and will also muffle street noise, increase your privacy, and hide unsightly views.

■ **Storage.** Make a list of yard implements you will need to store, and plan storage that's easy to access. Attach a small shed to the house if you don't have room for a separate structure.

Plan your patio to take advantage of elements in your landscape and build additional structures when necessary. This patio uses the shade cast by mature trees, and the lanai offers an outdoor respite in rainy weather.

This airy setting, open to sunlight and breezes, is designed to offer an area for relaxation and—separated by the stone-edged steps—room for larger gatherings.

Your patio area can serve the whole family if you dedicate a portion of it to children's play. Mulch reduces injuries and keeps maintenance to a minimum. Paved walkways are great for riding toys, and nearby seating offers a restful place for supervision.

and their number. Sandboxes are great for toddlers, but as they grow they'll need tree forts and things to climb. Plan your space so you can add these elements as children grow.

CONSIDER THE GARDENER

Patios offer endless opportunities for the family gardener. If space doesn't permit flower beds, container gardens are great substitutes.

This quiet setting is flexible enough for many uses. Movable furniture and flowerpots allow a fresh look for every season and every occasion.

How Will You Use Your Patio?
continued

Good News for Old Patios

Even a patio in the most beautiful location will go unused if cooking space is cramped, guests have to sit sideways, or if it sports a surface of unadorned concrete. If your patio doesn't call you to it, don't dismay. Enhance it strategically.

Often, adding just a small piece of the same paving can increase your comfort and improve the looks of your landscape. Don't be afraid to mix materials. A ground-level redwood platform goes well with flagstone or brick. And if there's no room immediately adjacent to the patio, build a detached area and unify the two surfaces with a river-rock path.

Whatever the nature of the improvement, build on what you have. Wouldn't new paving stones on top of the old slab do nicely? Could you extend the patio into the yard, creating room for a fire pit? How about recycling the concrete by breaking it up and using the pieces for a garden wall?

Don't overlook small spaces when planning your patio. Create a cozy spot like this one, by laying pavers in unusual patterns—circles within an octagon, for example.

The materials you choose should suit the use of your patio. Here, saltillo tiles set in concrete make a durable surface smooth enough for dancing.

Outdoor Rooms

Planning a patio is really not much different than planning a family room. Although it might not be apparent at first, your outdoor room will have a floor, ceiling, and walls.

An outdoor floor, of course, is the paving—brick, stone, or concrete—and it defines the purpose of a room.

An outdoor ceiling can be anything that protects you from the elements and provides a sense of enclosure. It also increases privacy, blocking the view from second-story windows. You might already have an outdoor ceiling and not know it. That old oak tree in your yard is nature's own ceiling structure. It casts welcome shade on your retreat and gives a sense of protection. If nature hasn't provided the site with such a ceiling, you can make your own with a pergola or arbor.

Outdoor walls do the same thing indoor walls do—they separate one space from another. They also create a sense of enclosure, add privacy, help show off decorative accents, screen out views, and soften harsh winds. Solid walls or fences do the job. Also shrubs, hedges, and plants set out in containers function well as outdoor walls.

This patio was designed for small groups and quiet brunches. Note how the different shapes separate one space from another and create an inviting environment.

Brick, tile, casual furnishings, and background plants bring warmth and comfort to this entertainment area.

Who says outdoor walls have to stand above the patio surface? These wood dividers act just like solid walls, separating one space from another. Moving furnishings in and out of the squares offers endless possibilities for large and small group gatherings.

An overhead structure such as this pergola can expand the use of your patio, providing visual interest and welcoming shade.

GATHER THE FAMILY

Planning a patio should be a family matter. Get the whole family together to discuss how everyone wishes to use and enjoy the patio space. List everyone's wishes and be prepared to make compromises. Start with a list of absolute necessities, then add elements that are desirable but not required. Cooking and eating areas are primary. Parties will need extra seating and conversation areas. Plan for use first, add aesthetic touches to incorporate your patio with the rest of the landscape.

HOW WILL YOU USE YOUR PATIO?
continued

Inspired by the terraced gardens of the Mediterranean, the dry-stacked stone walls and sand-set pavers create inviting spaces for both small and large groups.

PAVING OPTIONS

Your paving options fall into two broad categories—dry-set and wet-set—and each comes with its own advantages.

Dry-set paving means any material—bricks, pavers, stones, stepping-stones and loose gravel—laid on a carefully prepared bed of well-tamped soil and sand. Wet-set paving is any material mortared to a concrete base. Concrete slabs also fall into this category.

Because dry-set paving sits on a porous base, you might find it the best choice for hard-to-drain soils and patios set near trees. A dry-set bed requires less excavation than a mortared surface, so you don't run as much risk of damaging tree roots. The sand base also allows moisture and oxygen to reach the roots. Dry-set materials are easy to install and repair. Just pry out the damaged section and replace it with the new.

Wet-set paving, on the other hand, typically remains stable because it is supported by a concrete slab. It's less likely to heave and buckle as the supporting soil freezes and thaws, but if it does, repairs can prove costly. For formal areas where you want to move chairs around easily and where the wheels of children's tricycles should move smoothly, wet-set brick, cut stone, and tile will suit your needs better than their dry-set counterparts.

A well-designed patio begins with an attractive floor. Here, exposed aggregate edged with brick makes a classic, yet economical, surface. The low stone wall and variegated foliage add a touch of dramatic privacy to this small-group setting .

BE FLEXIBLE

If you have an ideal patio concept in mind, it's wise to give extra thought to your climate and budget. Some flexibility in your plans may pay big dividends in the enjoyment of your patio.

If summers where you live are short, consider adding an enclosure to your landscape plans. A summerhouse or gazebo will let you entertain when the weather turns chilly.

Contain your costs by using materials that are local to your area. For example, where native stone is abundant, a stone retaining wall may be less expensive than natural timber.

Don't base your plans on budget alone, however. Balance budget, structures, and materials to meet your needs.

A Juggling Act

Maximizing the enjoyment from building and using your patio means you might have to juggle a variety of factors—how you intend to use the space, the complexity of any structures you plan to construct, your skill level, how much time you have, your materials, and your budget. The photographs above and below offer excellent examples of how these elements can come together to produce designs that are dramatically different, yet perfectly appropriate.

In the patio above, an uncomplicated, two-level paver surface accommodates the family's entertainment and leisure requirements. The low-cost design features storage for a barbecue grill and idle garden equipment, keeping the patio clean and uncluttered.

This simple design could have been accomplished as well with patterned concrete. Design and material costs of such a project are well within most family budgets, and costs are further reduced because its construction is easy enough for the average homeowner.

In the patio below, the stone-lined reflecting pool sports exotic fish and creates an interesting focal point in the overall design. A masonry wall adds color and texture and separates the surface from the rest of the landscape. The multi-tiered tile paving sets up different areas of use—small-group gatherings are made more intimate by the sheltering overhead structure. Areas for larger groups are open to the sky. This patio was designed with an eye toward comfort and visual impact but with little concern for economy. The space conveys the feel of professional design and execution.

Both patios will serve their intended purposes, both are attractive and useful additions to their respective homes, and both have been planned by homeowners who paid careful attention to their individual needs, abilities, and budgets.

SIZE AND SHAPE

How much space will you need? Some designers say a patio should be the same size as the interior room it adjoins. Others suggest it should be one-third the size of the main floor of the house. And, of course, in many houses, calculations using these rules of thumb might well yield about the same amount of space. The primary guideline? Make your patio large enough to accommodate all of the functions you want it to serve.

FUNCTION FIRST

How many functions will your patio serve? List the activities you want to hold on your patio. Assign different activities to different parts of the area, allowing ample space for the activity itself, traffic flow through and around the area, and outdoor furniture (which tends to be larger than indoor furniture).

Perhaps you'd just like a place for family dining. In that case, you might get by with an area as small as 6×10. But soaking in a hot tub will call for a substantial addition. Relaxation may not fit well in the same space where children play, and a basketball hoop could be disastrous near a dining area.

Where different functions must take place close to each other, separate their spaces with planters, trellises, benches, or even a change in paving patterns. Or employ structural solutions to separate one area from the others. Build a T-shaped patio or set the surface on different levels and connect them with stairs or sloping pathways.

PLANNING TO SCALE

Once you've determined the approximate size of your patio based on its intended uses, step back and consider its scale. The patio should be proportionate to the house and grounds. A small patio can be overwhelmed by a huge house, and a lavish site will likely seem out of proportion to a modestly sized home. Your budget and lot size may provide the most help in solving this problem. Start with a design that fits the uses you envision and then scale back to fit the limits of your budget and terrain.

TESTING THE SITE

The best way to find out if the size of your proposed patio will meet your needs is to rope off the area and move in the furniture and equipment you will use— tables and chairs, barbecue grill, lounges and recliners.

If you haven't purchased the furniture yet, use interior furnishings and add about a foot more space for each item. You can generally figure about 2 feet square for each outdoor chair, plus about a foot or do to push it back from a table. Tie helium balloon in places where new trees and shrubs will go.

Adjust the size of the space until you get it right for your needs and then draw the plan on paper.

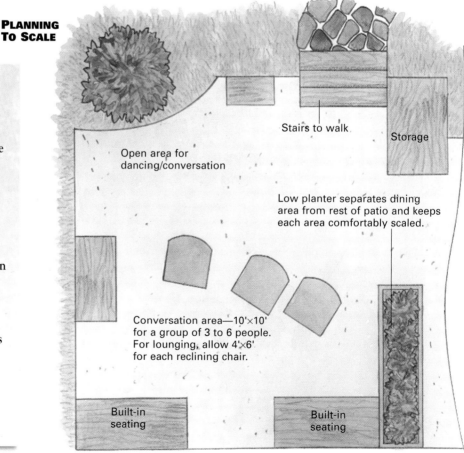

PLANNING TO SCALE

Stairs to walk

Storage

Open area for dancing/conversation

Low planter separates dining area from rest of patio and keeps each area comfortably scaled.

Conversation area—10'×10' for a group of 3 to 6 people. For lounging, allow 4'×6' for each reclining chair.

Built-in seating

Built-in seating

LEGALITIES

Your patio will be affected, of course, by your lifestyle and budget—things you can control. But it may also be affected by legalities outside your control—building codes, zoning ordinances, deed restrictions, and easements. These regulations can have a major effect on where and how you build. A little preliminary research will save time, effort, and frustration.

■ **Building Codes.** Communities enact building codes to ensure the safety of their residents. You may find regulations that define footing depths, material choices, and fence heights. Check with your building department before you start, then submit your plans for approval.

■ **Zoning Ordinances.** These provisions govern the use of property and the placement of structures. They can establish minimum setbacks from property lines,

easements, and the size of your patio. In recent years, many communities have become strict about the size of patio surfaces because they increase runoff into storm sewers.

■ **Deed Restrictions.** These regulations control local property values or architectural style. You may find restraints on the kind of patio you want to build, its style, and the materials you want to use.

■ **Easements and Right-of-way.** These rules guarantee access by local utilities to their service lines. If a utility company has a line running through your yard, you might not be able to build a patio over that line. It is possible, however, that a sand-set patio, which allows quick access to utilities below it would be permitted in areas where a concrete patio would be forbidden.

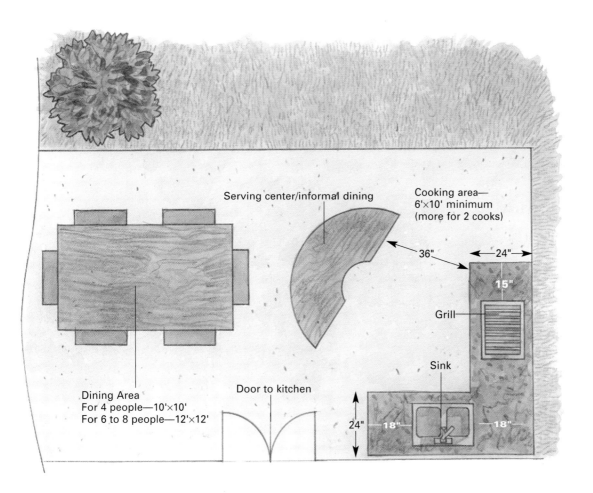

Serving center/informal dining

Cooking area—
6'×10' minimum
(more for 2 cooks)

36"

24"

15"

Grill

Sink

Dining Area
For 4 people—10'×10'
For 6 to 8 people—12'×12'

Door to kitchen

24"

18"

18"

SIZE AND SHAPE
continued

The sweeping curves of the patio contour, the low walls, and the small pool all combine to make this patio well suited to formal and informal gatherings, both large and small.

THE SHAPE OF YOUR PATIO

Once you have settled on an approximate size for your patio, it's time to address its shape. Start by revisiting the contours of your house and yard. There are things you may not have noticed the first time that may affect where you put the patio.

First, the shape of your house may suggest a configuration for your patio. Second, you may have overlooked areas of your yard that are largely unused.

Front-yard patios can extend the driveway or open up the area around the entrance to your home. Patios on the side of the house can turn wasted space into more space for outdoor living. Of course, in any area, a patio makes an excellent location for situating flower beds and plantings.

ATTACHED PATIO: The typical attached patio is located next to the house with direct access to the interior—usually the kitchen or family room. U-shaped or L-shaped houses come with built-in walls that offer ready-made opportunities for maintaining privacy, but that doesn't mean that the contour of the patio has to be uniformly rectangular. Round off the corners, create flowing patterns with your paving, and add shrubs to soften hard edges.

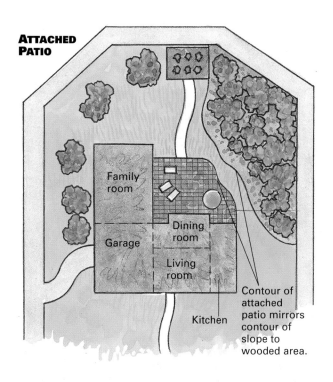

ATTACHED PATIO

Family room

Garage

Dining room

Living room

Kitchen

Contour of attached patio mirrors contour of slope to wooded area.

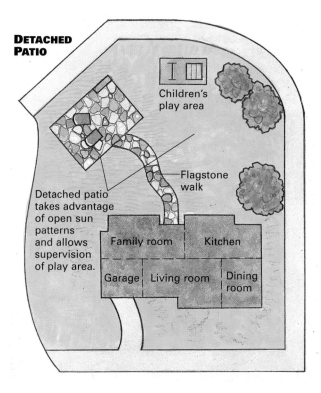

DETACHED PATIO

Children's play area

Flagstone walk

Detached patio takes advantage of open sun patterns and allows supervision of play area.

Family room

Kitchen

Garage

Living room

Dining room

DETACHED: A detached patio offers a quick fix for sun and shade problems. Move the patio away from the house and into the natural surroundings to take advantage of the changing shade patterns cast by existing trees. A detached patio also makes a good retreat, allowing you to separate yourself from the business of the household.

Even though it's situated away from the house, your detached patio should have the same general architectural tone as the house. Its very distance from your home lets you create stunning patterns on its surface that harmonize and contrast with the property's overall design. But be sure to connect the patio to the house with a path or walkway that complements the looks of your overall landscape—formal brick or rustic wood chips, for example.

COURTYARD PATIO: A courtyard is a great solution for townhouses, condos, apartments, or any home with a small lot. A courtyard needs walls, of course, but if you don't have them, you can make them with fencing or tall hedges. Garden beds or planter boxes will make this spot your private oasis, but if garden beds won't do, use potted plants or small trees to bring greenery and flowers into the space. Install trellises and let vines climb the walls. You can even add the splash of falling water by installing a small recirculating fountain available in most garden centers. If running water lines and putting in a pump isn't feasible, consider an ornamental wall fountain. If the courtyard is small, keep the paving subdued and the furniture simple so you don't overwhelm the space.

WRAPAROUND PATIO: A wraparound patio is a made-to-order option for the family that wants patio access from several rooms or has plans for multiple uses—a quiet retreat outside the master bedroom, family dining off the kitchen, and parties that flow from the family room.

If the size of your patio won't quite fit the open areas of your yard, this style is for you. It allows you to keep space for smaller gatherings on the least-used side of the house and still have enough room for large parties. Curved corners, garden beds, planter boxes, and low walls—independently or in combination with each other—will separate each area and give each space its own character.

COURTYARD PATIO

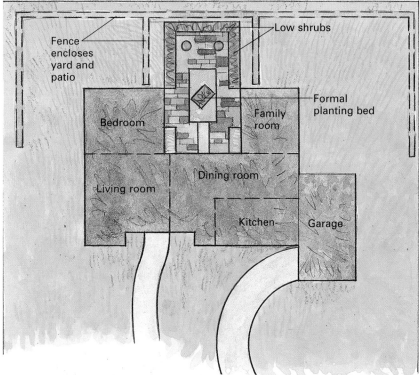

WRAPAROUND PATIO

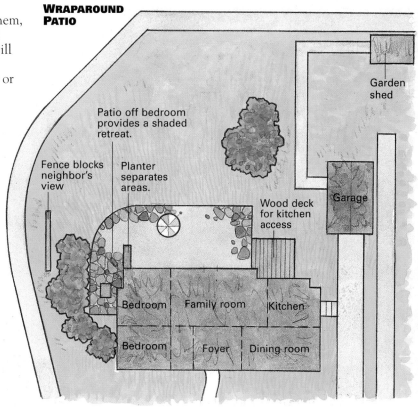

SOLUTIONS FOR SMALL SPACES

If your proposed patio seems like it will look cramped in your small yard, don't throw away your plans. There are numerous ways you can make small spaces seem larger and feel more secluded and comfortable. The key to small-space design is simplicity.

■ Create one large area from two smaller ones. If, for example, your patio spills out into your yard, it will seem larger.

■ Draw attention to the patio, not the property line. Instead of letting the lawn end undramatically at the property line, sculpt the perimeter of the lawn with planting beds. This will redirect attention to the patio, where you want it.

■ Use plants with interesting textures to focus attention on the surrounding landscape rather than on the limits of your property.

■ Concentrate color in a patch instead of scattering flowers throughout the landscape. Groups of flowers create more impact than scattered blooms. If you use color in more than one location, repeat two or three colors to tie the areas together.

■ Whenever possible, borrow nearby views. For example, if you live next to an attractive pond or rolling lawn, make the most of what that surrounding scenery has to offer by leaving the view open.

Reclaim a small area, above, with judicious pruning, paint, and detail. Painting the wall and fence a neutral color pulls the area together. Lattice and vines camouflage the fence planks, and the fountain helps "enlarge" the area by drawing attention outward.

Oversize pavers make the "floor" space of this patio seem larger than it is, and the statue draws attention away from the narrow edges.

Leave room for greenery in small spaces. Here, a patch of grass and a vine clinging to the wall keep a small patio looking fresh.

This small patio gives the illusion of being deeper than it is because plants and containers not only conceal part of the view, they hint at another destination.

■ Instead of walling off the patio entirely, place screening strategically to enhance privacy and block only those sights that are distracting.

■ Hang wind chimes or install a fountain. The soothing sounds will subdue any close-by neighbor or street noise.

■ Install built-in seating. It takes up less space than freestanding furniture. The same goes for round tables. They'll leave you more room than rectangular ones.

■ Keep paving patterns scaled to the size of your patio. A lot of small patterns and contrasting textures will leave you feeling dizzy and hemmed in.

DETAILS... DETAILS...

Details—those special decorative touches—must work extra hard in small spaces because there's no room for clutter. Finishing touches—artwork, found objects, or architectural salvage—give small spaces personality. And your small patio might just be perfect for an object that would get lost in a larger setting.

Too much of a good thing, however, can ruin an otherwise artful patio. To avoid overwhelming the space, step back and view your patio in its entirety. Look for noticeable bare spots. Do they function better as empty areas that draw attention to your decorating scheme, or would a potted plant, artwork, or other accent improve the setting?

Leave room for each detail or collection to breathe. For example, if you line a wall shelf with shells, don't put a lot of small items on the table below it. And if you have more things to display than you have space, store the surplus for a while and rotate it with other elements of your decorative stock every two or three months.

Connecting small spaces but limiting the view from one area to another makes a small city courtyard seem bigger and more secluded than it is.

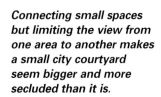

FORCING PERSPECTIVE

Forcing perspective is one way to make a small area seem larger. Narrowing the line of sight through a small space, as shown in the illustration at left, is a technique that goes hand in hand with this optical space saver.

The stepping-stones that curve around the house make this space seem larger by seeming to connect it to a hidden area. Small plants in the background and large ones in the foreground would enhance the effect, as would placement of coarse textures in front and fine textures to the rear.

In this way, empty side-yard space becomes a cozy garden getaway.

This little patio looks comfortable. Tucking large items off to the sides keeps the center space open and avoids crowding.

ACCESS AND COMPATIBILITY

You'll dine alfresco more often by locating your patio table within a few steps of the kitchen and within view from indoor rooms.

No matter how complete your design scheme, you won't use even the most luxurious patio if you can't see it from the inside, if you don't provide an easy way to get to it, and if its uses conflict with the uses of the adjacent interior room. These factors—visual access, actual access, and compatibility—can be the difference between a successful and an unsuccessful design.

EASY AND INVITING

A patio that's difficult to get to probably won't be used. Start by making sure the main door to the patio is wide enough to permit an easy in-and-out traffic flow and will provide an inviting view from inside the house.

French doors, atrium doors, and sliding glass doors work especially well because they give a sense of continuity between indoors and outdoors. If your house does not have such doors, consider including them in your patio plan and budget.

Patios adjacent to the house should be as close to the level of the house floor as possible. If winter brings snow, set the patio 3 inches lower than the floor to keep snow out of the house. If rain is your primary concern, build the patio about 1 inch lower than the house floor. If the drop to the patio level is greater than 3 inches, build steps.

VISUAL ACCESS

At its most basic level, visual access means that you can see the patio—or a portion of it—from the inside. Ideally, however, visual access should also extend a palpable invitation into the space.

Windows and see-through doors provide visual access, but you don't need to see the entire patio. Just a glimpse of the space can draw you there more effectively than a complete view. In landscaping your patio, include ways to entice guests outdoors by providing visual hints of the destination. At least some of the area should be visible from more than one interior room. The most complete view of your patio should be from the room that adjoins it.

ACTUAL ACCESS

Actual access refers to the physical method by which you get from inside your home to the patio outside.

Actual access should be easy. Whenever possible, avoid having to step up or down to move from inside to outside of your home. That means that the level of your patio should be as close as possible to the level of the interior floor. (From the doorway to the edges, however, the surface should slope slightly for proper drainage.)

If the patio is significantly lower than the bottom jamb of the door, add a landing or an entry deck to avoid having to step down immediately as you go outside. Such a threshold gives you the opportunity to get your bearings as you move from indoors to outdoors. If a landing is out of the question,

Make the most of the views from your patio. If your site offers a panoramic view such as this, design your seating and railings to keep visual access as open as possible from all angles.

REVISITING ACCESS

If you don't use your patio as much as you thought you would, perhaps it's because the design doesn't allow sufficient visual or actual access.

Inconvenient access from interior rooms can reduce the use of your patio. If getting to your patio from inside is difficult, rearrange the furniture. Add a landing to even out the levels of the patio surface and interior floor. Improving access is often all it takes to turn an underused outdoor room into a popular destination.

If you feel you're on display while meditating on the patio, the site probably allows too much visual access. Look for ways to shield the area by adding a fence, shrubs, or an overhead structure. Areas for private use require limited visual access. Areas for public use can afford to be more open to outside views.

Without the easy access these French doors provide, this brick patio would have been pretty but probably underused. Always consider traffic flow to and from the patio when you design it. It is, after all, another room of the house that just happens to be outside.

build steps and make them wider than the doorway to create an illusion of spaciousness. Each tread (the part you step on) should be no less than 12 inches deep so the stairs aren't too steep.

Build access into the house from the start. Adding a patio to this Spanish decor required opening up the exterior wall to accommodate four multipaned doors, which provide ample accessibility. Opening all the doors allows the interior space to flow outdoors.

THE ART OF REARRANGING

When actual or visual access seems confined and unwelcoming, it may be the furniture, not the amount of access itself, that is the culprit.

Examine the placement of both interior and exterior furnishings. Can you see at least a portion of the patio from indoors? Is there a welcoming path from indoors to outdoors, or do furnishings impede the progress of guests on their way outside? Rearrange inside furnishings so you can see some of the patio from the family-room table or your favorite chair.

Outdoors, if a large table limits movement around your patio or deck, think about replacing it with smaller tables that can be scattered among chairs in less dominating locations.

Use accessories in moderation. Too much of a good thing becomes overwhelming, especially in a small area. If your love of collecting exceeds your display space, alternate what you exhibit. This keeps the outdoor room from becoming crowded and also gives it a fresh look from time to time.

ACCESS AND COMPATIBILITY
continued

COMPATIBILITY

Even when all of the other design elements are complete, the success of your patio may depend on how you use the nearest indoor room. That's because you'll most likely use your patio more often when the general purpose of both the indoor and outdoor spaces is similar. If the primary purpose of the outdoor area differs substantially from its connecting indoor room, you're less likely to make full use of the space.

A small patio for coffee and the morning paper, for example, will feel just right if it's adjacent to your bedroom. But the same site would be disastrous for party traffic. For frequent dining, put the patio close to the kitchen, even if you plan a completely self-contained outdoor cooking area. And don't forget to include trash storage in your plan to avoid carrying it inside, only to have to carry it outside on collection day. For entertaining,

Patios can bring the interior of a home into the outside world—and vice versa. Here, the brick pattern flows smoothly from the family room into the patio, creating a natural extension of the indoor space. The large windows and open doorway make indoors almost indistinguishable from outdoors.

plan a location that's close to the public rooms of the house. Make patios that serve more than one function large enough to be accessible from several rooms.

For private areas, look for ways to limit access—shield your patio behind hedges or fencing. For entertaining, look for ways to increase access, with doorways from rooms where you will entertain guests and with interior "walkways" that allow guests to move to and from your patio without traipsing through the house.

Although the small shift in the surface level and the doorways separates this sheltered space from the interior room, the large multipaned glass doors and the comfortable furniture extend the family room into the outdoors.

Same-floor access may not be possible for all patios. Here, a short flight of stairs links a small dining patio with an upper-story kitchen, and a wooden landing links it all to a ground-floor family room.

EVALUATING COMPATIBILITY

To evaluate the compatibility of your indoor and outdoor rooms, consider how they relate to each other. Take a careful look at your floor plans and then note how you use each room. Label each use as active (such as entertaining) or passive (such as reading). Although each room may be home to both passive and active uses, one type of use probably dominates.

Where an active area meets a passive area, either change the use of the indoor room to better suit the nature of the outdoor area or change the outdoor room so it complements the interior use. For example, a patio favored by the kids riding tricycles sees lots of active use. This patio would be compatible with an active playroom, family room, den, hobby room, or kitchen. It would not be compatible outside a quiet area such as a bedroom, study, bath, or formal living room.

Potential solutions include converting the bedroom into a playroom until the children are older, finding another place for tricycle riding or limiting outdoor access to the patio by adding a gate, blocking off the route with planters, or replacing a paved walkway with stepping-stones to discourage the use of riding toys.

DESIGN TIP

To create a visual flow between an indoor room and patio space, select a paving material with a color and pattern that resembles the interior flooring. The similarity establishes the indoor–outdoor connection at a glance.

If immediate access to the kitchen won't fit your budget or the floor plan of the house, consider altering an existing kitchen window to link the two areas.

CREATING A STYLE

Adobe walls reflect the color of the desert soil and "imported" stones, a theme carried out in the lightly tinted concrete. Well-placed cacti and native plants make this patio seem as if it emerged on its own from the landscape.

■ Curved lines, irregular and often free-flowing shapes, and odd-numbered groupings characterize informal patio designs. Balance and informality are the goals instead of symmetry. A typical informal patio might even employ loose materials—small stones or wood chips—in its surface, but many successful informal patios have brick in curving layouts. Informal patio designs often interweave gardens with paved patio areas.

HERITAGE

Style can be further categorized as traditional or contemporary.
■ Think Greek or Roman and you'll conjure up an approximate image of what traditional means. For example, a formal courtyard accented with urns, fountains, columns, and lush foliage would look traditional. A traditional patio usually comes dressed

Formal and informal design elements come together in this hideaway for two. Natural foliage and flowers soften what might otherwise be a stark wall and offer a pleasant contrast to the nouveau-style table and chairs.

Your patio needs to be practical, of course, but patio design shouldn't stop when everything is perfectly functional. You'll enjoy your outdoor space and use it more when its style appeals to you and reflects your personality. One of the quickest ways to develop an understanding of style—and to get you going in a direction that reflects your individuality—is to look at style in two ways: formal and informal.

FORMAL AND INFORMAL

The chief difference between formal and informal styles is their use of lines, shapes, angles, and materials.
■ Formal designs employ straight lines, right angles, regular geometric shapes, and decorative objects arranged in even numbers. For example, a formal layout might feature a patio surface paved with a central circle surrounded by rectangular planting beds. Pairs of classic urns or columns would enhance a patio in this style because formal designs tend toward symmetry. If a line were drawn down the center, you would find that one side mirrors the other.

MATERIALS AND MOOD

Different paving materials will create different stylistic results.

For a formal setting, select smooth materials with sharp edges and well-defined shapes—brick, slate, tile, precast pavers, and patterned concrete, for example. Mortaring enhances their formality—the mortar lines create visual appeal in the surface.

If you're looking for informality, get materials with rough surfaces and irregular shapes—weathered brick, irregular pavers, and flagstone, for example. Let plants creep between the stones. Dry-set paving often shifts and settles a bit over the years, adding to its casual charm.

Vines and an oval planting bed provide a backdrop for this formal courtyard. Brick set in sections of alternating patterns add interest to this symmetrical scene.

This zigzag bench brings movement to this outdoor composition. Smooth flowing lines suggest stability.

What could be more inviting than this hidden sanctuary? Notice how the irregular flagstone pattern contributes to the comfort of the design, making it an ideal setting for quiet conversation or reading.

Casual chairs and used brick—some with a bit of mortar still on the surface—balance the formality of a raised pool in this patio.

in formal lines, but informal styles can be set traditionally as well. For example, in a formal garden, you might find steps built with brick set with clean orderly edges. In an informal traditional setting, the same steps might be stone.

■ Contemporary patios are cool, serene, and comfortable. A contemporary patio probably could include bolder shapes and colors, sleeker lines, and unusual combinations of materials, such as colored concrete inset with bright, glazed tile. Decorative items in a contemporary design will tend toward the abstract, with emphasis on color, texture, and light instead of representational forms.

FINDING YOUR STYLE

The best way to discover your personal style is to tour your neighborhood and mentally note things you like. Then jot down your impressions. Clip photos and diagrams from magazines. File them all in manila folders. When you're ready to make your final design decisions, take the folder and spread its contents before you. Discard what doesn't appeal to you. You'll notice a general consistency in the images left over. Use the elements of that style in your paving patterns, fences, and overall landscape plan.

CREATING A STYLE
continued

REGIONAL FLAVORS

Some patio styles transcend formality and informality, evolving with the local climate and culture. Regional styles can offer a handsome solution to patio-design problems because they fit their surroundings. They also make budget sense—local plants and materials are easier to find and less expensive than imports, and native plants require less care and maintenance.

Elements endemic to other parts of the world can also add interest to a patio design. Include unusual items from distant places that don't require extra cost and maintenance. One bonsai tree won't transform your patio into a Japanese garden but will add a harmonious contrast to a Southwestern theme. Adobe pavers and cacti—inexpensive and easy to care for—can add a touch of the Southwest to a Midwest patio.

CREATING HARMONY

A successful patio design will combine all its various elements into a unified whole.

Like most successful patios, this rustic desert one is built to fit its surroundings, not contradict them. Here, the house and pool accent the patio's style. The design is formal but uses organic shapes as accents.

Achieving harmony requires an artful blending of many diverse elements, primarily the shape of the patio and its paving materials. The shape and materials give the patio its form, mass, and texture and define its relationship with the house and landscape.

To achieve a sense of unity, the contour of the patio should repeat or blend with the dominant forms of its surroundings. These often are the rectangles of the house but may also include curves, angles, and free-form shapes suggested by swimming pools, garden beds, or sloping lawns.

The type of paving can radically affect the appearance of the patio. Select a paving material that complements the style of your home in the context of the yard. For example, a quarry-tile patio might look out of place with a Victorian house but would be perfect with a Southwestern adobe home. The paving material does not necessarily have to match the foundation, but it should not conflict with it either. For example, a flagstone patio next to a concrete foundation will work fine, but next to a red brick foundation it might look discordant.

Set in a web of intersecting arcs, these pavers provide a fanciful complement to the curved wall. The overall style looks formal, but the paving pattern, loose pottery, and potted plants keep it from appearing severe.

Select accessories and furnishings that harmonize with the patio and tie together the house and yard. Fortunately, styles of patio furniture exist for every taste and budget, from sleek, contemporary pieces to classic cedar or charming, old-fashioned wicker.

GUIDELINES FOR DESIGN

Don't be a slave to stylistic categories. Combine classic and modern styles to create a patio with old-style charm and modern convenience. Mix in different regional accents to spice up the outdoor space with surprises. Use the following guidelines to help harmonize your patio, home, and garden.

UNITY AND CONTRAST: Create a sense of continuity between your house and patio by using materials, colors, shapes, and textures in both. Use small, carefully placed patio elements to contrast color, shape, or texture. Gardens, edgings, walls, colored concrete, stones, tiles, bricks, logs, gates, furnishings, lights, and decorative pieces all add pleasing and lively accents.

Interweave trees and plants with your patio, or formally contain them on the perimeter with edging, fences, hedges, or planters. Don't crowd the paved areas—paving is for people.

As you consider various plants, think about how their textures, shapes, colors, and mature size will complement your structural materials.

CENTER STAGE: Arrange walls, plants, and walkways so they lead to a focal point, a destination— any object or view to which you want to call attention. Place furniture around focal points to give them greater definition.

If your patio is large or is made up of many smaller paved and garden areas, position smaller groupings of furnishings and decorative elements in ways that won't clutter your central area.

How will you know when the design you've created is harmonious? It will look soothing rather than jarring. It will present a cohesive blend more than a jumbled clutter of parts, and its general impression will be inviting and comfortable.

Flagstone and potted plants dress up this portico so effectively that you almost don't notice the rear wall. Its function is to provide a neutral backdrop to the scene, screen the view from the neighbor's yard, and buffer prevailing winds.

A stone and log bench rise up from limestone surrounded by a paver border—circular elements that in another setting might look formal. The careful selection of materials and patterns, however, makes this eclectic design endlessly interesting and a fun place to be.

FURNISHING YOUR PATIO

An outdoor living area isn't truly inviting without good seating. Choose outdoor furniture for durability as well as comfort and style.

Every patio, no matter how beautiful, is incomplete without furnishings. Furnishings give outdoor living space its style. They make a patio feel comfortable and inviting. Your patio furniture will influence how you feel about the space and how often you will use it.

JUST RIGHT

Outdoor furnishings should be proportionate to their setting. If your patio is small, use round tables, which take up less space than square or rectangular ones. In larger spaces, establish conversation areas with groupings of tables and chairs or lounges and side tables. Include a serving cart and leave plenty of room to walk around the furniture.

accessories to get the most out of your patio. You'll find there are plenty of ways to get the most out of the space and put your personal stamp on it.

Investing in well-made stylish garden furniture and accessories will do more than decorate the space. It will help create an enjoyable retreat for yourself, your family, and your friends.

UPKEEP AND PORTABILITY

Outdoor furniture represents an investment, so choose durable materials that offer year-round usability. If you can answer yes to the following questions, it will help you narrow down your choices.
- Is it weatherproof?
- Are the pieces heavy-duty enough to wear well but light enough to move easily?
- Are cushions removable?
- Can the furniture be stored outdoors over winter?
- Can you maintain or repair it yourself?

STAIRS

In crowded settings, where seating is limited, people will sit on stairs if they're available. So if your patio will be small, build steps. Make the tread (the part you step on) at least 18 inches deep. Be sure to install a handrail, which may be required by local building codes, for safely walking up and down the steps.

FURNISHINGS AND LIFESTYLE

Make sure your patio furnishings both complement your overall landscape design and fit your lifestyle. Your choices should reflect the purposes of the patio. For example, chairs for a patio that adjoins a small gardening area will likely be different than for one that is used primarily to give the kids a resilient place to play.

Take time to think about seating arrangements, lighting, cooking facilities, and

Flat stones topping this low river-rock wall offer informal, built-in seating.

Fit furniture to the space. The bulky chairs (left) dominate the patio and leave little room to walk. The chairs and table (right) are a better fit and the bench increases seating capacity without crowding the space.

FREESTANDING SEATING

Freestanding seating comes in many forms—from hammock chairs and lounges to dining sets with cushioned chairs. It also increases the flexibility of your patio, allowing you to move seating around to change the setting or change traffic flow.

Look for seating that suits the style of your outdoor room: painted or stained, wood or resin, iron or aluminum, wicker or twig. Choose from rockers and recliners, gliders and chairs. Remember, the more you pay for comfort, the more likely you'll be satisfied.

You probably need little encouragement to set out enough lounge chairs for everyday seating. But go beyond that and consider what the space will need when you entertain. Keep a stack of folding canvas chairs handy for impromptu parties and guests.

BUILT-IN SEATING

Built-in seating may not be portable but it has a couple other distinctive benefits.
■ It takes up less floor space than freestanding chairs
■ It can also serve as storage.

Attached benches might be the first form of built-in seating that comes to mind, but there are other choices. Raised planters and retaining walls can fill in as benches when built wide enough.

Choose flat stones for the final course of a wall that will double as seating. Top the wall with finished bench slats or pillows for extra comfort. If the wall borders a raised

planter, install low-growing, soft-textured groundcovers, perennials, or shrubs next to the sitting area. Put taller, stiffer plants farther back in the bed so they don't discourage people from sitting on the wall.

Color and style go hand in hand in furnishing this conversation area. The gray tones in the stone and the weathered fence are repeated in the fabric and chair frames, tying the composition together. The simple furniture style seems right at home with the offset paver pattern.

DIMENSIONS FOR BUILT-IN SEATING

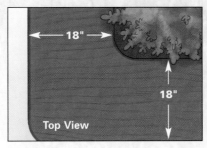

18"

18"

Top View

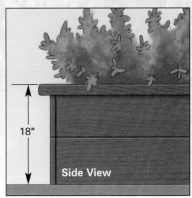

18"

Side View

For comfortable built-in seating follow the 18-inch rule: The top should be 18 inches above the finished surface of the decking and at least 18 inches deep.

DECORATING WITH PERSONAL TOUCHES

Outdoor seating is one of the first aspects of decorating you should consider. This area could have been made simply functional with an ordinary slat bench, but this "new" Spanish revival bench (found at a local import shop) gives the space a touch of antique charm.

Spending time on your patio will be more enjoyable if you're surrounded by a few of your favorite things. But like all aspects of good design, decorating a patio can profit from a little advance planning.

SURVEY THE SCENE

Relax in a comfortable chair and survey your space. Let yourself go, and without consciously trying to plan the space, notice where your gaze rests—those are the places that need details.

Choose one good-sized item per seating area for emphasis. For example, a smooth, round granite or concrete ball or colorful bowling ball perched beside a bench adds a focal point by creating a juxtaposition of objects. If floor space is limited, mount your largest object on the wall.

COLLECTIONS

Grouping related objects, such as birdhouses, folk art, or finials, invites comparison and draws attention. Small pieces take on greater importance when displayed together.

Walls, ledges, windowsills, empty corners, and even flower beds are good places for displaying collections. Because a collection forms a single focal point out of several objects, choose its setting carefully. Avoid placing collections together or near other accents that compete for attention. Neutral backgrounds, such as walls, fences, and green plants, show off collections to their best advantage.

INDIVIDUAL PIECES

When setting out decorations individually, it helps to establish a theme—for example, using star-shaped objects, rabbits, or things that are blue—so the space maintains a unified look. Avoid cluttering the space by allowing enough room between items so that each one can be properly showcased. Displaying accessories at various heights also helps avoid clutter.

ADD PERSONALITY

There is no right or wrong way to display personal details in your outdoor room. However, consider these suggestions:
- Mount driftwood on a blank wall and tuck orchid plants into its crevices during warm months.
- Set seashells on top of rafters so they're visible only if you're looking upward.
- Prop a shell-shaped fossil or other salvaged artifact against a pot of flowers at floor level.

A would-be dull corner is a lively little scene when dressed up with outdoor art, a few old tools, and a potting bench.

OBJECTS D'ART

Beauty is in the eye of the collector. Whatever catches your fancy and can withstand the elements has potential as a decoration for your outdoor room.

Place objects such as old doors where you need something special to fill a dull spot. Consider these items or think of your own.

- Pottery
- Keys
- Old tools
- Canoe paddles
- Shells
- Fossils
- Birdhouses
- Marbles
- Antique signs
- Folk art
- Architectural salvage
- Watering cans
- Sun motif
- Fishing gear

- Nail or glue old bottle caps across the foot of the screen door.
- Paint a prominent fence post a different color from the rest. Or paint a face and attach arms, wings, or a hat to create your own garden sculpture.
- Spike a weather vane in a pot of flowers to draw attention to the seasonal color.
- Open air serves as a gallery itself. Hang mobiles or wind chimes to catch the breeze.
- Suspend unexpected objects such as old silverware or prisms.

Above all, look for ways to make your outdoor room more comfortable. Soften furniture with plump cushions. Keep a stack of books or magazines handy. Add an ottoman. Then put your feet up and enjoy!

An old ornament provides a wonderful focal point for a secluded spot. Lattice creates a backdrop with warmth and texture instead of a stark concrete wall.

Look for unusual items, such as this moss-filled topiary resembling a shoe. Then find the right spots on ledges, shelves, walls, and tabletops to set your found treasures.

PLANTS IN ALL THE RIGHT PLACES

Plants bring patios to life. What's more, they help solve design problems in a way no other element can. Container plants with bright colors create a pretty view from the house. A nearby hedge screens an unattractive view. Potted trees provide shade, privacy, and perhaps fruit. Large planters help control traffic patterns. Well-placed planting beds, trees, shrubs, perennials, and groundcovers blend your patio into the landscape, making the entire scene a single attractive composition.

When you're ready to integrate plants into your patio plan, first decide where they should go. Use your design concept as a guide (see pages 94–103). It will tell you where you need shade, privacy, and shelter. Then pick plants which do the job in style.

MAKING GARDEN BEDS

Before you decide what to plant in a bed, first decide on the shape. Remember, the edges of a garden bed also shape adjoining lawn areas.

If you don't have your plans on paper yet, experiment with a garden hose, creating outlines in keeping with your overall style choices. Most homeowners find that curved lines—even bordering the square corners of a patio—give their landscape a professionally designed look.

Once you're happy with the contour, mark the hose outline with flags or flour, pull the hose off, establish the outline with spray paint, and cut the bed from the soil. Plant beds in tiers, placing the shortest plants toward the front and gradually increasing the height of the plants toward the rear. Plants right next to the patio should be no more than eye-level when you're seated, unless you're using them to screen out a view or increase your privacy.

TREES

Trees can do more than grow upright in your landscape. They provide shade, reduce erosion, keep homes cooler in the summer, and help keep the air clean. If you expect your trees to do all these jobs, research your choices and plant species that will adapt to

Accent plantings draw attention to themselves. Enhance their effectiveness by placing them beside a door or gate. Notice how these geraniums and stand seem to pop forward from the neutral background of the wall.

ROOM FOR VINES

It only takes a small opening cut into paving to grow plants within a patio. Vines thrive in openings as small as 8 inches across.
A single vine can cover the face of a wall with a cloak of leaves. Or plant one at the foot of an arbor to twine up a post and grow overhead.

BASKET TIPS

Before hanging a basket, make sure it's in a spot where people won't bonk their heads. Then use the following "recipe" for sure-fire success.

■ Start with a 12-inch or larger basket.

■ Purchase three trailing plants (in 3-inch pots or six to a pony pack).

■ Position the trailers in the basket of soil as the three points of a triangle, spaced equally apart and a few inches from the edge.

■ Place the upright plants similarly in the center of the basket.

■ Randomly tuck in a few filler plants.

Coarse-textured shrubs contrast boldly with the smooth adobe walls and tile surfaces of this enclosed patio. Such variety reduces attention to the confinement of the space.

the seasonal extremes of your climate as well as to soil and drainage constraints. Don't worry about existing trees unless they affect the placement of your patio.

When choosing new trees, use the following as a guide.

■ Choose between deciduous trees, which lose their leaves in the winter, or evergreen species, which keep their leaves.

■ Consider the growth rate and mature size of the tree. The 6-foot sapling at the nursery may root into your foundation if placed too close to the house.

■ Check out the tree's "personality." Some species have all the attributes of the perfect botanical addition to your landscape, but they may be messy, dropping seeds, foliage, and blossoms.

SHRUBS

The mid-size stature of shrubs make them good plants for transitions between larger elements, such as trees, sheds, or decks. They're great in places trees won't fit.

Before you head for the nursery, list the qualities that will meet the needs outlined in your plans. Explore your neighborhood or go on garden tours for ideas. Be sure to include these factors in your decision.

■ How much care the shrubs require.

Only inches high, variegated hosta surrounds a brick patio, forming an attractive living room divider.

Without the plantings, this setting would be a stark patio surface that would probably be uninviting to family and guests. Plants help soften hardscape designs, and their colors add interest to the entire setting.

PLANTS IN ALL THE RIGHT PLACES
continued

■ How high and wide they will be when mature. A full-grown shrub on your patio will prove to be an unwelcome guest.
■ How well it matches your landscape style and how well it takes to pruning.

CONTAINER GARDENS

Container gardens dress up a dull spot with living color or allow easy rearrangement of your setting. Almost any kind of plant can be grown in a container, even in hot, dry weather. Also, you can move plants around and change them from season to season.

Before you decide what to grow, determine where you'll put the plantings. Here's how.
■ Sit on all of the benches, chairs, hammocks, walls, and steps of your patio and look at the view. Also check the view from any adjoining rooms inside.

Design window boxes to look good from inside the house as well as out. Decorative brackets and painted trim below the boxes add eye-level interest outdoors.

Container gardens garner attention. Here, you might not even notice the street in the background.

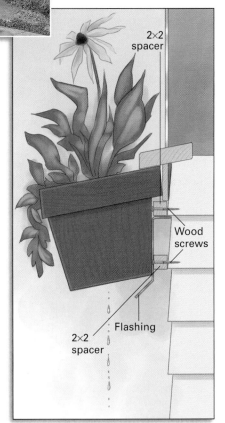

To protect siding from stains and water damage, install a 2×2 spacer and flashing behind the window box and pitch the box forward for proper drainage.

2×2 spacer

Wood screws

Flashing

2×2 spacer

Container-grown plants clustered at the foot of steps lend color, texture, and importance to the entrance of a raised deck without getting in the way.

Lobelia, begonias, sweet alyssum, and browallia thrive in a basket, showing off their contrasting foliage and pleasing blossoms.

Grouping similar containers adds unity and interesting texture to the otherwise flat surface of the fencing.

■ Note any distractions in the background, such as utility wires, heating and cooling units, meters, outlets, and tools. Then place the containers to block these views.

■ Pay attention to any areas that may need more privacy. Plants can add perceived height to a wall without creating a walled-off feeling.

■ Look for empty corners or blank walls, then liven up these areas with container plants.

WINDOW-BOX TIPS

■ The deeper the window box, the healthier your plants will be. Boxes at least 10 inches deep allow room for adequate root growth.

■ Be sure your window boxes have at least two drainage holes in their bottoms.

■ Slide a sheet of foam inside the front of your window box before filling it with soil. The foam insulates roots from heat and reduces evaporation of soil moisture.

■ Before planting, mix water-retaining polymers in the soil. These tiny pellets swell when wet and hold moisture in the soil.

■ Water window boxes daily (or sometimes twice a day) during hot weather. If soil is dry to the touch, it's time to water.

BOXES AND BASKETS

Window boxes and hanging baskets offer an opportunity to create a self-contained composition on a small scale. A window box or a basket filled with a row or circle of clipped topiaries or tumbles of bright flowers will always add cheer to your patio.

Generally speaking, all the plants in a window box or a basket should have the same requirements for sun, water, and fertilizer. For reliable results, combine plants of similar colors or contrasting textures. For variety, look for contrasting textures, colors, and shapes. Billows of fine-textured plants, such as baby's breath, make fine companions for plants with spiky foliage, such as rosemary. Upright forms accent a composition when surrounded by trailing flowers.

Window boxes and baskets offer a perfect place for tiny gardens, too. Include lettuce, herbs, and edible flowers.

Extenders with built-in pulleys let you hang baskets at the desired height and lower them easily for watering.

PRIVACY
CREATING A SENSE OF ENCLOSURE

Combine fences or walls with plantings for the best of both worlds. Walls offer instant privacy, and plants soften their hard surfaces. Use vines for a quick cover.

A privacy fence covered with dense foliage solves two problems at once. It creates privacy and helps to muffle unwanted noise.

Without visual cues to suggest the edges and a sense of height for your patio, your outdoor living space can leave you feeling exposed and slightly uncomfortable. *When relaxing on your patio, you'll want to feel a sense of privacy and enclosure. If your site lacks natural attributes that enhance this sense, create it yourself.*

Consider privacy first. Screen your patio from the street and from your neighbors' views. If your proposed site is tucked behind a retaining wall or hedge, you may have already solved any privacy problems. But if you need to increase your privacy, add a fence, a wall, or trees and shrubs to your plans.

These elements will also provide a sense of enclosure. So can benches, garden beds, and other features. And remember to look up. Overhead space affects comfort, too. You may like the view of the open sky while roaming your landscape, but above your patio it may make you feel unprotected. That's when you need an outdoor "ceiling"—an overhead structure, such as an arbor or pergola, or tree limbs.

In this chapter you'll find a host of ideas to increase your privacy and create comfortable space on your patio for years to come.

Tree branches, arbors, roof overhangs, and sunshades help provide a sense of shelter. This arbor and latticework screen beckon you into the patio space. It also cuts the glare from the sun and helps define the patio space.

Even an umbrella can cure a case of too much open sky and bring outdoor space down to human scale. It also adds much needed shade to a spot that might not be used on sunny days.

Walls don't need to be towering structures to increase privacy. This low stone wall is just high enough to separate this patio area from its surroundings without isolating it.

WALLS AND FENCES

A cut-stone wall forms a large planter, with enough room for a small statue. It also helps separate formal areas of the patio from the informal spaces.

W alls and fences make beautiful additions to a patio, connecting it to the larger landscape and adding an important vertical contrast to the horizontal expanse of lawn. They can solve design and environmental problems, too.

Walls and fences can give each space an identity that suits its purpose, whether it be lounging, gardening, or children's play. They can hold back a slope, adding space for a new or expanded patio or open up larger outdoor living space by closing off unsightly views. They can make large areas seem less imposing by dividing them into smaller ones. They can knock down annoying winds, form backdrops for decorative accents, and hide utility areas.

DEFINING SPACE

Without definition at its perimeter, your patio may seem open and flat—just an extension of the lawn. Without something to set apart your family dining space from entertainment areas, your weekend brunch area can feel exposed. Both inside your patio and out, you need something that visually separates one area from another.

There are obvious walls, such as fences, hedges, and the sides of the house. There are also walls that are not so obvious, perceived walls—ankle-high hedges, built-in seating, planters, posts for an overhead roof, even plants and trees. Anything that separates your patio from the rest of the world—or one area from another—is acting as a wall.

A low hedge, for example, becomes a living wall, dividing the patio from the rest of the lawn. A row of trees can do this, too, their trunks filtering the views, not blocking them.

Built-in benches and raised planters can keep your party space from encroaching on the private areas of your patio. Freestanding benches create the suggestion of a wall or fence and divide areas without completely enclosing them. They're especially useful when you need to separate two spaces that have closely related purposes.

Erecting a maze of solid walls, fences, or closely knit hedges to divide your property into bits of space can result in separate, but isolated areas. Perceived walls, on the other hand, create an implied separation without leaving areas feeling isolated from one another. They interrupt both visual and actual movement but don't block views, so they direct traffic effectively and define space without creating a claustrophobic feeling.

CONSIDER THE VIEW

Open up your landscape by removing trees or shrubbery that block pleasant views. Raze or repair unsightly sheds instead of building fences to hide them. Weed out overgrowth. Replace out-of-control shrubs with low-growing varieties, and substitute well-behaved species for pod-bearing trees.

When you need to separate your outdoor living space from neighboring high-activity areas, erect a tall fence in a style that compliments the landscape.

Redwood fences and planters create a sense of privacy and enclosure and do so in style.

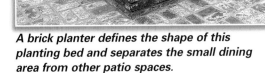

A brick planter defines the shape of this planting bed and separates the small dining area from other patio spaces.

LOCATION AND PRIVACY

Defining space and creating privacy often go hand in hand. Where lots of foot and vehicle traffic passes nearby, it might take a solid brick wall or board fence to provide enough privacy. Where the patio is visible from only a few vantage points, a couple of ornamental trees or a latticework fence might be all that's required to stop prying eyes.

A patio in an urban yard is exposed to more noise, traffic, and neighbors than one in the suburbs. Here, it may be best to fence off all sides of the lot rather than isolating the patio. In most suburban areas, the expansiveness of the lots creates enough separation, so you can be more selective when choosing where walls and fences will go.

A high brick wall effectively separates patio space from the noise and activities of a busy neighborhood.

WALLS AND FENCES
continued

SCREENING

Screening means strategically placing plants, fences, walls, trellises, and other structures to block views and provide privacy. As a result, screens boost your comfort level while using your patio.

To determine the amount of privacy screening you need, take a moment to go outside and sit in the proposed location of your patio (or the present patio if you have one already). Note the levels of privacy and exposure from different vantage points. Then sit in the same locations and make a list of any unsightly or unattractive elements you want to screen out.

A solid wall, softened with latticework and flowers, offers maximum screening and blocks unsightly views without making the space feel confined.

SCREENING FOR PRIVACY: When taking notes on privacy, follow your instincts. If you feel on display in a space, it's not private enough. How much privacy you'll need will depend on how you'll use each of the areas you've designated for a special use.

Cozy, intimate spots and areas for reading, conversation, sunbathing, or meditation should provide plenty of privacy. Screen these areas with high walls, fences, or plantings.

Active areas for parties, family gatherings, or children's play require less privacy. Here, partial screening should do the trick, such as latticework, airy trees, or seat walls.

Where you put privacy screens matters, too. The closer to the patio area, the more privacy you'll get. The farther from the surface, the less privacy.

Very few patios will require screening around the entire perimeter. So before you decide to plant a hedge around your patio, figure out the angle from which other people can see you. Then plan the screening to block the most revealing views first. Lattice, picket and ornamental iron fencing form a friendly, see-through screen.

SCREENING OUT VIEWS: When you're enjoying your outdoor room, you won't want to be looking at the garbage cans, the dog run, a heat pump, your neighbor's open garage, or parked cars. Consider the angles from which you can see these unattractive sights; then strategically place screens to hide them from view. Take care to not box in your outdoor room, obstructing all views.

SOLID-WALL SCREENING: For a strong sense of permanence in your landscape, think about height and

Waist-high fences and walls offer a touch of privacy without totally enclosing an area. Sturdy, low walls, such as this one, seem more inviting than solid, high fences.

HOW HIGH?

The purpose of a wall or fence should dictate its height. A structure for security, a windbreak, or total screening can be 6 to 8 feet high. Walls built solely to separate spaces can be as low as 6 inches or as high as 3 feet. In general, any wall or fence should be either well above or well below eye-level. There's nothing worse than having a wall or fence cut your view in half.

density—a wall, solid fence, or dense hedge. These barriers provide maximum privacy and security, in addition to screening views.

Solid walls and fences have a number of advantages. They can function as effective boundaries that keep children and pets in the yard and unwanted visitors out. They can also provide an ideal backdrop for garden beds, supplying a level of protection to the plants and creating a nurturing microclimate— the extra warmth and shelter they need to survive outside the limits of their usual hardiness range.

A wall of any sort provides an instant visual backdrop for an outdoor setting—whether it defines the boundary along all sides of an area or simply encloses part of a patio. Flower borders, ponds, and sculptures show off nicely against both walls and screens. If your yard has an old wall or fence that you'd rather hide than display, disguise it with climbing plants.

MATERIALS: Choosing materials for outdoor walls and fences offers yet another design opportunity. You'll find vast choices, but the main goal remains the same. Select materials that suit the style of your home and landscape.

Perhaps you'll decide to build a solid wall of brick or stone for a classic and imposing look. Interlocking concrete blocks, designed for building retaining walls, suit most home styles. Another possibility combines a simple fence with a hedge of evergreens or roses for a decorative look that's fairly impenetrable. Or you may live in an area where adobe offers the most appropriate building option.

EVERGREEN OR DECIDUOUS?

If you need continuous, year-round screening and you've chosen trees or shrubs to do the job, you'll need evergreens, which don't lose their leaves in the fall. Deciduous species drop their leaves and grow dormant, which can be an advantage in winter climates. A tree without leaves lets in the sun and can help warm any interior rooms next to the patio.

Fences and walls can separate without isolating your patio. Here, a brick wall and a low, white picket fence define spaces without blocking sunlight and desirable views.

DON'T BUILD A FORTRESS

To avoid turning your yard into "Fort Patio," beware of building barrier-style screens, such as solid walls, high fences, and dense, straight hedges. Use these only in areas that require absolute maximum screening.

SCREENING WITH SOIL

Berms, or mounds of soil, can block views and deflect noise. To keep a berm from resembling an awkward bump, build it several feet wide and no less than 30 inches higher than the existing grade. To minimize erosion, the berm should slope gently upward. As the roots of plants on the berm grow, they'll help stabilize the soil and prevent erosion.

OVERHEADS AND SHADE STRUCTURES

If an open roof doesn't fit your landscape design and the cost of shingles isn't in your budget, let vines grow up and over the roof.

Enclose an area to create a courtyard that directs attention inward, making the space feel more private.

Whether you call it an arbor, pergola, lanai, or canopy, an overhead will enhance your patio with a minimum of materials and work.

FUNCTION FIRST

Let the use of your patio determine whether it needs an overhead. The sky might be the ceiling for the outdoors, but many times it's simply too high for a patio. Active areas for hosting large parties or for children's play can function well if left open. But intimate areas planned for dining, talking, or relaxing will feel more inviting and cozier with an overhead.

Protection from the elements is also a reason for an overhead.

STYLE

No matter what your reason for building an overhead, make sure its design reflects and complements the overall architecture of your home. An overhead structure should appear to be an integral part of the design and not as an add-on. Repeat a detail of the house—a molding or post style, the pitch of the roof, an accent color, or a building material—to link the overhead to your home.

Curved overheads lend a romantic, cottage style to an outdoor space. Dressed and painted lumber suggests formality. Rough cedar lends a rustic air. A masonry arch adds a touch of old-world charm.

COMING TO TERMS WITH OVERHEADS

Technically, an arbor is a freestanding structure and a pergola is attached to something, such as the side of the house. A lanai (a Hawaiian word) is a porch or veranda, uncovered or covered, and a canopy is a general term for any overhead cover.

"UP" SCALE

Overhead space, both indoors and out, has a psychological impact. Indoors, we feel most comfortable in rooms with 8- to 10-foot ceilings. Outdoors, we're accustomed to higher ceilings, but we still feel more comfortable when the overhead space is somewhat closer to the indoor standard. In general, make sure that space for intimate activities has some kind of cover over it, from 10 to 12 feet high. Areas for parties will feel more comfortable with ceilings up to 20 feet high. A rule of thumb for covering your patio from above: shelter at least a third of the surface.

WORKING THE ANGLES TO GET THE BEST MIX OF SUN AND SHADE

If you want an overhead to provide shade, take the time to find the maximum amount of shade in the heat of a summer day and the minimum amount when it's cooler.

Monitor your proposed deck area to see when the sun makes the deck site too hot and bright to use. Note the season, the time of day, and the angle at which the sun shines on the area. Then position the overhead and design it to block the sun's rays from that angle by shading the areas where it's most needed.

Control the amount of sunlight reaching a sheltered area by varying the size, spacing, and orientation of framing members. Build the structure and then experiment with different slat configurations before attaching them.

Slats oriented east to west will shade the area underneath for most of the day. Oriented north to south, they will provide the same amount of shade as east-to-west slats in the morning and evening but will allow some sun through at midday. Setting rafters at a 30-degree angle blocks more sun. Spacing slats close together will also provide more shade.

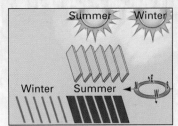
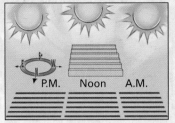
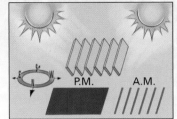
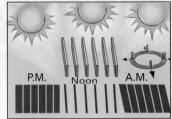

Attach louvers or lattice to the sides of the structure to filter low-angle rays on late summer afternoons, or plant vines to sprawl across the top and the sides.

ROOFED STRUCTURES

Structures with a solid roof made from corrugated metal or plastic, cedar shakes, asphalt shingles, or slate tiles offer more physical protection than open roofs. They keep you dry when it rains and completely block out the sunlight. They're especially helpful above outdoor cooking areas, keeping both the cook and the equipment dry.

Solid-roofed structures create miniature environments underneath them. Shadows cast by the roof may cool nearby uncovered paving but may also darken the interior of your home if not positioned carefully. If possible, locate solid roofs away from the main portion of your patio so that the space can be used in both fair and inclement weather.

This patio seems like a natural extension of the landscape, thanks to an analysis of sun and shade patterns and close attention to elements of style. Simplicity and cohesive materials are key to this design.

GROWING PRIVACY AND ENCLOSURE

Should you build a wall or fence to increase your privacy or let plants do the job? The answer depends on your budget, your patience, and the look you desire.

Planting for privacy doesn't have to mean formal, clipped hedges. Flowering trees and shrubs can add intimacy to a seating area. Combine deciduous plants with fences or evergreens. You'll have both seasonal interest and year-round structure.

Plants grow. Fences and walls don't. For that reason, privacy plantings make good economic sense. If you have the patience, you can start with small plants and wait for them to grow. Or you can start by investing in a few large plants to block critical areas and use smaller plants to fill in places where you don't mind waiting for a living screen to mature.

Then there's the neighbors. A substantial fence can create sore feelings next door. Trees, shrubs, and other plants create a softer look than fences or walls so it might not be as evident to the neighbors that you're putting up a privacy screen. Plantings also remove the possibility that your neighbors (or you) won't like looking at the back side of a fence. If your yard already has a lot of paving or decking, using plants instead of fencing keeps the hardscape from overwhelming the space.

SELECTING PLANTS

If you want to plant a screen but don't know which plants to grow, consider the amount of privacy you need. Evergreens will yield year-round and complete privacy; deciduous species, seasonal screening. Evergreens, however, grow more slowly than deciduous plants.

Some trees, such as serviceberry, feature multiple trunks that lend themselves beautifully to separating areas and creating a sense of enclosure. They offer a measure of privacy, too. Deciduous trees permit winter rays to warm your patio and allow sunlight to reach inside your home. Mixing evergreen and deciduous trees and shrubs together gives you the best of both types.

The hedge, perennials, and small tree combine to block the view of a compost bin (on the left) and direct attention to the small built-in pond.

EVERGREEN SCREENS

Common Name	Botanical Name	Zones
TREES		
Canadian hemlock	*Tsuga canadensis*	3–7
Colorado blue spruce	*Picea pungens glauca*	3–7
Douglas fir	*Pseudotsuga menziesii*	4–6
Eastern red cedar	*Juniperus virginiana*	3–9
Eastern white pine	*Pinus strobus*	3–8
Leyland cypress	*× Cupressocyparis leylandi*	6–10
Loquat	*Eriobotrya japonica*	8–10
Norway spruce	*Picea abies*	3–8
SHRUBS		
American arborvitae	*Thuja occidentalis*	3–7
Hick's yew	*Taxus × media 'Hicksii'*	5–7
Inkberry	*Ilex glabra*	3–10
Leatherleaf viburnum	*Viburnum rhytidophyllum*	6–8
Luster-leaf holly	*Ilex latifolia*	7–9
Nelly R. Stevens holly	*Ilex 'Nellie R. Stevens'*	6–9
Oleander	*Nerium oleander*	8–10
Yew pine	*Podocarpus macrophyllus*	8–10

PLANTING TIPS

■ Research growth rates before buying plants.
■ Plant selectively. Three large shrubs or trees grouped together will block a specific view.
■ Plant large evergreen shrubs at the back of a flower bed for year-round privacy.
■ Place plants away from the patio by half their mature spread to avoid crowding later.
■ Mix plants and hardscaping. Install fences or walls to block the worst views and add plants to blend in with the fence.

Use your house as one border and a high hedge as another to turn your patio space into a private courtyard.

PLANTING STRATEGICALLY

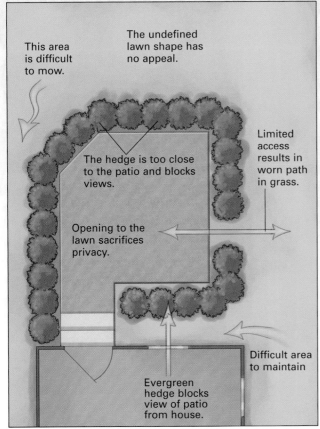

This area is difficult to mow.

The undefined lawn shape has no appeal.

The hedge is too close to the patio and blocks views.

Limited access results in worn path in grass.

Opening to the lawn sacrifices privacy.

Difficult area to maintain

Evergreen hedge blocks view of patio from house.

BEFORE

Ringing a patio with shrubs provides privacy but closes in the area, making it uninviting and difficult to maintain.

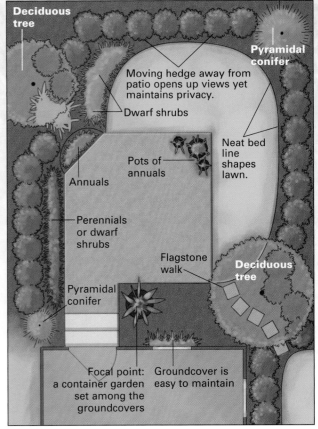

Deciduous tree

Pyramidal conifer

Moving hedge away from patio opens up views yet maintains privacy.

Dwarf shrubs

Neat bed line shapes lawn.

Annuals

Pots of annuals

Perennials or dwarf shrubs

Flagstone walk

Deciduous tree

Pyramidal conifer

Focal point: a container garden set among the groundcovers

Groundcover is easy to maintain

AFTER

A more inviting solution comes from thinking strategically: Block unwanted sights, then develop and accentuate the yard's better views.

GROWING PRIVACY AND ENCLOSURE
continued

TREES

There are many species of trees to fill the role of sentry beside or within your patio. Even a small tree, one that matures at 10 to 20 feet, adds shade and a comfortable sense of height to your patio area. Keep in mind that deciduous trees shade outdoor rooms in summer, lose their leaves in fall, and allow sunlight to reach the interior of your home in winter, brightening and warming it.

When planting new trees near your patio, select a species that matures between 30 and 35 feet or less. Trim the lowest branches of mature trees, allowing a minimum 6-foot clearance so you can walk under them without getting poked in the eye.

Look for hardwood species that don't drop messy fruit or twigs. Avoid planting too close

An overhead structure like this pergola can provide shade, but if its linear architecture doesn't suit your taste or the style of your landscape, soften the lines with vines.

to pavement and foundations; tree roots can buckle them. Position trees where they'll frame (not block) views and protect your home from winter winds and summer sun. Good patio species feature neat and trim silhouettes that suit confined spaces.

Be sure to include a variety of trees and create a landscape that offers beauty and

GOOD PATIO TREES

No tree is completely mess-free, but these trees come pretty close. They mature at 30 to 35 feet tall or less and adapt to confined conditions.

Common Name	Botanical Name	Features	Zones
American yellowwood	*Cladrastis lutea*	Fragrant flowers	5–8
Amur maple	*Acer tataricum ginnala*	Shade, fall color	3–8
Apple serviceberry	*Amelanchier × grandiflora*	Spring flowers, fall color	3–8
Chinese elm	*Ulmus parvifolia*	Interesting bark	4–9
Crape myrtle	*Lagerstroemia indica*	Summer flowers, sculptural form	7–9
Eastern redbud	*Cercis canadensis*	Spring flowers	4–9
European mountain ash	*Sorbus aucuparia*	Fall color	3–6
Japanese maple	*Acer palmatum*	Fall color, sculptural form	5–8
Sargent cherry	*Prunus sargentii*	Spring flowers	5–8
Sweet bay magnolia	*Magnolia virginiana*	Fragrant summer flowers	5–9
Washington hawthorn	*Crataegus phaenopyrum*	Winter berries	4–9
Wax myrtle	*Myrica cerifera*	Fine-textured, evergreen foliage; prune into tree form	8–10
Wax-leaf privet	*Ligustrum lucidum*	Glossy evergreen foliage; prune into tree form	7–9
Yaupon holly	*Ilex vomitoria*	Winter berries; prune into tree form	7–9
Yoshino cherry	*Prunus yedoensis*	Spring flowers	5–9

MORE FOR THE MONEY

When you use plants to increase your privacy or create a sense of enclosure, you're also making a design statement.

Plants help soften the hard edge of an overhead structure. Leafy canopies offer dappled shade, whether you opt for a vine-covered pergola or the shelter of large trees.

Mature trees spread a high-domed canopy over an outdoor room. They define the upper limit of the outdoor ceiling, filter sunlight, and offer a sense of protection.

Small plants work well, too. Plant small trees in pots to set beside your patio or vines that will scramble over the top of an arbor. Train potted shrubs into the shape of small trees. Be sure to select dwarf-type plants that won't outgrow the space allotted them.

Even a small climbing vine will provide a sense of overhead security when the constraints of space or budget won't permit a larger structure.

a haven for wildlife year-round. Choose trees that thrive in your area. Look around your neighborhood to see which trees appear to be thriving in the climate. Then visit a local nursery and consult the experts; verify the hardiness of your favorite trees before making a final selection. A little homework now avoids costly mistakes later.

VINES

Vines add leafy layers and colorful blossoms to posts, arbors, and trellises. Plant vines at the base of supports and let them grow up and over your patio. Plant them in ample containers, taking care that their roots have plenty of room to grow. Use fast-growing varieties, such as trumpet vine and clematis, to provide a quick umbrella. Some vines offer greenery year-round; others lose their leaves in the fall, letting the sun's warmth reach the interior of your home during the colder, winter months.

VINES FOR ARBORS AND PERGOLAS

Common Name	Botanical Name	Features	Zones
Armand clematis	*Clematis armandii*	Fragrant flowers, evergreen foliage	7–9
Bougainvillea	*Bougainvillea glabra*	Winter flowers	9–10
Carolina jessamine	*Gelsemium sempervirens*	Spring flowers	8–10
Climbing roses	*Rosa* hybrids	Showy flowers	Varies
Confederate jasmine	*Trachelospermum jasminoides*	Fragrant flowers	8–10
Coral vine	*Antigonon leptopus*	Summer flowers	8–10
European hop	*Humulus lupulus*	Bright foliage	5–8
Hyacinth bean	*Lablab purpureus*	Purple fruit; rapid-growing annual	7–10
Clematis	*Clematis* hybrids	Spring flowers	4–8
Moonflower	*Ipomea alba*	Summer flowers; rapid-growing annual	8–10
Morning glory	*Ipomea tricolor*	Summer flowers; rapid-growing annual	4–10
Silver lace vine	*Polygonum aubertii*	Summer flowers	4–8
Sweet autumn clematis	*Clematis terniflora*	Fall flowers	6–9
Trumpet honeysuckle	*Lonicera sempervirens*	Summer flowers	4–9

SMALL TREES FOR PLANTERS

Many of these trees can grow for years in a container if provided with adequate water, fertilizer, and drainage.

Common Name	Botanical Name	Features	Zones
Australian tree fern	*Cyathea cooperi*	Fine-textured foliage	9–10
Japanese maple	*Acer palmatum*	Fall color	5–8
'Little Gem' magnolia	*Magnolia* 'Little Gem'	Summer flowers, evergreen foliage	7–9
Rose of Sharon	*Hibiscus syriacus*	Summer flowers	5–9
Tree-form wax myrtle	*Myrica cerifera*	Fine-textured, evergreen foliage; prune into tree form	8–10
Wax-leaf privet	*Ligustrum lucidum*	Glossy evergreen foliage, multiple trunks; prune into tree form	7–9
Windmill palm	*Trachycarpus Fortunei*	Fanlike fronds, hairy trunk	8–10
Yaupon holly	*Ilex vomitoria*	Winter berries; prune into tree form	7–9

Mix plants with structure. Build a fence or wall to block the worst views and add plants that will enhance the structure as they grow.

ADDING AMENITIES

This fully equipped outdoor kitchen has a high counter that can serve as a buffet or dining area and helps keep small children safely away from a hot grill.

Amenities bring many of the comforts of the indoors into the beauty and spaciousness of the outdoors. Which amenities you choose will depend on how you want to use the space.

Outdoor kitchens allow the cook to escape the heat and isolation of the indoor kitchen and enjoy more time outside with the guests. An outdoor cooking area with a propane grill and some cabinetry can be as easy to use as the indoor kitchen. With a working sink outdoors, you can cook entire meals without dashing in and out of the house.

Outdoor lighting adds decorative beauty as well as extra hours to the enjoyment of a patio or deck. Easily installed low-voltage systems can set just the right mood.

Consider including a fireplace, chiminea, or fire pit in your patio plans. Just as a fireplace inside provides a cozy gathering point, firelight outside draws guests and family to its dancing flames and crackling embers.

Just off the patio or deck, a small pool with a fountain adds charm. So does a container or tabletop fountain, which are available at home centers. Research a water feature first to find suitable plants and fish—species that require minimal maintenance.

If your design includes any of these amenities but your budget doesn't, plan for them now and add them later. At a minimum, you'll probably want outdoor electrical receptacles and running water.

PLANNING FOR AMENITIES

Many patio amenities require plumbing, electrical, or natural-gas installations, and all of them should be included in your plans before you start building your outdoor living space.

For example, a spa requires running water and a drainpipe. Spas, ponds, fountains, and waterfall pumps require electrical outlets with ground fault circuit interrupters (GFCIs). Lighting systems require electric lines. A permanent natural-gas line for a gas grill might be preferable to propane tanks. An exterior phone jack is useful for households that haven't yet gone wireless. If outdoor activities include watching TV, you'll need an electric outlet and perhaps an exterior cable connection.

Utilities are best run underground to the site— both for safety and to avoid clutter. Plot the utility run so that it does not interfere with anything else in the area. Rough-in the systems after excavation, but finish them before laying any foundation.

This pool and waterfall only look complicated. Their installation requires a few basic skills. Start with a pool liner as shown on page 171 and place the pump outside the pond. Surround the liner with mortared flagstone. Slightly angle the flagstone steps toward the pool to direct the water downward.

Soft low-voltage lights scattered among the plants provide just enough light on this patio for late-night conversations. The standard-voltage lights flanking the house door provide additional illumination and safety.

OUTDOOR KITCHENS

Everyone knows how much better food tastes when it's cooked and served outdoors. Incorporating an outdoor kitchen in your patio plans requires only a little creativity and perhaps some minor modifications to make the space easy to use, efficient, and pleasurable. You can equip the space with facilities ranging from a plain charcoal grill to a fancy gas range and complete the kitchen with an outdoor sink.

LOCATION, LOCATION

Because a moveable grill—gas or charcoal—will fit just about anywhere, you might think it doesn't make much difference where you put it. But portable or permanent, a grill can have disastrous consequences if its location is poorly planned.

First, find the safest spot. Convenience is important but safety is a higher priority. Locate a portable grill so it's far enough away from flammable surfaces and little ones' hands. Construct a built-in with fire-

Your patio will become a favorite dining room if it offers plenty of room for preparation, sheltered seating, and a great view.

prevention methods that conform to your local building codes.

Whether portable or permanent, put grills out of access routes and views. Take care that they don't pose other safety issues—you don't want anyone to get smoked out. Consider installing a small overhead shelter with a vent above the cooking area or locate the grill under overhanging eaves. This way, you can continue grilling if it starts to rain. And if your unit is portable and you don't have room to store it somewhere, you'll need a waterproof cover when it's not in use.

Your outdoor kitchen should include enough room for preparing and serving food as well as storage space for utensils. If you're adding a portable grill to your plans but lack space for full-blown serving areas, keep cooking items handy but out of sight by tucking them inside a potting bench or other cabinetry or behind a screen. Large potted plants will do a good job of hiding the grill too. Set them on platforms with casters for easier maneuverability.

BUILT-INS

Permanent fixtures, such as outdoor cooktops, ovens, and refrigerators, offer options that can turn your patio into a summer kitchen. You'll find compact cooktop-only units as well as combination units with a built-in rotisserie, grill, or griddle that fit into a relatively small space.

Look for outdoor-grade equipment that meets building codes and withstands all weather conditions.

Choose from cooktops fueled by wood, charcoal, electricity, or natural gas. Have electric or gas lines installed before setting up the unit.

Even weather-resistant outdoor appliances need shelter and waterproof countertops. Marble, metal, or tile countertops provide plenty of elbow room for preparing meals. Have your contractor help calculate the expense of building the countertop large enough to form a 15- to 18-inch overhang opposite the cooking area for a bar or buffet. Waterproof cabinets prove useful too. So will storage made for a kitchen-size garbage can. Close cabinets with screen door hooks or a sliding bolt to keep critters out.

Cooking out is easier when your outdoor room contains built-in cooking space. Whether it's simply a spot for charcoal grilling or a gas stove top, there is a wide variety of equipment available for fresh-air use.

ADDING AN OUTDOOR KITCHEN

When retrofitting a patio for outdoor kitchen space, think small. You may need only a modest extension to the patio surface. Build a grill-size spot from the same paving materials as your patio. Concrete stepping-stones or precast pavers on a sand base will go with almost any design scheme.

The best outdoor cooking areas offer plenty of weatherproof storage as well as room to prepare and serve meals. After all, you don't want to tote supplies in and out every time you cook.

Arranging an outdoor kitchen is similar to arranging one indoors. You may need extra countertop space for shared work if family members enjoy cooking together outdoors.

LIGHTING

Lighting extends the use of your patio into the evening hours and makes it safer and more secure at night, even when you're not using it.

Adding lights to a patio takes planning and care, but it's not difficult. Choose the lighting system you prefer, review the installation guidelines, and prepare to enjoy your outdoor living space any time of day or night.

Lighting extends the use of your patio, increasing your enjoyment with minimum investment. It also creates an ambience, such as the subdued glow from these elevated fixtures.

LIGHTING SOURCES

Decorative and concealed light fixtures lend style and atmosphere to outdoor space and bolster home security.

BEWARE THE GLARE

Artfully placed fixtures cast gentle pools of light that transform your patio in to an evening-friendly space. Choose lighting that improves the setting and helps guests feel comfortable. Mounting bright spotlights to shine on the patio will provide plenty of light, but that's all. Your guests will feel uncomfortable under the glare.

CONCEALED: Concealed light sources focus attention on an object or area, not the fixture itself. Tucked among plants, in a tree, or at ground level, their strong bulbs typically cast their beams a long distance. Place the fixtures carefully so the bulbs aren't readily apparent.

DECORATIVE: Decorative fixtures throw a more diffused and weaker light than concealed fixtures. You should be able to look at them without squinting. They come in two forms—either as freestanding units mounted on short pillars or ones made for mounting on posts or walls. Decorative fixtures should fit their setting. For example, small lanterns perched on chunky pilasters or hanging on a large empty wall will look out of proportion.

LIGHTING STRATEGIES

Getting the right light in the right places on your patio means combining light from various sources in different strategies.

UPLIGHTING: This technique, in which a concealed fixture casts light up into an object from its base, adds drama to your patio. Use uplighting to draw attention to an area or

NEW LIGHT FOR AN OLD PATIO

When building a new patio, lay PVC pipes through the area before installing the paving so you can run electrical wires easily.

If it's too late to do that, hide the wiring by attaching it to the underside structures.

Low-voltage perimeter lighting can be installed at any time. If the space receives at least six hours of sun, consider installing solar fixtures, which require no wires.

Low-voltage lights can transform your landscape, giving outdoor spots an after-hours appeal. Uplighting highlights trees and shrubs. Downlighting illuminates pathways and steps.

decorative object. Position the fixture so its beams graze trees or artwork to highlight their shapes. Aim the light toward a wall or fence silhouetting the shapes of plants, trees, sculptures, or fountains.

Position the fixture in front of the object so that the beam shines away from viewing areas. Or use can lights, which are recessed into the ground and shine upward at an angle while shielding the bulb from view.

DOWNLIGHTING: Downlighting casts a soft, indirect glow on horizontal surfaces, such as steps, paths, floors, balconies, and tabletops. Mount the fixtures on tree trunks, branches, or overhead rafters. A special type of conduit is available for running wiring up trees without harming them. On arbor rafters, thread wires through the center of hollow columns or cut a rabbet along the length of a solid post to create a channel for the wiring.

Keep downlighting fixtures out of sight so they don't draw attention from the illuminated object. As with other lights, aim them to illuminate your yard and outdoor rooms, not your neighbor's.

PATH LIGHTING: These low-level, decorative fixtures cast light directly along a walkway, linking your outdoor room and other parts of your yard, such as the driveway, parking area, or pool. Use a single or matched pair of path lights to illuminate short flights of exterior steps or to mark points of entry.

Conventional path lighting (far left) operates on an electrical-wiring system. Wireless solar fixtures (left) gather and store the sun's energy during the day.

TIPS AND TRICKS

Remember, it's not necessary to light the entire floor of your patio for safety. There are better ways to illuminate the space. Enhance the night with ambience; don't conquer it with brightness.
- Uneven walking surfaces require the most light to keep them safe. For the rest of the patio, use lighting to highlight accents.
- Set underwater lights in a pond to make it more attractive.
- Don't overestimate the amount of light it takes to make a space useful. Entry points, changes in floor surfaces, and food-serving areas should be well lit. Sitting areas and other gathering spots will feel more intimate with subdued lighting.
- Keep fixtures above or below eye-level and far enough apart so the pools of light fade into one another.

CHOICES: LINE VOLTAGE AND LOW VOLTAGE

Lighting systems come in two forms: line voltage, which uses the 120-volt AC power in your house, or low voltage, which uses power reduced by a transformer to 12 volts of direct current. Working with line voltage is easy enough for homeowners with experience doing their own electrical work, but it can be dangerous to use outdoors; you may want to hire professional electricians.
- Most outdoor line-voltage installations require approval from a building inspector. Because low-voltage systems are safer for outdoor use, they seldom require inspection unless you add a new 120-volt circuit to feed the low-voltage system. Even with low-voltage circuits, you need to use care and follow all manufacturer's instructions carefully.
- Low voltage is safe, easy to install, and inexpensive to operate. Line voltage is compatible with the wiring you already have, and it's useful for outdoor appliances and power tools as well as lighting. If you can't decide which

system to use, think about which one matches your needs best.
- A line-voltage system requires conduit, fittings, junction boxes, receptacles, fixtures, bulbs, wire, and connectors. Your supplier can tell you what other materials, tools, and hardware you'll need. Low-voltage systems are designed for use outdoors and require fewer accessories.
- Several kinds of fixtures are available for both systems, but low-voltage systems generally offer more options. You can find lights to illuminate patio surfaces, walkways, and stairways. Others are made to show off plantings, walls, fountains, and other special features. Fixtures are available in a wide variety of materials, from molded plastic to hand-finished teak to cast bronze.
- A retailer who handles outdoor lighting may offer free design advice to customers. Take your plan along in case you need to ask for help.

FIRELIGHT

Outdoor fireplaces bring warmth and intimacy to fresh-air space. The style of the outdoor fireplace, especially if it's near the house, should match the style of the home. It shouldn't look like you tried to use up leftover brick.

No artificial light source can match the comforting glow of a controlled fire. Firelight brings instant coziness and extends your patio's potential for use.

Firelight is most appealing at night, encouraging after-hours use of the outdoor room. Fires also take the chill out of spring and fall evenings.

Most homeowners don't think about including a fireplace or fire pit when planning their patio. But it's easy enough to do, in either new or existing installations.

FIREPLACES

Unlike interior fireplaces, which are built into a wall, most outdoor fireplaces are freestanding, although you can build a fireplace into a wall or use it to accent a retaining wall against a hillside. Made of mortared brick or stone, outdoor fireplaces resemble the indoor variety. A hearth provides a fireproof safeguard against burning embers that tumble out. Andirons hold logs in place, and fire screens contain sparks that

fly from burning logs and exploding embers. Control the fire's draft with a damper. If you like, include a rotisserie and a brick-lined warming oven in the plan and use your fireplace for cooking and keeping food hot.

Build the outdoor fireplace so it will suit the way you use your outdoor living area, as a warming place near the pool or the backdrop for an outdoor room. Whether you construct your fireplace of masonry, firebrick, or other material, it should match the style of your home. Choose a rustic look with a wide stone ledge mantel for a log home. Or design a neat brick structure if your home is more traditional. Cover masonry with a stucco finish, if you prefer, but consult a contractor about fire retardation before applying finishes. Cap the chimney as you would a house

FIRES AND CODES

Before including a fireplace or fire pit in your patio plans, check local regulations first.

Many communities have setback and construction requirements as well as seasonal burning rules. Arid fire-prone areas may restrict outdoor fires altogether.

SOFT LIGHT

Don't despair if fires are not allowed in your community or your patio space is too small. Even the tiniest patio has room for candles, no matter where you live. Their glimmer transforms the plainest spot into a magical world. Lighting groups of candles gives you the satisfaction of settling into your own little retreat. Candlelight sets an intimate mood for dinner under the stars. Candles also complement a low-voltage lighting system and offer just the right touch for nighttime outdoor entertaining.

Once exclusive to the Southwest, chimineas are now available just about anywhere. These wood-burners cost less than a fireplace and are convenient for open or roofed areas. Use a vent pipe in closed or roofed areas.

Build a raised pit for safety. Raised pits prevent accidentally stepping into the fire and also contain sparks.

Candles set a magical, intimate mood, almost like starlight. Choose from pillar candles, votives floating in water, luminarias, lanterns, or outdoor candelabras.

chimney and screen it to keep out birds and other animals. Dress up the mantel with potted greenery, flowers, and natural treasures, such as driftwood and attractive stones for summer appeal when the fireplace is not in use.

CHIMINEAS AND FIRE PITS

Chimineas, a portable fire source, resemble potbelly stoves. These kiln-fired ceramic pieces, which originated in Mexico, spread first through the southwestern United States and have become increasingly popular in other regions. A chiminea holds a fire in its rounded base, which has an opening for feeding logs (and showing flames). It has a chimney tapering upward from the base. Usually chimineas sit on a metal stand to prevent overheating any underlying paving or decking.

These decorative fireplaces add comfort with their heat and provide the sound and scent of burning logs. But they are not designed for cooking. Store them indoors when temperatures fall below freezing. If moisture held by the porous surface of the terra-cotta freezes and expands, the chiminea can crack, flake, or begin deteriorating.

As an alternative, other styles of free-standing gas and wood-burning fire pits are widely available. Classic in-ground fire pits open to the sky. Lined with firebricks and surrounded by a wide fire-resistant coping,

such as stone, their open flames resemble campfires. What's more fun than gathering around an inviting fire to toast marshmallows or even cook a meal?

Plan carefully before constructing a fire pit. Provide plenty of floor space on all sides of the pit to keep people a safe distance from the flames. Provide seating nearby so you and your guests can gather for conversation in the firelight and warmth.

Like other fireplaces, fire pits require common sense. Make safety a priority; instruct every family member what to do if a fire grows out of control and keep an extinguisher handy. Also have a cover for clamping over the pit to smother flames should they grow too large. This also helps contain sparks, which could blow out of the pit after the party is over.

WATER FEATURES

Want your patio to really sparkle? Just add water! Even if you don't need to subdue distracting sounds from beyond your yard, the gentle splashes and trickles of water in motion will make your patio seem a world apart.

Still water in a shallow reflecting pond, with its glassy surface, acts as a natural mirror and creates a contemplative, calm setting. You can shape your design with brick or have a professional pour a concrete base for the pool.

Moving water plays with light, catching it, refracting it, and casting it about. Fountainheads spurt water in several basic patterns: glassy mushrooms, multilevel tiers, gurgling bubbles, and simple streams from a spitter. Some fountainheads offer several patterns in one unit.

INSTALLATION OPTIONS

Putting in a water feature can be as simple as setting up a small pond using a preformed, rigid liner. Leave room in the paving for excavating and either set the liner in, or on

For a natural-looking pond, edge it with materials native to your region. Keep edges irregular to make it look like the water has cut its own channel through the soil. Set water plants around the edges and stock the pond with fish.

top of, the patio surface, camouflaging it with landscape timbers or rocks. Alternatively, dig a hole for a pond next to your patio and form the base of the pond with a flexible liner.

All water features must follow one basic guideline: The water should be aerated. Stagnant water breeds mosquitoes, smelly bacteria, and algae. It also collects silt and debris. Water spilling over the edge of a waterfall or splashing out of a fountain picks up air, which helps it stay fresh.

To keep water moving, install a submersible pump that recirculates the water, sending it to the top of a waterfall, out of a fountainhead, or simply back and forth in the pond. As the name suggests, a submersible pump operates underwater. It must be submerged at all times so it doesn't pump air, which burns out the motor. You must also keep intake filters clean so that debris doesn't clog the pump. Skimming the surface of your pond to remove debris helps prevent clogging as does setting the pump on a stone or brick on the bottom of the pond.

Liners, submersible pumps, and fountainheads are readily available at home centers, aquatic shops, and nurseries. Ask an employee to help you select the right materials for your water garden and ensure that everything is correctly sized for the volume of water.

ADDING WATER TO AN EXISTING SITE

To build a pond on an existing patio, you'll need to cut through the paving. When installing piping to the pond, pry up sections of dry-set paving. Replace the paving when you're done.

For mortared surfaces, you'll need to cut through the paving to install the sleeves. Patch it by laying a band of stone, brick, or other material in the cut (a concrete patch will be obvious). Repeat the banding as a decorative element elsewhere on the patio. If you don't want to cut through the concrete slab, hire a contractor to jack and bore under it to install piping. A trencher pushes and screws its way through the compacted soil beneath the paving, creating a tunnel. Expect to pay per linear foot of tunnel.

DRAINING THE WATER FEATURE

You'll need to drain your pond periodically for cleaning, maintenance, and winterizing. With a small pond or fountain, simply bail the water by hand. For larger ponds, install a drain valve and a drain line that empties into a storm system or natural drain area; the chore of emptying the pond will be much easier. In areas where ponds can freeze solid, remove the pump and store it temporarily in a bucket of water in a basement or other area where it won't freeze. Once a pump has been used, it's important to keep it wet to prevent the seal from drying out and shrinking.

The formal grace of a traditional garden fountain presents the sound of water with classical elegance.

MAKING PLANS

When including a water feature in the construction of a paved patio, plan for the installation of a pair of 2-inch schedule-40 PVC pipes across the patio site. Draw them in your plans so they run like tunnels under the paving—from one end of the patio to the other. These pipes—called sleeves—will provide a route for electrical wires and smaller pipes connected to a water source. They also protect wires and pipes from the pressure of paving, especially if it settles and shifts. If a water line or wire breaks, you can replace it without digging up the patio by snaking the replacement through the sleeve. Any water leaking from a break flows through the conduit and out the ends beyond the paving instead of seeping directly into the soil under the paving and weakening it. Always run power and water lines through separate sleeves.

CONSTRUCTING A POND

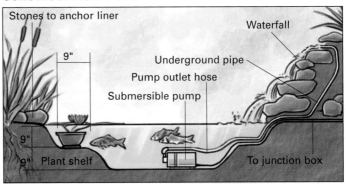

Create an enticing sense of discovery for your outdoor living space by installing a water feature in a far corner. That way you'll hear it before you see it. The sound of the water will lure you and your guests into the space.

The sound of splashing water can soothe and cheer you. Moving water also muffles the noise of air-conditioners, traffic, and other annoying neighborhood sounds.

WATER FEATURES
continued

Pedestal fountains draw attention to their form, not just their sound. Most suit small spaces beautifully.

Look for a fountain that reflects your home's style. The wall-mounted fountain in this courtyard splashes gently into an elegant reflecting pool.

FOUNTAINS

Wall-mounted fountains catch trickling water in prefabricated basins. Because their weight is borne by a wall, not the floor, you can put them virtually anywhere. And because the walls on which they are mounted shelter these modest-size features, overspray rarely causes problems.

Wall-mounted fountains require a power source to run the pump that recirculates the water. Have an electrician install an outlet on an exterior wall of your house so you won't have to disturb the existing flooring.

Running a pump without adequate water will damage the pump, so whether yours is wall-mounted or freestanding, you'll need to regularly replenish its water in a fountain during hot, dry weather, when evaporation occurs. Simply pour water into the basin of the fountain.

Supply large water features with a source of water that's controlled by a float valve. The float valve automatically monitors water levels so the pool is always full. It turns on the water when levels fall below a preset mark and shuts it off when the fountain is refilled. Installing one slightly raises the cost of the fountain, and you might need to hire a plumber to do the work.

FINE-TUNING

It takes only a moderate volume of moving water to mask unpleasant sounds such as traffic. Just a small trickle or drip will buffer noise from the outside world. If you have to shout to be heard over your waterfall or fountain, too much water is moving through it too quickly. Adjust the flow valve on the pump to reduce the flow and soften the sound.

This simple bamboo pipe connects to a hidden water source; a recirculating pump moves the overflow back to the source. The pattern of stones in this shallow pond is a feature of Japanese-style fountains.

WATER FEATURE SAFETY

All pumps require electricity—but mixing water and electricity is dangerous. For that reason, you should only plug pumps into waterproof exterior outlets that connect to a power source with a ground fault circuit interrupter (GFCI). The GFCI helps prevent electrical accidents.

Most building codes classify water features in a special category called "attractive nuisances." That means you'll be held responsible if anyone falls into your pool or pond. Rules regarding attractive nuisances vary locally, so check with the building inspector in your city or county to see whether you need to include a fence in your plans.

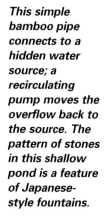

STORAGE

Anything you plan to keep on your patio—garbage cans, firewood, furniture covers, pet supplies, garden tools, or barbecue utensils—needs a spot to call home. Finding places to put such items—and keeping the living space from looking like a giant storage box—takes a little creative thinking.

NIFTY STORAGE PLACES

■ When adding a privacy wall, build it with space for firewood.

■ Paint a child's toy box with weatherproof exterior paint and use it as an outdoor coffee table with built-in storage.

■ Keep pet supplies and birdseed in watertight plastic bins, which protect them from weather and pesky critters looking for food.

■ Buy an extra mailbox or decorative bin to provide a dry place for storing small hand tools and garden gloves.

■ Place a baker's rack against a blank wall to store empty flowerpots, harvest baskets, and watering cans.

■ Use everyday yard tools as outdoor art. Mount hooks or handle holders on walls for hanging shovels, rakes, and hoes. The back or side of a garage, where the roof overhangs, provides a protected place. If you have a wall but no eaves, mount a shallow awning overhead to shelter the tools from weather and help prevent rusting.

■ Buy freestanding benches with lids, or build them into the perimeter of your patio.

■ Prefabricated fence sections or lattice panels mounted on posts conceal garbage cans as well as heating and cooling units without obstructing airflow.

■ Mount a trellis to support vines on the side of your home to hide exterior conduit and wires. If a utility meter spoils the look of your outdoor room, build a box around it with a hinged door for the meter reader to open. (Contact your utility company first; some have rules against this.)

This brick patio hides garbage cans behind a lacy, lattice-topped fence. Latched doors provide access.

If your home has deep eaves, consider hanging a cupboard from them. This one holds yard tools off the ground, away from water damage.

Garbage cans and yard tools can be close at hand without spoiling the view. This stone wall and wooden gate blend in handsomely with the adjacent patio. Screen out utility areas or other unsightly elements by planting shrubs or erecting fences, trellises, or walls.

ASSESSING THE SITE

Behold the vast wilderness of your yard! Numerous limitations and countless possibilities lie there. You'll want to know exactly what these are before you begin building your patio.

The features of your landscape can affect both where you put your patio and how you design it. Now is the time to assess your site to determine any modifications it will require.

Terrain is perhaps the most important feature. Although no site is perfectly level, a flat yard will keep your job uncomplicated. A slope, especially one that falls off sharply, might call for grading the soil and installing a retaining wall to hold back the remaining soil. A steep slope might mean locating your planned patio to another spot.

Drainage, existing vegetation, views, and climate should be considered. After a rain, is there a newly carved canyon or a sparkling lake now marking your lawn? Are your trees providing shade or just blocking a view. Or is the view undesirable anyway? How about street noise and privacy?

Many of these features, of course, are beyond your control, but ignoring them can result in an unused and unattractive patio. If you design your outdoor living space with them in mind, you can minimize their effects. The key is working with nature and not against it.

ON-SITE PHOTOS

Take photos of your yard when assessing your site. The camera is less forgiving than your eye. Because it's easy for you to overlook things you see everyday, you'll be surprised how much the photos call attention to details you may have missed.

Perhaps you forgot that the neighbors can see right into your window. Or you may not have noticed how unattractive your shed is. Photos allow you to bring landscaping problems indoors to your kitchen table.

The photo, left, shows a sideyard with a significant slope. Sketching on the photo with a marker—or using a digital photo and computer software—can help you envision what a terraced patio might look like here.

This patio was designed with the site's elements in mind. Its placement takes advantage of the shade cast by existing trees. A lattice fence helps define the edge of the yard, providing privacy without blocking the breeze. The colorful table umbrella supplements the natural shade and acts as an overhead structure in miniature. Finally, the curved brick wall follows the contour of the gentle slope, containing the soil and providing space for a well-defined planting bed.

CLIMATES AND MICROCLIMATES

Your patio should offer more than privacy, protection, and plenty of seating. It should take advantage of the natural surroundings, such as cooling breezes, warm sun, shade, and subtle garden fragrances. Paying attention to weather patterns and designing your patio for maximum comfort in a range of conditions can extend its usefulness.

SUN AND SHADE

As the sun travels overhead throughout the day and year, it casts varying amounts of warmth and light. Shadows cast by trees, walls, and rooflines will also shift with the

If you can't find the perfect patio spot that offers both sunlight and shade, create separate areas for each. As shown here, an open table and chair and a covered lounge chair would allow you to sit in the sun on cool days or to recline in a shady spot when it's hot.

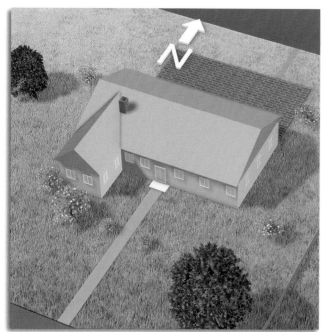

Most north-side locations will be in almost constant shade and will probably be cool on all but the hottest days. If you're planning a north-side patio, you may want to build it some distance from the house or large enough to reach beyond the shadow line of the house. That would provide both shady and sunny areas in the summer. This site would work well in a climate that is hot year-round.

Southern sites get sun all day and may need added shade from trees or an overhead structure. Although the south side of the house receives sun most of the day, it does so from different angles, depending on the season. The summer sun arcs high in the sky, but a winter sun arcs low. A south-facing patio with a lattice-covered pergola would have filtered sun in summer and full sun in winter. Outdoor space on the south side will have the best chance of getting winter sun in mild-winter climates.

sun. Place your patio so this natural effect corresponds to the times of the day and the seasons when you'll use it.

Take an inventory of how much sun and shade your yard receives during the day, especially during the warm months. Keep track of shifting shade patterns with stakes driven in the ground. Note the patterns on paper and refer to it when you begin to draw your plans.

If your proposed site is already shaded during the times you'll use the patio, then locating it is not a problem. However, if you are limited on where your patio can go and shade is what you desire, these tips can help you find shelter from the sun:

■ Trees and other plants can shade a site that gets too much afternoon sun.

■ A pergola helps filter hot sunlight as can a roll-out awning, which can also be retracted when it's not needed.

■ Let roses or vines climb an arbor to create a private shaded spot that doesn't block cooling summer breezes.

■ Vines climbing up a lattice wall can cool off a site that gets hot in the late afternoon.

■ Or you could find a location that features both partial shade and partial sunlight during the hours of greatest patio use.

OFF THE AXIS

Many homes are not situated on a true north–south, east–west axis, and a patio on such sites will get a mixture of sun and shade patterns. For example, a patio on the southeast side of a house will get sun much of the day, but escapes the hot late-afternoon sun.

To get an idea of how your site will be affected, make a rough sketch of your home and experiment with different patio locations, shading in the shadow patterns illustrated on these pages.

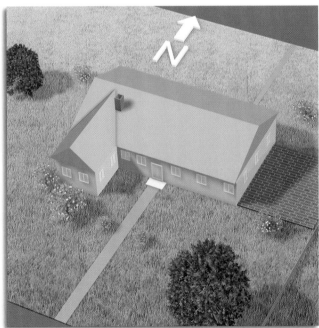

For breakfast in the early light or a cool spot for evening meals, an east-facing patio is ideal. The eastern sun warms the cool morning air, but an east-side site will also be shaded sooner than any other location. For example, by 5 p.m., an east side-location will be shaded for several feet. By 7:30 p.m., even in the summer, it will be engulfed in shade. Depending upon your climate, such early shade can be an asset to your patio or restrict its hours of use.

A west-facing patio will get the hot afternoon sun and, without natural or added shade, may become unbearably hot in the afternoon. The west side starts the day in shade, but gets the hot sun from early afternoon until sunset. Of course, patio surfaces will radiate heat long after dusk. To create a patio site that's enjoyable from early afternoon to evening, you may want to consider a wraparound style that takes advantage of both western and northern exposures.

CLIMATES AND MICROCLIMATES
continued

An evergreen hedge helps deflect the wind from this patio. The tall trees behind it form a larger windbreak.

Although this fence, built for privacy and to reduce prevailing winds, is tall, its latticework admits sunlight, controls the view, and tames the winds into gentle breezes.

WIND

The wind will affect your outdoor comfort as much as the sun. A pleasant breeze may bring welcome relief on a hot day, but gusting winds can make it impossible to enjoy the space.

Study the wind patterns in your yard and learn to make a distinction between prevailing winds (the general direction of wind currents) and seasonal breezes (those localized to a time of day or season).

If possible, locate your patio in a spot that's sheltered from the effect of strong prevailing winds. If your site is exposed, a slatted fence or windbreak (trees and hedges) can transform a strong wind into a breeze that flows across your patio, cooling and freshening the air.

RAIN AND SNOW

You can't stop the rain, but you can build yourself some shelter. A solid roof over part of your patio can keep you dry outdoors in rainy weather. So can a gazebo or retractable awning.

If you live in an area with strong winters, construct overhead roofs so they won't be vulnerable to snow buildup or ice dams. And be sure to retract the awning before the first snow. Rain will also affect the relationship of your patio surface to the indoor floor. Build your patio about an inch lower than the floor inside to keep rain from seeping in.

In snowy climates, you'll want to keep the snow from becoming an uninvited guest in your family room or kitchen. Build the patio 3 or 4 inches below the interior floor. Heavy snowfalls might mean dropping the patio to about 8 inches below the inside room; but you can ease this drop with an outdoor landing.

CREATING A MICROCLIMATE

Did you ever notice that the air on a patio feels a bit different from that a few feet away? That's because the materials that go into a patio create what's called a microclimate.

Different paving materials absorb different amounts of heat and light from the sun each day. For example, a light-colored concrete slab in full sun reflects a lot of heat. Although its surface may remain comfortable, it can reflect harsh, glaring sunlight. On the other hand, a dark brick surface won't reflect the brilliance

TREES, PLANTS, AND MICROCLIMATES

Unless you're building a brand-new house, your choice of patio sites will be affected by your landscape: Your yard will be either hilly or flat, sunny or shaded. And although you have very little control over the terrain, you can moderate temperature extremes around your patio by carefully planting trees and shrubs.

Trees can add welcome shade and break up harsh winds. Deciduous trees—oaks, maples, and walnuts— are quite bushy in the summer but lose their leaves in the winter, shading your patio in the summer and warming it in cooler months. That makes them a practical

investment in areas where the patio is in use most of the year.

No matter where you live, your yard will have prevailing winds— most often coming from different directions in the summer and winter. Plant to take advantage of the wind. In summer, you'll want to channel the wind toward the patio; in winter you'll want to block it.

As you design your site, minimize the variety of trees and bushes to unify the design, and don't plant deep-rooted trees or bushes too near the house or patio; their roots can undermine the foundation and patio surface.

of sunlight but will absorb a tremendous amount of heat. This can make the patio uncomfortable underfoot during the day, but the stored heat radiates during the cool of the evening, prolonging the daytime warmth.

Likewise, a hilltop patio will feel warmer on a calm day than one at the base of a hill because cooler air flows downhill. What's more, if you trap the cold air at the bottom of a hill with a retaining wall, a fence, or a house wall, you might make your patio quite cool in the evening.

The construction of a wall or fence can also create a microclimate. Don't expect a solid structure to help reduce winds. Wind-control research shows that solid fences create low-pressure pockets that pull the wind down into the very area you want protected. The wind swirls over the top and drops back down at a distance roughly equal to the height of the fence.

This means that if your quiet site is "protected" by a solid 6-foot wall, the force of the wind on your patio at about 12 feet from the wall is roughly the same as on the other side. Build louvered fences or walls with open areas on top to filter the wind; let the wind through instead of causing it to vault over the top and come down with a vengeance.

COOL AIR MOVES DOWNHILL

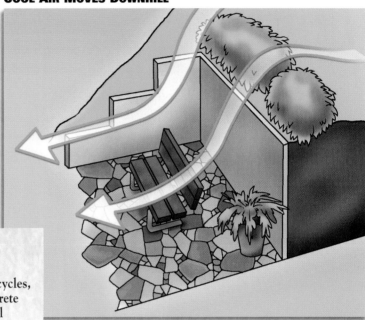

Because cool air is heavier than warm air, it will flow downhill, making a patio site at the bottom of a slope cooler than one situated on higher ground.

FROST AND FOUNDATIONS

In climates that experience frequent freeze-thaw cycles, a mortared patio will require excavation and concrete footings. Without this extra support, the frost will heave the soil and crack the patio surface.

SUN AND HEAT REFLECTS DURING THE DAY

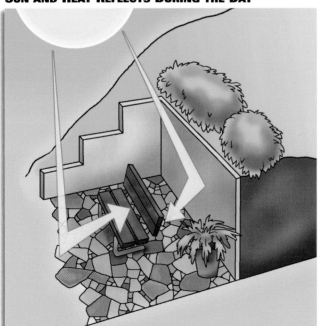

Walls and patio surfaces constructed of light-color materials will reflect both light and heat, making an otherwise pleasant site uncomfortable.

ABSORBED HEAT RELEASES AT NIGHT

Dark materials absorb light and heat, which can make their surfaces uncomfortable during the day. These same materials, however, will release some of the stored energy at night and can help extend the use of your patio into the evening hours.

SLOPE, SOIL, AND DRAINAGE

Not all slopes require retaining walls. A gentle slope with good soil can be kept in place with groundcovers and other plantings.

Sloping sites, such as hillsides, banks, ravines, and drainage swales, often pose a problem, but they may offer more opportunities than you think. If you ignored a slope when developing your design concept, take a second look.

Land sloping away from a high spot offers a view to the area below. Land that slants uphill generally creates privacy and shelter from harsh winds. A seemingly problematic area might turn out to be the best spot in your yard for a new patio. Where there's a slope, there's usually a way to grade it level.

LEVELING THE SOIL

To level a slope, cut into its side to remove soil and form a flat plateau, or fill in a low point, or do both.

Both methods will create a level surface suitable for your patio, but fill dirt is not stable and will settle unevenly, causing your patio to crack. You'll need to tamp and firm the loose surface of a filled area before paving

it. If you plan a paving project that requires more than 6 inches of fill, consider spanning the slope with a deck instead.

If soil sloughs off when you cut into a slope, you should build a retaining wall to hold it in place. Even if a retaining wall isn't necessary, building one will give you a cozy patio nestled into a hillside.

TYPES OF SOIL

All soil is not created equal. There are several kinds of soil, and each will have a different affect on your site and how you prepare it.
■ Loose, sandy loam absorbs water and drains well, is good for plantings, and is easy to grade. It erodes easily, however, and does not compact well. If you want a fence with your patio, set the fenceposts in concrete.
■ Silted soil is easy to dig and to compact, but posts for overheads and fences will need to be set in concrete.
■ Clay is compact and sheds water so easily that runoff can prove to be a problem. Fix it

Cutting into a slope created a level area for this snug patio. The brick retaining wall supports the hillside and creates an attractive, well-designed boundary for the patio space.

WHAT TO DO WITH EXCESS FILL DIRT

Put the soil removed from grading to the best use by filling in the area of your patio (but be sure to tamp it once it's laid). Or use the dirt to level other parts of your lawn. This procedure is called cut and fill and works best when grading removes an amount equal to the areas that need additional soil. Cut and fill also eliminates the expenses of disposing of excess soil, as well as the cost of purchasing fill dirt.

If cutting into a hillside results in more fill than you need, use the excess soil in your planting beds. Not all of the excavated dirt will be suitable for planting beds. Use it to construct berms, low mounds in a landscape. But don't spread soil around trees, even temporarily. Just a few extra inches over tree roots can suffocate delicate feeder roots and kill the tree.

with grading or with drains that terminate in storm sewers or catch basins.

Each type of soil has a different angle of repose, the steepest angle at which it will stay in place. In general, soils with a high clay content have a steeper angle of repose than loose, sandy soils, which readily give way.

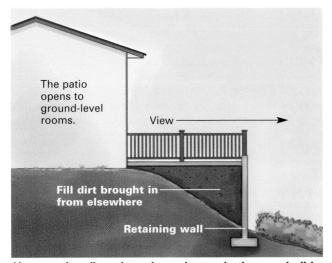

How you handle a slope depends on whether you build the patio above or below it. Above a slope (above), a patio will require additional fill dirt, compacted and held in place with a retaining wall.

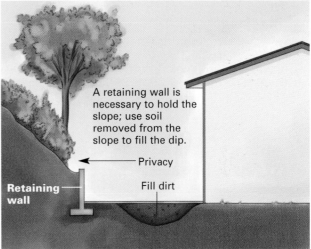

Below a slope (above), a patio will often require cutting into the soil and keeping the remaining dirt in place with a retaining wall. Be sure to plan for adequate drainage.

TIPS FOR RETAINING WALLS

Include weep holes in the design of your retaining walls so groundwater behind the wall can seep through its face. When the water has a place to go, it won't build up pressure behind the wall and crack or topple it.

In general a wall footing should be twice as wide as the wall, but if your soil is sandy or loose, consult a professional to help you calculate the size of footings.

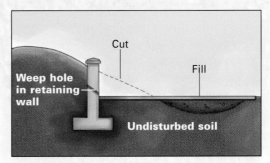

SLOPE, SOIL, AND DRAINAGE
continued

GRADING FOR DRAINAGE

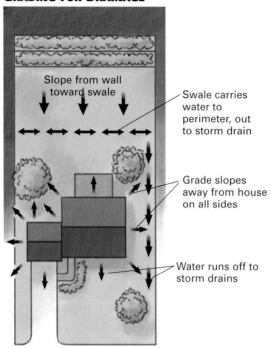

Slope from wall toward swale

Swale carries water to perimeter, out to storm drain

Grade slopes away from house on all sides

Water runs off to storm drains

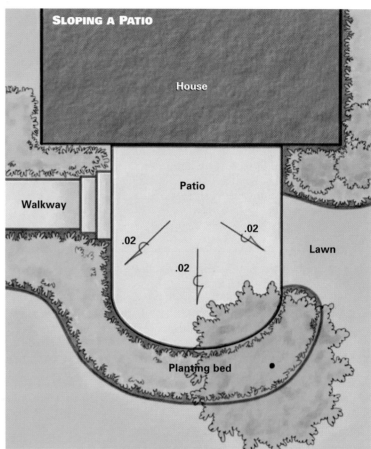

SLOPING A PATIO

House

Patio

Walkway

.02   .02

.02

Lawn

Planting bed

Sloping a patio toward its edges eliminates the need for a drain in the center of the paving. Never slope a patio toward your home. A 2-percent slope (1 inch of slope for every 4 feet of patio surface) away from the house will move runoff across most paving.

DRAINAGE

Improper drainage can damage hardscape and plantings. It can cause concrete surfaces to become slick with mud, wash out flower beds, seep into basements, and crack foundations. Where will the runoff go? You need to answer that question before beginning any grading. Fortunately, you can rescue almost any area in your yard from the threat of bad drainage.

POSITIVE DRAINAGE: Paved surfaces should slope slightly away from foundations and toward lower ground. Slope patio and concrete surfaces toward their edges, so water doesn't puddle on the patio. A slope of just 2 percent is adequate to move runoff. That's about 1 inch every 4 feet.

SWALES: You can intercept water and direct it around objects with these gentle surface ditches. A swale must slope continuously and

FOUNDATION DRAINAGE

If you have water in your basement, it may be caused by ground sloping toward the foundation. Here's an easy solution. Slope the soil next to the foundation away from the house for a distance of 1 inch for every 4 feet. Bring in new soil as necessary. Lay landscape fabric over the slope. If you're going to plant the area, cut holes in the plastic for the plants. Decorative rock or wood chips will camouflage the plastic.

Use a trench drain to catch and redirect water that would otherwise collect where horizontal and vertical hard surfaces meet, such as these stone steps.

BUILDING A FRENCH DRAIN

If you plan to use a planting bed to border your patio, install a French drain to carry excess water away.

A French drain is a fancy name for a 1-foot trench filled with gravel and containing a perforated drain pipe to eliminate areas of standing water. You can leave the gravel exposed at the surface or cover it with sod.

Most often the course of the trench runs parallel to an edge of the patio and terminates at an inconspicuous spot where the drain can emerge at the soil surface. The end of the trench next to the patio needs to be higher than its terminal point.

The gravel allows water to come off the patio and enter the drain pipe. Landscape fabric over the pipe keeps soil from washing into it and clogging it up. You can

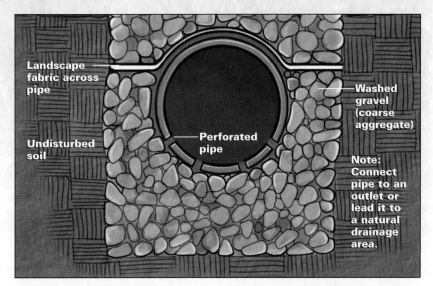

Landscape fabric across pipe

Undisturbed soil

Perforated pipe

Washed gravel (coarse aggregate)

Note: Connect pipe to an outlet or lead it to a natural drainage area.

also buy sock-wrapped drainage pipe, which will eliminate the landscape fabric, but you'll notice a substantial difference in the price.

When it rains, water running across the area of the drain seeps through the gravel. As it fills the trench, water will enter the pipe through the holes and flow away.

can be tiled or planted with grass. Water from a swale should empty on an open lawn—but never into the neighbor's yard. It is usually illegal and certainly inconsiderate to divert water so it flows onto adjacent properties.

FRENCH AND CURTAIN DRAINS: Easy to install, these are trenches with perforated pipe set in gravel to carry water away from structures or low spots (see above).

DRY WELLS: These gravel-filled holes serve as outlets for water from other trenches.

Typically 2 to 4 feet wide and 3 feet deep (check with local codes), they must be placed at least 10 feet from the house and covered with a concrete slab and planted soil. They are especially useful in places where water cannot be diverted to a storm sewer.

CATCH BASINS: These underground receptacles hold water from surface drains and direct it through underground pipes to storm sewers or other outlets. You can purchase precast units at your materials outlet.

DRAINAGE GUIDELINES

Standing water isn't welcome on any patio. It can be unsafe and can damage your handiwork. Misguided runoff from a patio adjacent to your home also can threaten its foundation. Here's a handy checklist to help minimize the damage caused by improper drainage.
■ Slope the patio gently away from the house—build in 1 inch of slope for every 4 feet of patio.

■ If your landscaping includes terraces or retaining walls, provide drainage for these features so water doesn't end up on the patio surface.
■ Plantings at the edges of your patio will absorb and slow runoff.
■ As you plan your landscape, don't create narrow channels anywhere in the lawn. They invite erosion.

Before you start thinking about the specifics of grading and drainage,

take a look at the big picture. Find out about existing grades and drainage patterns. Walk your yard during different times of the year and in different weather conditions. Talk to neighbors, the developer, the previous owner, if possible, and local building department officials.

Shaping the land to its best possible contours is critical to the success of any landscaping project.

SLOPE, SOIL, AND DRAINAGE
continued

RUNOFF AND PLANTS

Runoff from a patio can also wreak havoc with the patio's surroundings. Water moving across impermeable surfaces flows quickly. As it gathers speed and runs off the hardscape, it cuts channels through flower beds, washing away seedlings and topsoil.

Established plants with fibrous roots, such as lawns and ornamental grasses, will probably be able to stand up to this wash of water. But shallow-rooted plants, such as those in recently installed flower beds, will usually wash out of the ground. Runoff flowing into planting areas can also become trapped in puddles, and the overly wet soil drowns plants by suffocating their roots.

You have several options for dealing with excess water.

■ Redirect the water.
■ Plant annuals in raised beds or containers.
■ Choose plants that thrive in wet soil.

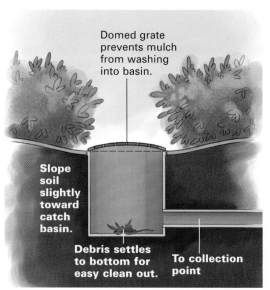

Domed grate prevents mulch from washing into basin.

Slope soil slightly toward catch basin.

Debris settles to bottom for easy clean out.

To collection point

Planting areas surrounded by paving can hold water. Install a catch basin before paving your patio. The basin collect excess water, and an underground pipe transports the water to elsewhere in your yard or a storm sewer.

RETROFITTING FOR DRAINAGE

After heavy rains, water can puddle on improperly drained patios. Perpetually damp spots provide the right conditions for slick moss to grow on walking surfaces and for mosquitoes to breed. Even if you've already built your patio or have inherited it as part of the property

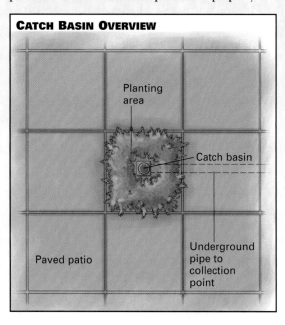

CATCH BASIN OVERVIEW

Planting area

Catch basin

Paved patio

Underground pipe to collection point

purchase, you can still remedy these problems.

To stop puddling, divert water away from low areas. During a heavy rain, observe the water's path. Almost anything—debris, excessive mulch, or a poorly placed plant—can block the flow of water and divert it where you don't want it. If the water originates from beyond the patio, change the direction of flow at its source. For example, relocate downspouts so they won't dump water onto the patio or other paved surfaces. Or install extensions to the downspouts to carry the water elsewhere.

Use curbing to block water that flows onto your patio from the lawn or a planting area. Or divert the flow with a swale, a slight depression made to channel water. When installing a curb to redirect storm water, dig a swale along the back side of it. Often, a shallow swale alone keeps water flowing in the right direction. Just don't build a walkway across a swale—it will form a dam and impede drainage.

Removing unused portions of paving is another solution because it reduces the amount of impermeable surface. Removing a section of paving can also pleasantly alter the shape or your patio and create room for planting within the space. This solution works best if the sections removed aren't part of the patio you use regularly. Be sure to leave enough paving for comfortable walking and sitting.

TREES, ROCKS, AND OTHER OBSTACLES

Many existing features of your landscape, such as flower beds, foundation plantings, fences, walls, and walkways, will affect the location of your patio. If you can't part with these things and are certain of your favorite spot, integrate them into your design. The same goes for trees, rocks, and other obstacles. Incorporating trees into your design, however, calls for some careful planning.

ENCLOSING A TREE: A patio built around a tree can appear as if nature put it there. Its height and mass will balance the horizontal expanse of your patio surface. But take care to avoid damage to the root system. The tree can be the life of your patio. Don't let your patio be the death of the tree.

Construction machinery can crush and tear roots, and a concrete slab can starve a tree of water, nutrients, and oxygen. The major root system of a tree is as broad as the spread of its branches and those roots need to have access to water.

Brick-in-sand patios or dry-laid flagstone patios permit rain to enter and reach the roots. Build an edging of 6×6 timbers around the tree base, well away from any exposed roots. Secure the timbers with 2-foot rebar driven into the soil.

Approach obstacles as if they were opportunities. Work around your trees to make them centerpieces that deliver both welcome shade and relief from the expanse of horizontal surfaces.

Think creatively when confronted with an obstacle such as these boulders. Rather than spend the time and money to remove the rocks, the homeowners incorporated them into the patio wall.

CHOOSING MATERIALS

Perhaps no other aspect of your patio project—with the possible exception of standing back and admiring your completed handiwork—will prove as rewarding as the selection of the materials you will use.

The right choice of materials, more than any other element, will help harmonize your patio with the overall architecture of your property.

You may be surprised—or even overwhelmed at first—at the range of options available in patio materials. If you stay flexible about your design, you can easily discover those that have the unique qualities—the shape, size, color, and texture—that will give your patio the look and feel you want.

SHOPPING FOR MATERIALS

Start your search for materials at their source—brickyards, quarries, cement plants, landscaping centers, and tile retailers. You'll discover a wide range of colors, textures, shapes, prices, durabilities, and installation levels. Seeing the materials first hand will also help you get a better feel for what you like best.

Once you've narrowed your decisions to a few choices, get samples (sometimes they're available for free) and bring them back to your patio site. This will help you visualize how the textures and colors will relate to your house and yard.

The Internet is also a good source for initial materials research. Many manufacturers and retailers now have websites that offer useful reference information about quality, uses, and cost.

**ESTIMATING
MATERIALS** Use these formulas to estimate the amount of materials you'll need, using the same units—inches or feet—for all measurements.

Rectangular solid

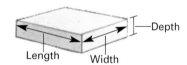

Volume = length × width × depth

Cylindrical solid Radius (½ of diameter)

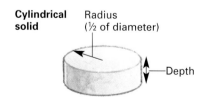

Volume = 3.14 × radius² × depth

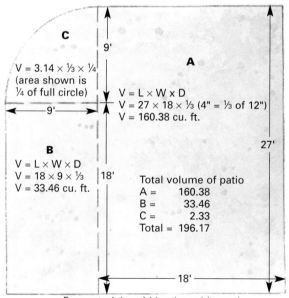

C
V = 3.14 × ⅓ × ¼
(area shown is
¼ of full circle)
9'

9'

A
V = L × W × D
V = 27 × 18 × ⅓ (4" = ⅓ of 12")
V = 160.38 cu. ft.

B
V = L × W × D
V = 18 × 9 × ⅓
V = 33.46 cu. ft.

18'

27'

Total volume of patio
A =   160.38
B =   33.46
C =   2.33
Total = 196.17

18'

For materials sold by the cubic yard, such as concrete, divide total cubic feet by 27.

HIDDEN COSTS

Remember that your patio will include costs not only for the surface materials, but also for the foundation, fillers, and shipping and delivery. Choose the look you want first; then adjust your materials selection if your initial design proves too expensive.

Materials make the difference. The rectangular cut stone (left), with offset corners and varying sizes, serves up a fitting formal contrast to the formality of the house and deck.

Mortared flagstone (below), set in a circular perimeter and with its interior edges selected for matching contours, complements the natural charm of this outdoor space for two.

MATERIAL MAKEOVER

When you want to replace an existing outdoor surface that's in bad shape or add an extension to it, you don't have to stick to the same paving. Such upgrades present opportunities for much latitude in design.

For example, when extending a patio, feel free to use a surface material that varies from the old one—a cut-stone addition to a brick or flagstone patio, for instance. Differences in material, pattern, and color often add character.

An ordinary-looking concrete slab can be a starting point for something new. If it is stable and strong, you can resurface it with tile, flagstone, or cut stone set in a mortar bed (see pages 118-119). You can even break up the surface of the concrete and reset the pieces as cement stepping-stones.

DESIGN PRINCIPLES

Tile and pavers combined with red, gold, and earth tones can be especially warm and inviting. They work well with redwood, shredded bark, and other natural materials.

Each material you pick for your patio has unique characteristics. Make sure your choices meet your design needs and that your skills are equal to the installation requirements.

COLOR

Color does more than establish a link with your home. It helps set the mood. Reds, beiges, rusts, browns, yellows, and oranges generally set a warm tone and complement traditional settings. Blues, grays, or black set cooler tones and work well with contemporary designs. Remember that fillers—mortar, sand, and groundcover—add color, too. So will furniture.

Scale also affects color: Color recedes in small quantities but can be overpowering in large areas.

TEXTURE

Surface textures also impact patio style and function. Glare, temperature, cleanliness, comfort and safety, all are influenced by the texture of the surface.

SMOOTH OR ROUGH: Smooth surfaces are great for dancing and also are less absorbent than rough materials, so they resist stains. However, smooth materials, such as glazed tile, polished stone, smoothly troweled concrete and even wood, become slippery when wet. Polished surfaces can assault you with glare in direct sunlight. The surface variation in natural stone will give your patio a natural or old-fashioned look. Poured concrete offers the flattest, least-varied surface, but even concrete can be textured.

HARD OR SOFT: Brick, tile, and concrete surfaces are hard, but alternatives such as loose gravel, rock beds, wood chips, and bark offer softer, more comfortable options that give way when you walk on them. They provide rustic complement to woodland or informal settings.

LOOKS AREN'T EVERYTHING

Don't choose a material for your patio just because you like the way it looks. Ask questions about how much maintenance it requires, how long it will last, and how suitable it is for your climate. The chart below lists several things you should consider when choosing materials and ranks them on a scale of 1 (least or shortest) to 5 (most or longest).

Material	Cost	Maintenance	Durability
Flagstone			
In sand	2	1	5
Mortared	5	2	5
Brick			
In sand	3	3	4
Mortared	5	1	5
Precast pavers	3	1	5
Concrete			
Natural	2	1	5
Tinted			
Integral	3	1	5
Stained	3	1	5
Stamped	4	1	5
Loose Material	1	4	2
Tile	5	1	5
Wood	3	2	3

SHOULD YOU HIRE A CONTRACTOR?

The explosive growth of the do-it-yourself industry shows that many homeowners can handle all but the most extensive landscape projects. When you're deciding whether to do the work yourself or hire it out, consider these points:

■ **DON'T KID YOURSELF ABOUT SKILLS:** Weigh your skill level and experience against the scope of the project. You can do minor excavating with a posthole digger or shovel. Slabs require heavy equipment. If your carpentry skills are weak, buy precut kits for fences and overheads.

■ **WILL FRIENDS HELP?** Many construction projects require at least two pairs of hands—lifting framing lumber into position on an overhead or pouring and leveling concrete slabs, for example

■ **POWER TOOLS:** Power tools save time. So does proper planning. Buy a power drill/driver if you don't have one. It will be a valuable addition to your tool kit. Rent a reciprocating saw for cutting posts or timbers.

■ **LOGICAL ORDER:** Don't build fences until the major projects are completed, and have materials dropped next to the project. Anything you can do to reduce your labor will make the job more enjoyable.

■ **ADD IT UP:** What will your total cost be? Make sure your materials list is complete and get prices for everything. Add subcontractor bids for any work you will definitely contract, such as excavation or electrical wiring. Include the cost of tools you'll have to buy or rent, as well as waste removal, permits, and inspections. Add these costs together and compare them with a general contractor's bid.

Are the savings large enough to warrant taking the project on? Even if the savings are small, remember that doing it yourself can be an enjoyable and rewarding experience.

CONTRACTOR CONSIDERATIONS

If you've decided to contract all or some of the job, how do you find a contractor? Friends and neighbors are good for references. So are local garden shops. But don't work with any contractor whose references you have not checked.

You may also need to enlist the services of landscape professionals such as:

Landscape architects: They completely design and plan your landscape, producing detailed drawings, plans, and written work descriptions. They will also supervise the construction.

Landscape designers: They will assist you with the design of your project and will provide drawings for your patio's general look. These drawings generally do not include construction details.

Landscape contractors: These builders have particular expertise in landscape construction. Some firms describe themselves as "Designers and Builders" and have professional architects, designers, and builders on staff.

The best way to find a reputable design professional is through the satisfied references of friends and family. Ask at work or parties: Anyone who has a new landscape will be happy to talk about it and the professionals who made it happen.

■ **NARROWING THE FIELD:** Once you've selected your prospective contractors, ask each one for job references; then check them. Visit job sites and inspect the quality of work.

Get several bids, and be wary of any that are significantly higher or lower than average. The bids of reputable contractors bidding for the same work with the same materials should be close.

■ **CONTRACTS:** Get everything in writing—everything. Read the contract carefully, and insert any information that you feel is needed. If you have any uncertainty, have a lawyer review the documents before you sign. The contract should specify the following:
• The work to be done.
• Materials to be used.
• A start date and a completion schedule.
• Procedures for making changes.
• Stipulations that the contractor will obtain building permits and lien waivers.
• Methods for resolving disputes.

■ **OTHER DOCUMENTS:** Often required by local laws, your contractor should provide evidence of the following:
• Licensing: showing government standards to do the work have been met.
• Bonding: evidence that if the contractor fails to perform the work, a bonding company will pay another contractor to finish the job.
• Insurance: liability for nonworkers and compensation for workers injured on the job.

■ **FINAL PAYMENT:** Before you make final payment, obtain signed lien waivers from the contractor for every subcontractor and supplier. You'll avoid liability in case the contractor fails to pay them.

When the job is completed, inspect it carefully. If anything looks questionable, make a note of it. Ask the contractor to do a walk-through with you so you can point out problems; then both of you can see firsthand what needs to be corrected. The contractor should either correct any defects or explain why they really aren't problems.

Many cities provide recourse for resolution of future problems—usually within a year. Check with your local building department. If problems arise, appeal first to the contractors involved; then allow a reasonable time for repairs. If the problem is still not resolved, appeal to the professional associations to which the contractor belongs or consult a lawyer.

COMBINE MATERIALS FOR STYLE

There's no design principle that says you can't put more than one kind of paving material on your patio surface. After all, inside your home, you wouldn't hesitate to use different flooring in different rooms—carpet in the living room, tile in the kitchen. Different interior flooring is appropriate when the use of the space is different.

The same goes for outdoor living space. Using different kinds of paving for the same patio can help you define different areas of use, separating quiet, intimate spaces from entertainment areas. What's more, combining materials does the job with style.

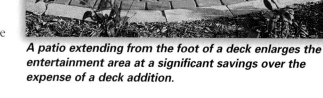

A patio extending from the foot of a deck enlarges the entertainment area at a significant savings over the expense of a deck addition.

This delightful creation is successful by any definition. Its bold mix of tile, brick, and concrete took daring as well as extra installation time. But it continues to reward the homeowners and their guests with its whimsical artistry.

TRANSITIONS: A mosaic of materials creates interest and can help you fit a patio into an odd-shaped lot or ease transitions between different spaces. Don't try to hide the division—a sharp contrast between materials works better than a poorly disguised boundary between them.

DECKING WITH PAVING: Patio and deck combinations work especially well for delineating areas of use. For example, locate amenities that appeal to children on a patio at the foot of the deck. Hang a swing from deck joists and give children a spot to play within sight of adults.

If the deck is slightly higher than the new patio, link the two areas with a few steps.

Build wide, inviting stairs to the deck, removing a section of deck railing, if necessary. Broad steps offer a welcoming transition between deck and patio. Steps that are 12 to 18 inches deep also double as seating during casual gatherings.

BUDGET-STRETCHER

Combining materials saves money. For example, gravel or river rock with pavers forms an attractive surface without breaking the bank. Concrete is a relatively inexpensive construction material. If your first choice is brick but your pocketbook says no, consider pouring a slab and bordering it with bricks. You could also cut a rectangle at the doorway in an existing slab (or leave a space open when you pour the concrete), and fill the space with a brick "rug." This dresses up your patio and makes the entry more dramatic looking. With either combination, you'll save on installation and still enjoy the beauty of brick.

Is your existing deck too small but you can't afford to enlarge it? Extend it with a patio. Paving offers a more affordable solution than decking, especially if you do the work yourself.

ENLARGING A PATIO

Deck and paving combinations also let you enlarge a patio on a difficult site. Decking swiftly spans slopes and rough or poorly drained terrain, making it a better choice than paving when such sites are the only ones available when you want to expand your patio. Combining new decking with old paving also keeps you from having to blend aged paving with the look of new construction.

When expanding either surface, select at least one that's already in use in your yard. Then, instead of looking like an afterthought, the new material will complement your home and landscape, and the new outdoor living space will seem to belong there.

Trim parts of the addition—borders, planters, entries, or conversation areas—with small insets of specialty material that resemble your old patio to help blend the old and new. If you can't match older paving, consider adding on with something completely different.

A mosaic of materials creates interest on a rejuvenated concrete surface. The subtle colors of masonry seldom clash, lending themselves to more creative design than you might think. Here, flagstone and brick—splashed with random pink pavers—provide an appealing patchwork that dramatically alters the drab expanse of an existing concrete slab.

CREATE A CASUAL COMBINATION

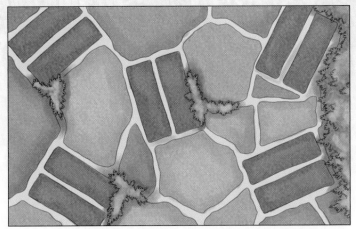

Combine brick, stone, and creeping groundcovers to build an inexpensive patio. Even when brand-new, the patio will have a been-there-forever appearance that's just right for cottage gardens or a casual outdoor style.

First, set pairs of bricks at random on a level base of crushed rock or sand. Old, worn bricks provide a rustic look; new bricks look more contemporary. Also set bricks at the edge of the patio.

Next, fill in between the bricks with flat stone. If the bricks are thicker than the stone (or vice versa), excavate under each thick piece so the patio surface is flush. Choose stones carefully for a tight fit. Because bricks are rectangular and stones are not, some gaps will result. Fill gaps with topsoil, and tuck in creeping groundcovers or herbs. Creeping phlox, Corsican mint, woolly thyme, and golden oregano are good choices.

Flagstone set in a bed of low groundcover adds a bit of patio space to the decking in this confined backyard.

BRICK

The bricks in this expansive patio complement the clapboard siding, cedar shakes, and rough stone wall. Traditional materials often are used to blend with an older home, but brick works well in contemporary designs, too.

If you're looking for a warm, earthy material that lends an old-world formality to your patio, brick is the perfect choice.

Most distributors stock a wide variety of sizes, colors, styles, and densities. And if you purchase a modular style—one with dimensions that are proportional—design becomes virtually goof-proof.

When shopping for patio materials, avoid common brick, face brick, and firebrick. These varieties are made for purposes other than paving. The following types are good choices.

■ Paving brick resists moisture and wear. Some types have rounded or chamfered edges, a feature which makes sand installation easier.

■ Brick salvaged from old buildings or streets may come with the mortar left on, which many designers feel adds to the charm of a cottage-style patio.

Depending on its original use, used brick may be softer than paving brick and may not wear as well. Many homeowners find that its worn appearance enhances its rustic look. You can approximate a used-brick look with manufactured salvage brick.

■ Adobe pavers, impregnated with asphalt, resist water almost as well as clay brick. They are not fired at high temperatures, however, so they won't stand up to hard use. Install them in sand in dry, nonfreezing climates.

ADVANTAGES

Brick has a range of appealing qualities, including durability, variety of color and texture, and adaptability.

■ Hardness: Brick is graded for hardness. The SX grade withstands the most severe weather conditions and costs more. If you live in northern climates, the extra cost may be worthwhile. In milder climates, the MX grade holds up to light frosts. Your supplier will be able to guide you in your selection.

■ Color: Colors range from white and light yellow to reds and dark browns.

■ Texture: Paving is slightly rough, but the

BUYING BRICK

■ Purchase brick from brickyards, lumberyards, or garden and home centers. Most suppliers will deliver for a small fee.

■ Some specialty-brick suppliers maintain websites.

■ Brick is sold individually or by the square yard. Order on pallets to reduce breakage.

■ Prices vary considerably with size, type, and color.

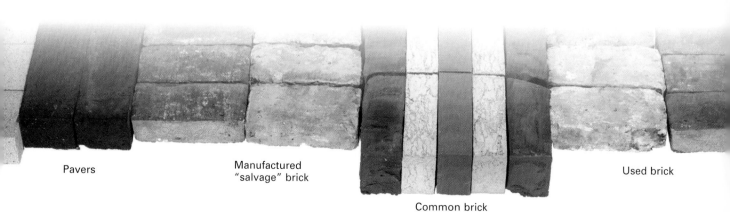

Pavers

Manufactured "salvage" brick

Common brick

Used brick

effect of texture depends more on the pattern and installation method than on the brick.

■ Siting: Most common in formal landscapes, brick can be cut and laid in gentle or dramatic shapes. Its modular dimensions fit almost any design.

■ Modular bricks are easy to lay in sand, requiring only basic skills and a little time. Mortared patios are more difficult.

■ Brick conforms to minor terrain variations.

■ It fits an array of designs, mixes well with other materials and is excellent for edging.

■ Mortared walkways need virtually no maintenance.

■ New pavers stand up to hard use.

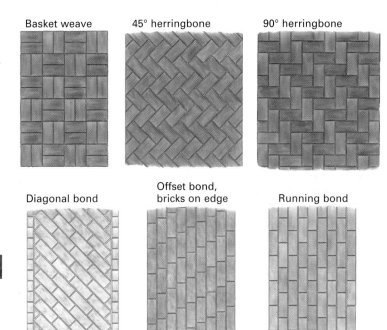

Basket weave   45° herringbone   90° herringbone

Diagonal bond   Offset bond, bricks on edge   Running bond

DISADVANTAGES

■ Salvaged brick may crack in winter and gradually crumble.

■ It can become a haven for moss.

■ Smooth brick surfaces get slick when wet, a danger on even moderate slopes.

■ Brick set in sand may require periodic weeding, resetting, and leveling.

■ Most brick will stand up to weather if properly bedded, but some porous brick may absorb water and crack when it freezes.

ESTIMATING QUANTITIES

■ Determine the area of your patio in square feet.

■ Multiply the area by 5. (About five standard 2×4×8-inch bricks cover 1 square foot.) Order 5 to 10 percent extra to allow for cutting and breakage. For other brick sizes, divide the path area by the face area of one brick.

HOW TO INSTALL BRICK

■ Remove existing sod and excavate. Install edging and landscape fabric. Pour and level base. Install paving. Mortared installations require a concrete slab and a mortar bed. (See installation instructions on pages 118–119.)

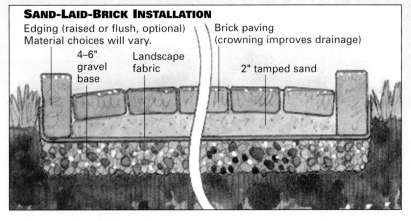

SAND-LAID-BRICK INSTALLATION

Edging (raised or flush, optional)
Material choices will vary.

Brick paving
(crowning improves drainage)

4–6" gravel base

Landscape fabric

2" tamped sand

DESIGN TIPS

Add interest to your brick design with alternating colors. Slight contrasts, a red-brown interspersed with dark red bricks, for example, look more pleasing than sharply contrasting colors. Bricks set on edge offer unusual design possibilities, but the smaller-edge surface will require more bricks and a larger budget.

Consider safety, too, when shopping for brick. Avoid material with slick surfaces.

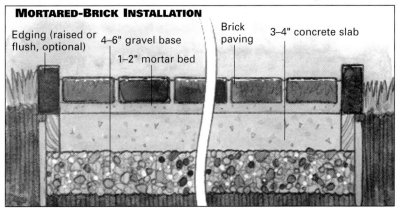

MORTARED-BRICK INSTALLATION

Edging (raised or flush, optional)

4–6" gravel base

1–2" mortar bed

Brick paving

3–4" concrete slab

FLAGSTONE

By using fewer and larger flagstones, the owner of this patio created a bit of drama in an unassuming corner of the yard. The size, color, and layout of the stone make the small patio inviting and attractive.

The general term flagstone refers to rock fractured or cleft into flat slabs two or more inches thick and used for paving. Flagstone most commonly used for patios includes bluestone, limestone, redstone, sandstone, granite, and slate. Its irregular shapes make it ideal, both free-form and geometric patterns—in an individual stepping-stone pattern or in stone-surfaces set in sand or installed over concrete with mortar.

CUT STONE

Cut stone originates from the same natural rock as flagstone. The difference between the two is in their shapes. Flagstone edges are natural and irregular. Cut stone is uniform, with straight edges and square corners. Cut-stone pieces range in size from about 1 foot to 4 feet and come in different thicknesses. Get paving at least 2 inches thick to avoid breakage under traffic.

Cut stone lends itself to the same kind of installation as flagstone—as stepping-stone or stone-carpet surfaces in soil, in sand, or mortared to concrete.

DESIGN CONSIDERATIONS

■ Color and texture: Flagstone offers an array of colors and textures. Colors range from blue-gray (bluestone) to various hues of tans and reds (limestone, granite, redstone, and sandstone), and deep, sometimes slightly iridescent black (slate). Textures vary from generally smooth to moderately rough.

■ Siting: Adaptable to both formal and informal styles; the final effect depends on the contours of the patio. Stepping-stone patios almost always look casual. Sand-laid and mortared installations can enhance both informal and formal styles, depending on their contours.

■ Random shapes and varied surface contours bring a sense of rough-hewn permanence to the landscape.

ADVANTAGES

■ Dry-set patios are among the easiest of hard-surface materials to install and require no specialized skills. Mortared surfaces are more difficult.

■ Flagstone conforms moderately well to minor variations in terrain, working well on gentle slopes.

■ It adapts to an unlimited number of design variations.

■ Properly prepared, a flagstone patio is not subject to heaving in freeze-thaw cycles and is virtually permanent.

Slate

Limestone

Marble

Sandstone

Granite

Bluestone

DESIGN TIPS

To increase the formality of a design, keep straight edges to the outside of the patio or use geometric edging, such as brick. Use large stones to pave large expanses of landscape, smaller units in smaller yards.

Lay out the general patio contour on paper and then carry the plans to the landscape to verify the practicality and aesthetics of your design. Unlike designing materials with shapes that are regular, design your flagstone patio on-site, laying the stones in a pleasing arrangement and experimenting with patterns at the side of the excavation.

■ Most varieties will stand up to hard use, continuous traffic, and wheeled garden equipment.

DISADVANTAGES

■ Large stones can be heavy and thus difficult to move and place.
■ A well-laid design will take time, especially if you're planning a stone surface set in sand or over concrete. Stepping-stone layouts require less precision.
■ Flagstone is more costly than loose stone.
■ It has pores that can collect water and become slick when frozen. Slate is slick when wet.
■ Sandstones wear with use.
■ Stepping-stone surfaces may require periodic

BUYING FLAGSTONE

■ Flagstone is generally sold by the ton or square yard.
■ Garden and home centers, landscape outlets, and building-supply retailers may carry individual pieces for small projects.
■ A bulk purchase from a local quarry or stone yard will save you money on a large project. Order bulk on pallets to reduce breakage. Hand-picking your stone increases costs considerably.
■ Prices vary with the size and type of stone. Stone native to your area will cost less.

weeding, resetting, and leveling. Sand-laid stone may need resetting from time to time. Mortared walks need little maintenance.
■ Climate conditions have little effect on most flagstone varieties—they endure the harshest of conditions. Some porous rock, like sandstone, may absorb water and crack in freezing temperatures.

INSTALLATION

■ Determine the square footage of your patio. Your supplier will convert this measurement to tonnage, if necessary. One ton covers about 120 square feet.
■ Remove sod and then excavate consistent with drainage needs and material thickness. Install edging (optional) and landscape fabric; pour and level base and sand bed. Lay out the trial pattern; install paving. Mortared installations require pouring a concrete slab and laying a mortar bed. (See illustrations and installation instructions on pages 120–125.)
■ Large stone will cover a surface more quickly than smaller stone but may prove harder to move, cut, and design.

SAND-LAID-FLAGSTONE INSTALLATION

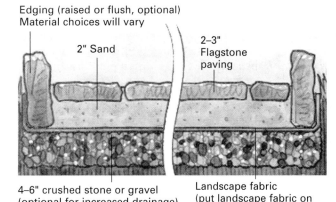

Edging (raised or flush, optional)
Material choices will vary

2" Sand

2–3" Flagstone paving

4–6" crushed stone or gravel (optional for increased drainage)

Landscape fabric (put landscape fabric on top of gravel if not using crushed-stone base)

MORTARED-FLAGSTONE INSTALLATION

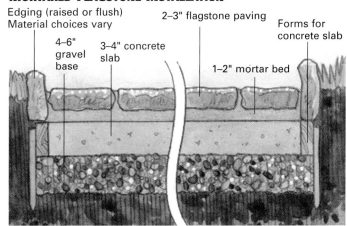

Edging (raised or flush) Material choices vary

2–3" flagstone paving

Forms for concrete slab

4–6" gravel base

3–4" concrete slab

1–2" mortar bed

CONCRETE PAVERS

Using only three shapes specifically designed for this purpose, the concrete pavers in this patio form an elegant circle. Notice the crown in the surface that tapers down from the center of the patio to its perimeter, allowing for quick drainage in all directions.

Concrete pavers resemble brick in their versatility and installation. Once made only as gray squares, they are now manufactured in various shapes and colors. In fact, rectangular pavers have taken a back seat in design to other shapes—circles, chamfered squares, diamonds, hexagons, octagons, crescents, and more.

Unlike brick, which is made of fired clay, concrete pavers are manufactured from dense, pressure-formed, cast concrete.

SIZES, SHAPES, AND TYPES

Concrete pavers are as durable as brick but lighter in weight and less costly. Many are thinner, too, running from 1½ inches to 2½ inches (the size of a brick) and larger. You'll find large rectangles measuring about 4×6, (and up to about 9 inches), geometrics about 2×4, and keyed varieties that you can lay in circles and fans.

Concrete pavers come in different categories, based on method of installation.

■ **Interlocking pavers** resist lateral movement because their sides—contoured, numbering more than four, S-shaped, or crescent-shaped—fit together and keep the units stable. They stay in place even under heavy use and dramatic weather changes. Manufactured corners and end pieces finish off the edges and don't need cutting.

■ **Standard pavers** are rectangular and not as stable as the interlocking variety. They may

SKIN DEEP

Look carefully at the depth of the color, and avoid pavers with shallow color. Colors applied to the surface only can wear off quickly, exposing bare concrete. Buy pavers that have pigment impregnated throughout their thickness.

DESIGN TIPS

Because of their regularity, many concrete pavers look best in formal design schemes. The paver itself creates the pattern.

Pay close attention to scale when you make your dimensioned plan. A small paver can make any patio look busy. Large pavers take less time to set because each unit covers more area, but their size can overwhelm your installation.

In the planning stages, if you sense that your design will end up looking too busy, enlarge the size of the paver or consider setting it with wider spacing. Planting groundcovers in the gaps can minimize the busy look.

BUYING PRECAST PAVERS

Building-supply centers, concrete suppliers, landscape centers, and home and garden centers sell concrete pavers individually, by the square foot, or in banded cubes (enough for about 16 linear feet).

MAKE YOUR OWN

You can make your own pavers with premixed concrete and homemade or commercial forms. Making them yourself might limit you to rectangular shapes. Commercial forms, available at garden and home centers, come in a wide variety of shapes and sizes.

shift over time, especially if your patio gets hard use or is set in poorly draining soil.

■ **Turf blocks** have an open design with holes designed for planting. They are even strong enough to be used in driveways. All varieties of turf blocks are weatherproof and extremely durable.

DESIGN CONSIDERATIONS

■ **Color and texture:** Colors come in a narrow range, typically reminiscent of brick—reds, browns, and earth tones—but also in black, grays, and off-whites. Textures also abound, from smooth to stamped to aggregate surfaces. Some pavers look remarkably like brick, stone, adobe, marble, or cobblestone.

■ **Siting:** Pavers are adaptable to both formal and informal styles. Although the regularity of their shapes tends to suit this material to formal designs, the final effect depends on the contours of the patio.

ADVANTAGES AND DISADVANTAGES

■ Pavers are modular and easy to lay in sand, requiring only basic skills and a little time. Mortared pavers are less common because pavers are manufactured for dry-set installations.

■ They conform well to minor terrain variations.

■ They fit an endless array of designs and mix well with other materials.

■ Standard pavers must be cut to fit geometric designs.

■ Pavers stand up to hard use, continued

traffic, and wheeled garden equipment.

■ Most paver patios will stand up to harsh weather if properly bedded.

■ Although not common because of their tightly fitting design, pavers may require periodic weeding, resetting, and leveling.

INSTALLATION

Compute the area of your patio and divide it by the coverage for the particular paver style recommended by the manufacturer or distributor.

Install concrete pavers using the same techniques as you would for brick. Sand-bed installations are more common, and some pavers are molded with built-in tabs that give consistent spacing in sand-laid installations. (Installation instructions are on pages 142–145.)

SAND-LAID-PAVER INSTALLATION

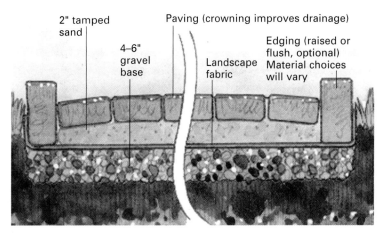

2" tamped sand

4–6" gravel base

Paving (crowning improves drainage)

Landscape fabric

Edging (raised or flush, optional) Material choices will vary

POURED CONCRETE

Concrete doesn't have to look institutional. Four poured slabs divided by single lines of brick make this landing a place to pause on the way in and out of the house. A carefully applied texture blends the concrete with the stone wall and wooden deck.

Because concrete goes on wet and cures to a hard, durable solid, it adapts easily to almost any design. You can pour it in gentle, meandering curves or in straight formal configurations. Modern concrete techniques, such as stamping, coloring, texturing, and embedding with aggregates, can create a dazzling patio surface.

DESIGN CONSIDERATIONS

■ **Color:** Gray in its natural state, but coloring makes your design possibilities almost endless.

■ **Texture:** Smooth or moderately rough when unfinished. Stamping, aggregates, and texturing create unusual likenesses to other materials.

■ **Siting:** It can be sited anywhere and in any design scheme.

ADVANTAGES

■ Poured concrete has unlimited design potential in both formal and informal installations.

■ It requires little maintenance.

■ It stands up to all climatic conditions.

WHAT'S IN CONCRETE

■ 1 part portland cement (a fine mixture of clay and limestone)

■ 2¼ to 2½ parts clean construction sand

■ 2½ to 3 parts coarse aggregate (gravel or rock)

■ ½ part clean water

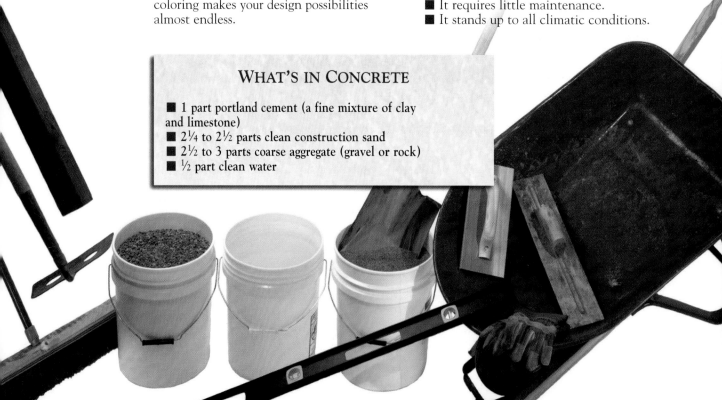

MIXING OPTIONS

BULK DRY INGREDIENTS: Refer to "What's in Concrete" on the opposite page. You can buy the first three ingredients separately and mix them with water by hand in a mortar box or wheelbarrow or mix them in a rented concrete mixer. Mixing concrete is a heavy job that requires a strong hoe and stamina, but for small jobs it's economical.

PREMIX: An easier but somewhat more costly alternative is to buy concrete in bags with the dry ingredients mixed in the correct proportions. You just add water, mix, and pour. Premix takes the guesswork out of mixing—but not the effort. It makes jobs under a cubic yard manageable (you'll need 40 to 50 bags for a cubic yard, depending on the weight of the bags), but for anything larger than that, order ready-mix.

READY-MIX: Ready-mix relieves you of the mixing process but requires a hardy and experienced work crew. Your site must be accessible to a large truck and be ready for the pour as soon as the truck arrives. Ready-mix has additives that make it workable in a variety of weather conditions.

ADDED INGREDIENTS

If your climate treats you to wide variations in temperature and strong or frequent freeze-thaw cycles, you'll need to add ingredients to your mix that will allow the concrete to expand and contract without cracking. Ask your vendor to recommend additives for use in your climate.

INSTALLATION

■ Determine the volume of your patio and add 5 percent to the total.
■ A 40-pound bag of premix makes ⅓ cubic foot; a 60-pound bag, ½ cubic foot; and an 80-pound bag, ⅔ cubic foot. A 4×20-foot walk 4 inches deep requires 26⅔ cubic feet of concrete—about 1 cubic yard (27 cubic feet).
■ Remove sod and excavate.
■ Build and install staked forms and tamp the gravel base.
■ Lay in any reinforcing wire mesh.
■ Order additives in the mix to adapt to hot or cold temperatures while curing.
■ Pour and finish. (See pages 126–135 for more detailed installation instructions.)

Concrete resists damage from freeze–thaw cycles if properly installed and is extremely durable if properly mixed and poured.

BUYING CONCRETE

■ Buy premix at hardware stores, home centers, lumberyards, or building-supply centers.
■ Order bulk concrete from a ready-mix concrete company.
■ Buy dry ingredients (portland cement, sand, and aggregate) at any of the above outlets.

DISADVANTAGES

■ It must be mixed to specifications or it will weaken or disintegrate over time.
■ Its very smooth finish can make a patio dangerously slippery when wet.
■ Broad concrete surfaces are not as resistant to cracking as stone, brick, tile, or pavers.
■ Large expanses of concrete reflect heat and can make your patio uncomfortable.
■ It requires careful planning and, on large projects, some heavy equipment.
■ Installation is hard work and can be exacting. Large projects require helpers.
■ Concrete has to be worked within specified time limits. It is unforgiving of mistakes.

INSTALLING A POURED-CONCRETE PATIO

3–4" concrete slab. (crown or slope to improve drainage)

Backfill

Reinforcing wire mesh (use depends on thickness of the surface)

4-6" gravel

Forms for concrete

DRESSING UP NEW CONCRETE

SCORE JOINTS

Score joints, cut partway through the slab, control eventual cracking. Instead of spreading like spiderwebs across a slab's surface, cracks follow the joints. Although score joints must be strategically placed, a skilled contractor can score the concrete in a pleasing pattern, along with other decorative lines. Request a sketch of the proposed score joints before you pour the slab.

Score joints differ from expansion joints. Score joints are like the lines on a sidewalk. Expansion joints are placed between pours to allow large sections of concrete to expand and shift with the weather. These joints usually incorporate another material, such as redwood strips, between paving sections.

Stamping concrete while it's wet results in a textured and patterned surface. Leave this job to a talented professional. Ask if score joints can be camouflaged in the pattern. Surface patterns accentuated by score joints add a touch of artistry and give concrete a predetermined place to crack.

Who says a new concrete patio must be stark and boring? Although poured concrete covers large areas quickly and cost-effectively, it needn't be glaringly unimaginative. Color or stamp new concrete for amazingly pretty effects. Plan ahead and choose from options available to create any of a variety of looks.

COLOR

You can color concrete paving with one of several techniques, but the following are the most common.

■ Spread colored dyes over the surface of a slab after it's poured. This method produces quick color, but it's only skin deep, and if the surface chips, you'll see gray beneath it.

■ Mix pigment into the wet concrete before you pour the slab. Because this method distributes color throughout the concrete, hues tend to have a uniform appearance even if the surface of the slab chips.

Ask the contractor to supply you with color samples that contrast or complement your home's color scheme. Choose a hue that's a little darker than what you ultimately want, especially if you live in a hot climate; bright sun will fade the color. Color hardeners applied to the surface will enrich their shades

but must be reapplied every few years.

Beware of trendy colors—you may tire quickly of gold or purple. Instead, consider the warm, natural look of adobe or slate.

Get several price estimates for pigmented concrete. Unless the supplier is sending out another order of the same color, yours will be delivered in a separate truck, which increases costs. Uncommon colors, such as clear blues, must be made with more expensive white portland cement to achieve the correct hue. Save money by choosing earth tones or shades of pink, which are made with gray portland cement.

PATTERNS

Freshly poured concrete, plain or colored, can be stamped with a pattern after troweling. Stamps are available to create patterns that resemble cobblestone, cut stone, irregular stone, brick, or precast pavers. Open-mold stamps simply outline the shapes; closed-mold stamps add surface texture as well, creating realistic-looking brick, cobblestone, slate, and paver patterns.

Stamping concrete requires skill. Each row of the pattern must line up with the next and follow curves neatly. Call around and interview several contractors who have experience with stamping concrete. Extra effort on your part at this stage will likely translate into extraordinary results.

Before deciding who to hire, ask to see examples of each contractor's work. Check out finished projects that are a few years old. Inspect each one for neatness, especially along curves, at paving intersections, and at the foot of steps.

TEXTURED FINISHES

The cheapest, easiest way to pattern new concrete involves tooling, or creating various surface effects by manipulating the wet concrete. There are several textures you can use. Try experimenting with the following four textures—offered in sequence from coarsest to smoothest—to see which you like the best:

TROWELED: Swirls made with a finishing trowel add interest to large expanses of flat concrete, giving them the hand-tooled look of an old-world material. An added bonus: the swirls increase traction for a more sure-footed feel when the surface becomes wet. A troweled finish isn't recommended for surfaces that freeze, however, as the texture can become icy, and be difficult to clear completely of snow.

BROOMED: A damp, stiff, coarse-bristled push broom of the type often used to clean garages can be pulled in long, even strokes across the concrete surface when it's still wet. The result is a patterned, slip-resistant surface that's still easy to clean. An added benefit: It prevents the glare that a smooth-finished slab can exhibit.

SEMISMOOTH: Dragging a wood float across a wet slab produces a surface that's a bit smoother than a broomed surface, but one that still provides an attractive, matte look and good skid resistance.

SMOOTH: Finishing the surface with a metal trowel, creates a marble-smooth finish. Such a surface is slippery when wet but is good for dance parties. An added benefit: it's the easiest finish to sweep clean.

Use a concrete stamp with a closed top when you want the textured look of stone.

Open-top stamps impress shape but not texture into concrete. Combine any stamp pattern with your choice of color.

These hexagonal shapes are newly stamped in tinted concrete. Other shapes mimic cobblestone, brick, cut stone, and pavers.

Aggregate concrete has a gravelly texture. Use it alone or combine it with other materials, as shown here.

Rock-salt-finished concrete appears aged. The pitted surface is unsuitable for cold regions with freezing weather.

FACE-LIFTS FOR OLD SLABS

Plain concrete slabs used to be the patio of choice. In fact, many developers still pour patio slabs when they build suburban homes.

If you have one of these slabs in your backyard, you know that white concrete reflects sunlight, causing glare, and over time discolors and develops fine cracks. You may have even thought about tearing out the patio and starting over. Don't reach for the sledge hammer just yet. If the slab sits in a good spot for a patio and is still in good condition, a couple of simple renovation techniques can improve its appearance.

Colored concrete is a good choice for outdoor flooring. Have new concrete poured with the color mixed in, or apply stain to existing concrete.

Transform a plain concrete slab into an attractive outdoor floor pattern by cutting concrete lines with a wet saw. Lines should be straight, not curved, and made by someone experienced with a wet saw.

COLOR

You'll get the biggest change and the quickest face-lift from staining the concrete. Concrete stain, a product available at most home centers, provides a dramatic change, resulting in an attractive, mottled finish. And if your concrete is discolored or streaked, stain will camouflage those blemishes, too.

Use darker colors to make spots and fine cracks less noticeable and to reduce the glare of direct sunlight. Natural browns, grays, and greens create an attractive surface that blends well with the landscape.

Surface stains require several coats for a rich color. To emphasize the mottled effect, apply the first coat evenly; then unevenly dab on subsequent coats, overlapping areas as in sponge painting. This subtle effect calls attention to the color pattern and hides imperfections. Use stencils to create a pattern of contrasting colors or sprinkle simpler designs here and there as accents.

CONCRETE FRAME

Another method of dressing up concrete uses stain to frame the perimeter of the patio surface. First, stain the entire patio. When the first coat of stain dries, measure in 6 to 10 inches from the outside edge of the concrete and apply duct tape to this area. Apply subsequent coats of the same color stain to the untaped area, letting it dry between coats until the desired intensity of color is achieved. When the final coat dries, remove the tape and you'll have an understated border.

This technique works better with single colors and straight edges than with curves.

CONCRETE STAINING TIPS

■ Chemicals in stains etch the surface of cured concrete and they will etch your skin, too. Protect yourself with gloves, work clothes, and safety glasses when using these products.
■ Use disposable foam or bristle brushes to apply concrete stain.
■ The stain may produce a greenish fizz when first applied, but the fizz will dissipate.
■ If you plan to stain new concrete after it cures, put a random broomed finish on the surface. The resulting pattern will complement the mottled appearance of stained concrete.

Because some stain always runs under the tape, when you use different colors for the border and the field, you end up with an obviously smudged edge. With a single color, a wavy edge goes unnoticed.

PATTERN

To completely alter the look of a plain concrete slab, cut lines into its surface with a wet saw. Measure your patio or landing, sketch it to scale on graph paper, then design a simple pattern. Small cuts are difficult to make, so think big. Plan on 1- to 3-foot squares. Or have lines scored on a diagonal to form diamonds.

Look under "Concrete Cutting" in the Yellow Pages to find a contractor. Although you can rent a concrete saw, it's better to hire someone with experience. There should be a garden hose within reach of the project to keep the saw blade wet during cutting.

To combine color and pattern, have your concrete slab scored first; then apply stain for best results. Cutting into stained concrete reveals the white concrete beneath the surface, so that the pattern looks like an afterthought. Staining concrete that has been scored in a pattern creates a finished look.

SPACE FOR PLANTINGS IN YOUR PAVING

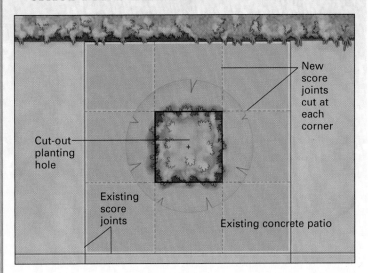

New score joints cut at each corner

Cut-out planting hole

Existing score joints

Existing concrete patio

Brighten up an old patio and break up a boring expanse of concrete with greenery. Make room for the plants in the interior of the surface by cutting out planting areas. Have a skilled concrete-saw operator cut out the areas and add score joints to prevent cracks. Scoring should extend perpendicularly from each corner of the planting hole until it intersects another score joint or the edge of the paving. Plant a small tree in each opening to shade the patio.

A NEW SURFACE

A Trowel Type-M mortar over clean slab

B Use spacers to set tile

C Grout

If your concrete slab has only hairline cracks and no section has settled unevenly, it's a good candidate for a new, dressier surface. Use brick, tile, or flagstone and mortar them to the old slab. Remember, the surface raises the patio, so you may need to trim screen doors or make other adjustments accordingly.
■ If grass or soil hides the edge of the slab, dig a shallow trench so you can work up to the edges. Refill the trench when you're done.
■ Clean the slab to remove moss or grime; let the surface dry.
■ Using 2×4s as temporary barriers, divide your patio into 3- or 4-foot squares. Then, working in one section at a time trowel on type-M mortar—it's made for outdoor use— and set your new surface material.
■ As you work, place ½- to ⅜-inch- thick spacers between the paving pieces and let the mortar dry.
■ Then force mortar or grout into the joints with a grout float or mortar bag. Use a concave jointer tool to strike the joints—that is, remove excess mortar and create a concave finish.
■ Clean the surface with a rag; then cover it with plastic for a day to allow the mortar to cure.

TILE

For this house with a clay tile roof and a colored stucco exterior, ceramic tile is the obvious choice for the patio. Beds and pots of flowers add contrasting shape and color.

With its regular geometric shapes and distinct edges, ceramic and stone tile make an excellent paving material. Its beauty and tactile appeal make it unique among materials. Made from thin panels of high-fired clay, ceramic tiles are extremely durable and offer more variety in colors, shapes, and sizes than any other material.

TYPES OF TILE

Four types of tile are made for outdoor patios.

■ **PATIO OR TERRA-COTTA:** Fired ceramic tile with earthen colors and irregular surfaces create pleasant, unobtrusive moods.

■ **QUARRY TILES:** Machine-made and formed from dense clay pressed tightly into molds, quarry tile is hard and is available with rounded or sharp edges and corners. Its appearance varies from one brand and firing to another—even within the same firing. Ask your dealer to show you how to judge quality. Then make sure all the tiles you buy have the same lot number—your best insurance for getting consistent tiles.

■ **TILE PAVERS:** These molded tiles are larger than other tiles and are made to cover larger areas. Some are designed to retain the deliberately imperfect look of a hand-crafted item. Mexican pavers, for example, are grainy and unglazed and have rough edges. The earthy colors work well outdoors. Others are regular and modern. Tile pavers are usually more expensive than quarry tiles.

GLAZED TILE

Glazed tile is for decorative uses only and are dangerously slippery when wet. However, its glossy look and bold colors make fine accents for edges and trim, raised beds, or wall decorations.

■ **SYNTHETIC STONE TILES:** As the name suggests, this type of tile is made of stained clay bodies that look very much like stone surfaces, such as granite or sandstone. Synthetic tiles are thinner, flatter, lighter, smoother, and more regularly shaped than natural stone and measure either 6 or 12 inches across. They offer a clever alternative for homeowners who want the practical qualities of a synthetic material yet prefer the look of stone.

No matter what type of tile you use, you will need to set it in mortar on a 4-inch concrete slab over a 4-inch gravel base. Make sure the base is absolutely smooth and level.

DESIGN CONSIDERATIONS

■ **Color:** Tile comes in an endless array of colors. Many varieties for outdoor use are available in earth tones, subtle tans, reds, and browns.
■ **Texture:** Tile for outdoor use is manufactured with a slightly roughened surface, but the effect of texture depends more on the pattern than on the tile itself.
■ **Siting:** It is excellent in formal landscape designs and it can be cut and laid in gentle or dramatic shapes. Its modular dimensions fit almost any design scheme.

ADVANTAGES

■ Tile absorbs very little water and resists cracking in changing temperatures. Once restricted to warm climates, newer varieties make tile practical in colder climates.
■ Unglazed tile is less likely than glazed tile to get slick when it's wet, which means a patio surface of unglazed tile will be safer after it rains. For best results, use unglazed, textured tile made specifically for outdoor paving.
■ Tile's high density will support heavy loads

and constant use (but only when properly bedded).
■ Tile stands up to hard use, continued traffic, and wheeled garden equipment.
■ Most tile will endure all kinds of weather.
■ Set properly on a mortared slab, tile needs virtually no maintenance.

DISADVANTAGES

■ Good tile is more expensive than other common patio surface materials.
■ Because it's most often square, it is more difficult to lay in brick-like patterns.
■ It's thin and susceptible to cracking on uneven surfaces. Repairing cracked tiles means chiseling them out.
■ Some porous varieties may absorb water and crack when temperatures drop below freezing.

INSTALLATION

■ Compute the area of your patio in square feet and add 10 percent for waste, mistakes, and cutting. Order cartons that have the coverage equivalent to the patio surface area.
■ Excavate and pour slab as you would for mortared brick or flagstone. Spread thin-set mortar on slab sections. Set tile, then grout and clean. (See pages 136–141 for specific installation instructions.)

BUYING TILE

■ Purchase tile at tile retailers, ceramic suppliers, home centers, and floor covering outlets. National retailing franchises specialize in tile.
■ Certain retailers may sell individual tiles, but most will sell it in cartons by the square foot or in boxes of large quantities.

TILE INSTALLATION

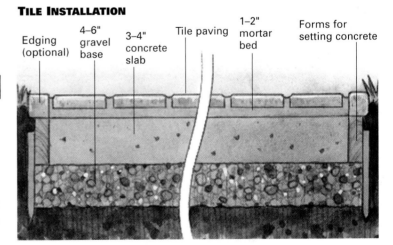

Edging (optional) | 4–6" gravel base | 3–4" concrete slab | Tile paving | 1–2" mortar bed | Forms for setting concrete

Cedar decking

Landscaping timber

Rounded landscape timber

Redwood decking

Railway tie

Treated 2×6 decking

Treated 4×4 landscape timber

WOOD

Wood brings a warmth to the landscape unmatched by any other material. Its appealing, organic look offers numerous design options. You can set it directly in the soil, in a sand bed, or in anchored frames.

Treated landscape timbers, wide wooden rounds, and end-grain blocks that look like brick are found in patio designs that have a woodland atmosphere. You can install wood decking squares (they look like parquet) in rectangular beds or use wood rounds in free-form layouts set within larger areas of loose materials.

CHOOSING THE RIGHT WOOD

Insects, rot, and mildew attack most wood. Redwood, cypress, and cedar, however, contain natural resins that resist insects and the elements. Get the heartwood only of these species; the sapwood is not resistant. Tropical hardwoods are durable, and their high cost can repay itself with years of freedom from maintenance. Make sure your tropical wood comes from sustainable-forestry sources.

Pressure-treated lumber offers a less-expensive alternative to resistant species. Treated wood is infused with chemicals (including arsenic, which will be phased out during 2003), which greatly reduces the wood's susceptibility to the ravages of nature. Treatment compounds turn the wood green or tan, but the color will weather to a gray within several months. You can special-order wood treated with colorless protectives (at a higher price), but you can also stain treated and untreated lumber to colors of your liking.

With a few weekends of work and a modest supply of redwood, the homeowners transformed this shady spot into a wooded hideaway.

Buy treated lumber rated for ground contact. Look for a "Ground Contact" or "LP25" stamp (or both) on the surface of the wood. Read the safety label attached to the lumber, and follow the instructions. Wear gloves when handling treated wood and a respirator or dust mask when cutting it.

No matter what kind of wood you choose, inspect each piece before you buy it. Don't buy split, cupped, or twisted pieces. Small knots won't cause problems, but large knots may work their way out after installation or cause the lumber to split, especially near an edge. Slight bowing will flatten if you fasten it in place.

INSTALLING DECKING ON SLEEPERS

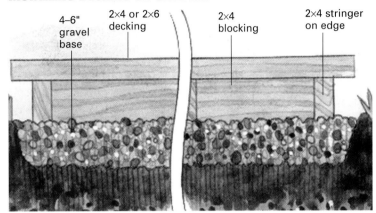

4–6" gravel base | 2×4 or 2×6 decking | 2×4 blocking | 2×4 stringer on edge

DESIGN CONSIDERATIONS

■ **Color:** Its natural colors range from light (cypress) to purple-red (cedar) to deep reddish-brown (redwood). The green cast of treated lumber turns gray in time. Stains, paints, and finishes will alter colors to suit your tastes.

■ **Texture:** Wood is generally smooth but this is conveyed more by pattern and design than by the material itself.

■ **Siting:** Wood will almost always look informal in the landscape but is suitable for formal, rectangular designs, especially as an edging and in modular patterns.

ADVANTAGES

■ Wood is less expensive than brick, flagstone, and cut stone (though more expensive than loose stone and organic materials).

■ Ease of installation depends on complexity of design, but wood generally requires only basic carpentry skills.

■ It mixes well with other materials.

DISADVANTAGES

■ It can become moss-covered when damp and slippery when wet, which can be especially dangerous on slopes and steps.

■ It does not conform as well to terrain variations. Changes in slope require posts or the installation of small sections.

■ You will have to occasionally replace worn or damaged sections and periodically reapply finishes and preservatives, even in mild-weather climates.

INSTALLATION

■ Determine square footage and structural requirements. Take your dimensioned plan to your supplier for assistance.

■ Remove sod and excavate. Install wood rounds or sections. For boardwalks, set posts or sleepers; then install decking as illustrated above.

■ Embed wood rounds and blocks directly in the soil or in a 2-inch sand base in places where better drainage is needed.

DESIGN TIPS

Wood can go almost anywhere but is especially suited to woodland-setting patio installations with boardwalks and footbridges.

Cut your own wood rounds with a chain saw. Embed them or lay 3- to 4-inch lengths of timber set on edge in loose stone or sand. Plant variety into the spaces with groundcovers or fill the gaps with bark or loose stone.

BUYING WOOD

■ Purchase wood from lumberyards or home centers.

■ Wood is sold by the piece or by the board foot. Prices vary with size and species.

LOOSE MATERIALS

Loose materials offer an alternative to hard pavements. Used by themselves or in combination with other hardscape, they offer an environmentally friendly means—many products are recycled materials—of creating a patio surface. Loose materials are generally available at low cost, and most require only moderate maintenance.
■ Unlike harder paving surfaces, loose materials will shift beneath your feet to enhance your walking comfort and to give your patio the feeling of a pleasant park or a spot in the woods.
■ The most popular loose materials for patio surfaces are easy to install and maintain and offer many appealing design possibilities.
■ Loose materials provide better drainage than any other surfaces. They help prevent erosion and, except for wood products, make the patio area easy to use after a rainfall.

Here are some of the more popular loose paving materials.

PEA GRAVEL: This material consists of medium-size stones that have been naturally smoothed by river or lake water. River rock is available in many colors, and it shifts easily underfoot. It also has a soft look and can be raked in interesting furrows and lines.

CRUSHED STONE: This is quarried rock that has been mechanically crushed and then graded so that most of the stones are of similar size but with varying shapes and colors.

WOOD BARK, CHIPS, NUGGETS, AND SHREDS: Several types of wood, including redwood, cedar, cypress, and pine are available in chipped and shredded forms. Redwood, cedar, and cypress are naturally resistant to weather and insects. Wood chips can serve a variety of landscaping purposes, particularly as mulch. They also are useful for cushioning surfaces under play equipment.

However, wood chips and other loose materials that are relatively light can be pushed out of place by footsteps. Add edging such as railroad ties, brick, pavers, or stone.

HOW TO ORDER

Redwood or cedar bark and chips are available in bags from your neighborhood home center, lumberyards, building-supply centers, landscape suppliers, and patio-supply stores. Or you may be able to get them from your local parks department for free. Local parks often recycle wood chips from the trees they remove and you may be able to have them for the hauling. Stone and gravel can be bought by the ton from quarries, stone suppliers, or patio supply stores. See the Yellow Pages for "Lumber," "Building Materials," "Landscaping," "Quarries," or "Stone."

MAKING A LOOSE-STONE PATIO

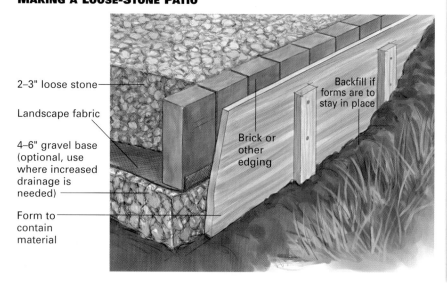

2–3" loose stone

Landscape fabric

4–6" gravel base (optional, use where increased drainage is needed)

Form to contain material

Brick or other edging

Backfill if forms are to stay in place

FOUNDATIONS, FILLERS, AND EDGING

Foundation materials provide drainage and support to keep paved surfaces from cracking under weight or the stress of freeze-thaw cycles. They are essential for the long-term stability of your patio.

Fillers between the joints secure the blocks, bricks, tiles, or stone, but they are more than functional. Their color and texture should be an integral part of your design.

Although not required for flagstone and mortared surfaces, edgings are a must for dry-set brick and concrete pavers. Edgings also serve an important design function—they set off and separate the patio from its surroundings. For specific installation instructions, see pages 111–130.

Brick

Plastic edging

SAND-SET FOUNDATIONS

■ Subbase: 4 to 6 inches of class-5 gravel. Fifty pounds will make a 1-square-foot-by-4-inch foundation.
■ Landscape fabric.
■ Base: 2 to 3 inches of fine sand. Twenty pounds will make a 1-square-foot-by-2-inch bed.
■ Filler: Washed sand.

MORTARED FOUNDATIONS

■ Sub-base: 4 to 6 inches of class 5 gravel.
■ Base: 3 to 4 inches of concrete.
■ Welded-wire reinforcing mesh.
■ Mortar (amount and types will vary with installation and materials).

MATERIALS FOR EDGING

Use edging materials that match or that tastefully contrast with the paving materials. Brick is naturally a great complement to brick, but it also provides striking contrast to a loose-filled or poured concrete surface.

Several common edging materials are described on this page but you can use practically anything you can think of. River stone, whole or broken shells, broken brick

or block and even reclaimed roofing tiles also make attractive and functional edging.

BRICK: Brick soldiers (set upright and on edge) and sailors (set flat and perpendicular to the pattern of the paving) enhance both formal and informal designs. Set bricks on an angle for an attractive edge. Use brick to edge curved patterns as well.

POURED CONCRETE: Poured concrete can be colored or textured to match or contrast with the patio. Installed in curbs, it requires strong forms and a little extra effort, but if properly installed, it will outlast many other edgings.

PLASTIC AND STEEL: Plastic edging is flexible and affordable and will conform to almost any curve. Anchor it with spikes driven through integral lugs. Use ¼-inch commercial-grade steel edging to contain concrete and other heavy materials. Both plastic and steel edgings are made to be buried below the edge of the surface materials so they will not show.

Wood

WOOD: Wood (2×4s, 2×6s, or 2×8s) and landscape timbers (4×4s or 8×8s) bring a pleasant contrast to brick or concrete patios. Stake wood in place and backfill with topsoil to hide the stakes. Predrill timbers and drive ½-inch rebar through the holes into the soil.

STONE: Both flagstone and cut stone make an excellent edging. You can purchase precut stone or cut the pieces yourself. Make sure to keep their width as consistent as possible.

PRECAST EDGING: Precast pavers or tiles are made by many manufacturers to match your paver pattern. They come in straight or curved shapes, many with sculpted designs.

Concrete pavers

KEEP YOUR FOOTING

Be careful with moss, plant, and grass fillers. They are very slippery when wet. Also remember that any living fillers will have to be weeded, clipped, or mowed.

PUTTING YOUR PLANS ON PAPER

You've pondered your patio's function and style, and you've chosen the materials you'll use to build it. Now you're ready for construction. Before you bring out the shovels and levels, however, it's important to refine your plan, to clarify and map out precisely where all the final elements will go.

This is the time for you to put your plans on paper. Detailing all the elements now will save you time in the long run, to say nothing of money and frustration. Paper plans also will help keep you on schedule throughout the construction process, and they will increase your satisfaction with your finished patio.

Drawing a patio plan first keeps you from having to make hurried decisions in the field. It allows you to experiment with the location of the patio, its contours, and the pattern of its materials. Paper plans also can give you a bird's-eye view of the landscape, helping you

discover design ideas you might not otherwise have seen considered. Even if you intend to contract all or part of the construction to a professional, a detailed plan will give you a basis for securing bids and will help your contractor build the patio exactly as you envision it.

If you suspect you could use a little help along the way, enlist the aid of design professionals to review your plans and offer suggestions.

On the following pages, you will find planning tips, as well as illustrations that demonstrate how professionals develop a complete landscape plan. If your project is small, you may not need to invest time in such an elaborate undertaking. But large or small, any patio project will profit from including each step of the design process.

Your plans need not be as detailed as those shown on the following pages. Simple projects can begin with a rough sketch, like this, but you should refine them and ultimately draw them on graph paper.

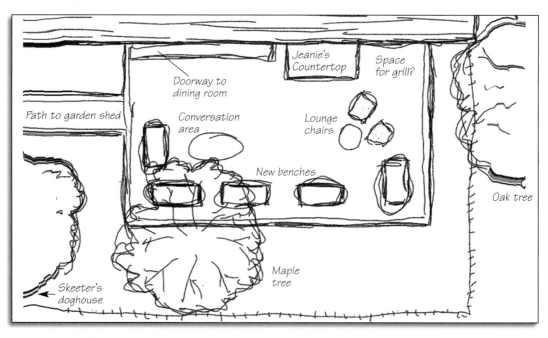

Jeanie's Countertop

Space for grill?

Doorway to dining room

Path to garden shed

Conversation area

Lounge chairs

New benches

Oak tree

Maple tree

Skeeter's doghouse

This seemingly elaborate woodland patio could not have been constructed without a detailed plan. All elements, from the flagstone paving to the wood steps and plantings, were carefully set out on paper before this peaceful setting was added to the landscape.

DRAFTING TOOLBOX

Here's what you'll need to get your plans down on paper.
- ■ An engineer's scale
- ■ Tracing paper (roll or sheets)
- ■ 2 circle templates ranging from ¼ to 3½ inches in diameter
- ■ Thick and thin black felt-tipped pens
- ■ Rulers (6-inch and 12-inch)
- ■ Pencils with erasers
- ■ Drafting or masking tape (drafting tape comes off surfaces more easily and doesn't leave marks)
- ■ T square
- ■ Pencil sharpener

MAKING A BASE MAP

As with any decision-making process, you'll simplify the task (and reduce your confusion) by taking the planning process one step at a time. The first step is to draw a base map of your property.

START WITH A SKETCH

Begin by walking around the outside of your house with a clipboard and a 100-foot steel measuring tape. You'll be measuring and sketching in the outlines of structures and plantings and other major details. Later you will transfer these sketches more exactly to a graph paper map. Even though you're familiar with your own house and lot, don't take anything for granted.

BOUNDARIES FIRST: Starting with the exact location of your property lines, (look for metal markers or use a metal detector to find them), sketch in the outline of your yard and house, noting its distance from all property lines. Take accurate measurements from both property lines. Measure and record the dimensions of each wall of your house and the sizes of other structures, such as detached garages or sheds. Your sketch should include how far structures are from one another.

LOOK AT SMALLER ELEMENTS: Include the little things on your sketch. They will matter when you build your patio. Here's a sample list of items to watch for:
■ Location of doors and windows, including width, height, distance from the ground, and what rooms they link to the patio.
■ Extension of roof eaves beyond the exterior walls of the house.
■ Location of downspouts and direction of runoff.
■ Where existing trees, shrubs, and gardens are planted.
■ Location of outdoor walls, fences, steps, walks, and driveways.

DRAWING A DETAILED MAP

Once your sketch is complete, transfer it to graph paper (24"×36" is a good size, with a scale of ¼" = 1 foot). Include all the elements on your sketch, and note all the dimensions you've recorded.

Be sure to include the locations of windows, doors, hose bibs, and electrical outlets. Use dotted lines for any buried cable.

This is the time for precision. If you're in doubt about any measurement, go measure again. Doing so can save you hours of actual construction time. When you're done, you'll have an accurate drawn-to-scale map of your property.

BASE-MAP SHORTCUTS

You may be able to shorten the base-map process by using existing maps of your property. Start with the existing legal maps and description of your house and lot. These documents—called deed maps, house plans, plat plans, or contour plans—are typically available from your title company, bank, mortgage lender, city hall, or county recorder's office. You may even have a copy filed in your records along with the other papers you received when you bought the house. Plot maps do not, however, show every measurement. You'll still have to measure the dimensions of your house and the elements outlined on the opposite page.

Another, though more costly, option is to have your property surveyed (a necessity if your plan includes extensive grading), but expect to pay several hundred dollars.

HIGH-TECH HELP

Computerized landscape-design programs take the pencil (and eraser) out of planning. They're easy to use, flexible, and can speed your progress from base plan to final design. One of a computer's more appealing features is deletion—an electronic eraser that allows you to change your design without redrawing it.

The features are slick: Programs calculate dimensions of each of your proposed structures and areas of use. Most programs have a number of symbols for trees and shrubs, as well as elements such as furniture, pools, and patios. Some will even create side elevations and three-dimensional views of your plan. Others can prepare material lists and cost estimates.

Check your home improvement center, too. Many offer computer design services. If you're not familiar with computers, you can take your rough drawings (including dimensions) and the store's staff will computerize your project and produce a materials list and cost estimates. Ask for extra copies—your local government building department will need them when you apply for permits.

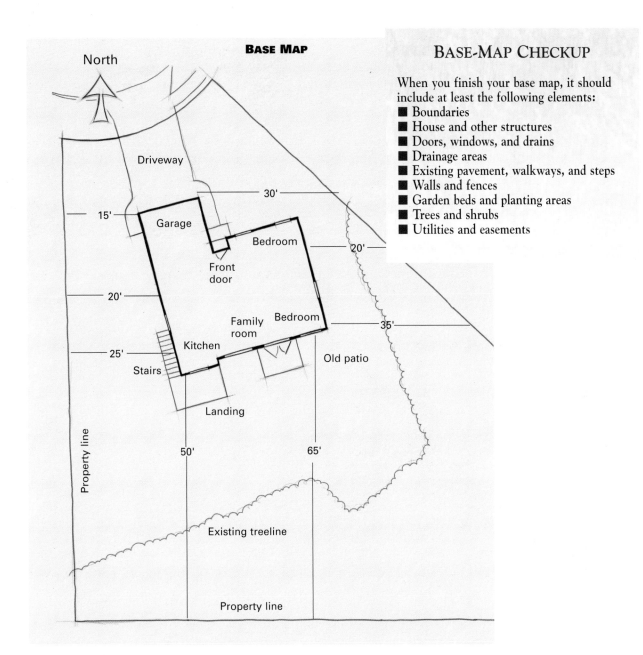

BASE MAP

North

Driveway

30'

15'

Garage

Bedroom

20'

Front door

20'

Family room

Bedroom

35'

Kitchen

25'

Old patio

Stairs

Landing

Property line

50'

65'

Existing treeline

Property line

BASE-MAP CHECKUP

When you finish your base map, it should include at least the following elements:
- Boundaries
- House and other structures
- Doors, windows, and drains
- Drainage areas
- Existing pavement, walkways, and steps
- Walls and fences
- Garden beds and planting areas
- Trees and shrubs
- Utilities and easements

WHEN IT'S TIME FOR A CHANGE

Did you inherit a dysfunctional patio or deck when you bought your house? Perhaps you built one years ago when your family's needs were different. When it's time for a change, here are some ideas for retrofitting a worn-out or out-of-date design.

- Is your patio larger than you need? Consider building raised planters to divide it into smaller spaces. Or cut through the paving and plant trees.
- Do you entertain on a regular basis but your patio is too small to hold all your guests? Convert a flower bed near the patio into lawn, where you can easily set up tents or party tables. Build a second patio and link the old and new spaces with a boardwalk or path so guests can move between the areas. Enlarge the space by

installing a brick patio at the foot of a deck. Extend a stone patio by pouring textured concrete at its edge and laying a border of stone that matches the existing one.
- Make the patio seem larger by removing hedges, fencing, or obstructions that are merely decorative. This will open up the view and make the space seem larger. Be careful not to take out plantings or structures that were put there to increase privacy.
- Improve the view. Bring compost bins, garbage cans, yard tools, and heating and cooling equipment into a single service area rather than leaving them scattered throughout the yard. Then hide them all behind an attractive screen.

ANALYZING YOUR SITE

A base map gives you a picture of the outline of your property and its contents just as they are. A site analysis takes that picture one step further.

A site analysis will enable you to view the components of your yard as if you were hovering overhead. It is primarily a tool that helps you evaluate the relationships between your landscape elements and to record what you consider to be its assets (the things you like and that work well with your lifestyle) and its liabilities (the things that don't).

CONDUCTING A SITE ANALYSIS

Take your sketch (not the base map) out in your yard and step back so you can evaluate its assets and liabilities (use the checklist on the next page as a guide). Ask yourself:
- What works well?
- What do I want to change?
- Is the route to the site pleasant?
- Is the site easily accessible, or will I have to take a circuitous route to reach it?
- Is the best part of the yard visible from the seating on the proposed patio space?
- Is this site private enough to feel comfortable when I relax?

Go through the checklist item by item and judge how each of these features of your yard will either enhance or detract from your comfort and convenience.

Make notes about your evaluation on your landscape sketch and include the following concerns.
- How does the distance from your proposed patio to streets, alleys, and sidewalks affect

CHECK FOR UTILITY LINES

No matter where you build, identify where all your utility lines lay. Call your local utility companies and find out where the gas, water, sewer, electrical, or communication lines are located on your property. Make sure construction won't cut in to them or that you won't cover them with the patio surface or accompanying walks.

Even if safety isn't an issue, you don't want your patio to prevent future access. Rights-of-access by utility companies are called easements, and easements apply whether or not you receive the service of a particular utility. For example, even if you use a satellite dish for television, you need to find out if the cable company uses underground lines. Note all easements on your base map or site analysis.

SITE ANALYSIS

Notes for Site Analysis
✓ Too much sun on patio space
✓ Don't block view to woods
✓ Yard slopes steeply at rear
✓ Deck will shade patio
✓ Neighbor has too much view of patio (screen view)
✓ Improve visual access
✓ Good view from kitchen window

your need for quiet and privacy?
■ Will streetlights and light from neighboring properties affect your use of the patio in the evening?
■ What views do you want to keep?
■ What views do you want to block?
■ Are there sources of noise nearby, day and night? Are there drainage problems you need

to correct? Are there neighbors' trees or bushes that overhang your yard?

Set your sketch and notes aside while you trace your base map on a piece of tracing paper. Label this first tracing "Site Analysis" and transfer your notes to it. When you're done, it should look something like the site analysis shown on the opposite page.

CHECKLIST FOR SITE ANALYSIS

Effective patio planning means more than simply drawing a plan and laying a slab or paving materials. A good plan should take into account the details of the total environment. When you are sketching your plans, it's easy to overlook details you may later find important. Here's a checklist for the elements to include while you're sketching your patio site. Use the list as a guide. Many items may not apply, and you may add other items not listed that are specific to your needs.

STRUCTURES
■ Dimensions of house, garage, and any other permanent buildings
■ Roof overhangs
■ Walls, fences, and trellises
■ Columns
■ Built-in furnishings and appliances (benches, tables, grills, and counters)

PAVED SURFACES
■ Existing and proposed patio pavings
■ Driveways
■ Walks and paths
■ Steps
■ Edgings

AMENITIES (DECORATIVE AND FUNCTIONAL)
■ Freestanding furniture and grills
■ Lighting
■ Play areas
■ Poolside areas
■ Birdhouses
■ Wind chimes
■ Sculpture and decorative elements

ACCESS
■ Foot-traffic patterns
■ Doors and windows

DRAINAGE
■ Spouts
■ Gutters
■ Current runoff areas and patterns

SLOPES OR STEEP GRADES
■ Dips in ground
■ Slope direction
■ Steep grades that may need retaining walls
■ Stairs and steps

PLACEMENT OF UTILITIES
■ Electrical supply lines, overhead or underground
■ Telephone lines, overhead or underground
■ Television cable
■ Natural-gas supply lines
■ Water supply pipes
■ Wastewater pipes
■ Hose bibs
■ Sewage pipes and catch basins
■ Septic tanks
■ Utility easements (access for utilities)

PRIVACY AND VIEW
■ Open and closed areas within your property
■ Views to preserve
■ Views to block
■ Privacy walls, fences, and plants

PLANTS (EXISTING AND PROPOSED)
■ Trees
■ Shrubs and bushes
■ Groundcover
■ Ground-level flower beds
■ Raised flower beds
■ Vegetable or herb gardens
■ Edgings

WATER AND ROCK
■ Erosion
■ Natural ponds
■ Streams
■ Constructed pools and fountains
■ Boulders or rock outcroppings

CLIMATE AND MICROCLIMATE
■ Prevailing winds
■ Precipitation
■ Sun and shade
■ Heating and cooling

CREATING A BUBBLE DIAGRAM

Your site analysis is a snapshot of the existing landscape with all its attributes and drawbacks. The next step—bubble diagrams—will reflect how things could be.

MAKING THE DIAGRAM

Making bubble diagrams means using more tracing paper. Lay a fresh sheet over your site analysis and retrace the basic outlines of your property, including the house, fence, property lines, and driveway.

Next, draw circles, like bubbles, on the tracing paper to represent various areas in your yard and how you want to use them. Label each bubble with a brief description of its intended use. If you don't like your first design, make another one. Repeat the process, overlaying the site analysis with new sheets of tracing paper to rearrange the bubbles. Try different schemes. Draw as many bubble diagrams as it takes to find one that works for you.

You don't have to be an artist to draw bubble diagrams. They are simply a tool to help you organize your ideas and get you going in the right direction.

BUBBLE DIAGRAM 1

Sketch as many bubble diagrams as you want before selecting the one that combines the best ideas for an attractive and practical landscape that works with your home. Compare this initial diagram with Bubble Diagram 2 on opposite page.

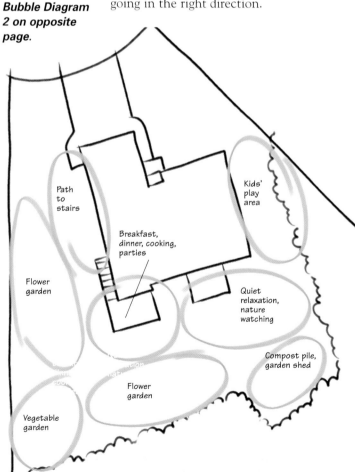

Path to stairs

Kids' play area

Breakfast, dinner, cooking, parties

Flower garden

Quiet relaxation, nature watching

Compost pile, garden shed

Flower garden

Vegetable garden

BRAINSTORMING WITH BUBBLES

Using bubble diagrams as a design tool works like brainstorming. Many ideas may seem extreme, but in the end you'll find a creative solution to your needs that contains practical and affordable elements.

Don't hesitate to move bubbles from place to place to explore different configurations. And don't think about budget limitations at this stage. Some ideas—such as moving the lawn—may require more effort or expense than you want to expend. Don't worry about that now; just let the ideas flow.

By allowing yourself to dream and scheme at this point, you might find other ways to achieve your goals. Perhaps you can't tear down an old patio and rebuild it in a new location, even if the new site is *the* ideal spot. But you might be able to put in an inexpensive sitting area.

Here's another possibility. Your existing patio opens to the lawn, but you want a more intimate space. Use bubble diagrams to find a way to separate the patio from the activities on the lawn and to open views. Perhaps you could leave the lawn and the patio where they are and draw a bubble to represent a privacy planting between the two. Or you could move the patio bubble to another part of the diagram or move the lawn to a different spot. Or how about adding a fence and planting along the outer edge of the lawn to give the entire yard more privacy?

REALITY CHECK

As you sketch bubble diagrams, watch for one that stands out as the most appealing and appropriate to your needs. Take time to study this "final" diagram thoroughly. Look at your site analysis and transfer the notes on it to your bubble diagram. Compare the proposed use of each bubble to the physical description of its location. Are they compatible?

For example, you may have picked the ideal spot for a new patio. You like the connection between indoors and out, the view from the area, and the size of the space. However, your site analysis reveals that this location slopes too steeply for a patio.

If you abandon this scheme for a flatter but otherwise less desirable area, you might not use the area as much as you like. Looking at site conditions before deciding on a final plan allows you to find a solution that works with existing assets or liabilities. In this case, the process could be as simple as building a deck—instead of a patio—over the slope.

BUBBLES FOR AN OLD PATIO

Sketching bubble diagrams is valuable even when evaluating an existing patio. You might want to change adjacent areas to complement your present space. For example, if you want flowers nearby when you relax or entertain outdoors, sketch a flower-garden bubble next to the patio. Rough out several schemes before selecting the sketch that illustrates the ideas that work best for your home.

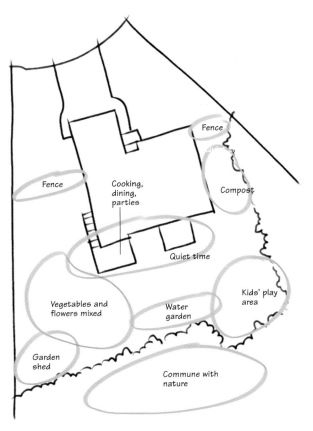

Fence

Fence

Cooking, dining, parties

Compost

Quiet time

Vegetables and flowers mixed

Water garden

Kids' play area

Garden shed

Commune with nature

BUBBLE DIAGRAM 2

Notice the changes from Diagram 1 (opposite page) to this plan. The areas for cooking, dining, and quiet relaxation are left pretty much unchanged—they are still accessible to compatible indoor rooms. But the children's play area is now moved to the corner of the yard, allowing easy supervision from the house and the dining and relaxation areas. Other areas have been rearranged for both functional and aesthetic reasons. However, this diagram is not the final plan. Note the differences between it and the Final Bubble Diagram.

Evaluate your entire scheme, bubble by bubble, considering the assets and limitations for each part of the site. Rearranging the bubbles may inspire a new strategy. For example, you might want to move a parking area because the cars ruin the view from a balcony. When you combine the notes from the site analysis with the bubble diagram, however, you realize that you'll have to cut down several lovely, mature trees. In this case, the bubble diagram was a good start, but the site analysis reveals that it's back to the drawing board. Thinking about the trees, however, could lead you to consider using foliage to screen the parking lot. However, another solution comes to mind: building a plant-covered arbor over the parking area.

While you may not use all of your ideas, your efforts won't be wasted. The process usually leads you to as many ideas as you'll need.

FINAL BUBBLE DIAGRAM

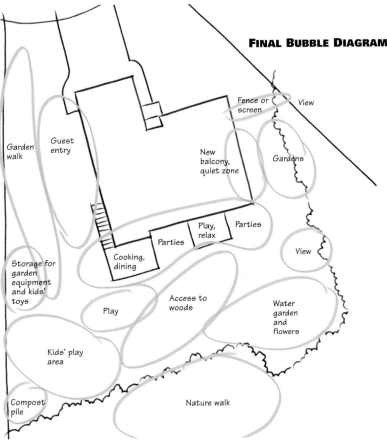

Fence or screen

View

Garden walk

Guest entry

New balcony, quiet zone

Gardens

Storage for garden equipment and kids' toys

Cooking, dining

Parties

Play, relax

Parties

View

Play

Access to woods

Water garden and flowers

Kids' play area

Compost pile

Nature walk

Sketch as many bubble diagrams as you want before selecting the one that combines the best ideas for an attractive and practical landscape that works with your home.

MAKING A MASTER PLAN

Now that you're sure where everything in your new landscape will be, it's time to get a little more specific.

THE DESIGN CONCEPT

A design concept includes every decision you've made about your landscape—for example, where you intend to add shade, wind protection, privacy, or overhead shelter. In one way, it is the final bubble diagram with instructions, and they will be the key to drawing your master plan.

Note the differences between a concept diagram and a bubble plan. The design concept tells you specifically what you need to build or add to accomplish the goals you've set out in earlier plans. To make a concept, trace your house and property on a fresh sheet of tracing paper and write descriptions of plantings and construction.

DESIGN CONCEPT

Combining the ideas of your favorite bubble plan with the realities shown on your site analysis will yield a design concept—a diagram of your landscape with instructions about what you plan to build, plant, or add to your site.

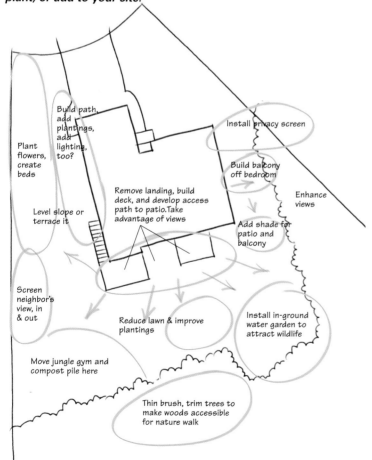

Build path, add plantings, add lighting, too?

Plant flowers, create beds

Install privacy screen

Build balcony off bedroom

Remove landing, build deck, and develop access path to patio.Take advantage of views

Enhance views

Level slope or terrace it

Add shade for patio and balcony

Screen neighbor's view, in & out

Reduce lawn & improve plantings

Install in-ground water garden to attract wildlife

Move jungle gym and compost pile here

Thin brush, trim trees to make woods accessible for nature walk

THE MASTER PLAN

Lay a piece of tracing paper over your base map and trace the outlines of your house and other existing features. Then make rough drawings of the new structures you will build, using your bubble diagrams to help you decide where everything will go.

STRUCTURES FIRST: Start with the patio and other structural elements—decks, parking areas, landings, and pathways. Designers call this hardscape. Play with different shapes and lines, but keep the basic configurations to scale.

There's still time to explore some ideas freely. If a square-cornered patio now doesn't look just right—or if it won't quite fit the space—round the corner. This is still a time for experimentation, and things are easier to change on paper.

PLANTS AND TREES: Once you draw in the hardscape, add lawn and planting areas with their bedlines. Because they are used as separations, bedlines shape two adjacent spaces at one time. You can make them formal and geometric or curve them with a flowing informality.

Next, sketch circles to represent any trees you plan to plant, referring to your design concept to remind you of any view you want to frame or areas that need privacy or shade.

Finally, label your renderings and the interior rooms of your home. Make one last check on the relationships each area has with the interior of your home. You may have forgotten that you had planned to remove a tree to open up a view or add high shrubbery to make an interior room more private.

DO A WALK-THROUGH

Now take your plan outside and walk its perimeters on your property. Make sure you haven't forgotten anything.
■ Are all the access routes to your patio workable?
■ Have you accounted for screening?
■ Do the axis lines call attention to the right focal points?
■ Can you move a structure within your plan to a spot where you won't have to excavate, without botching the rest of your design?

Even if you intend to build your landscape in stages over a period of years, the master plan will keep your design unified, both now and in the future.

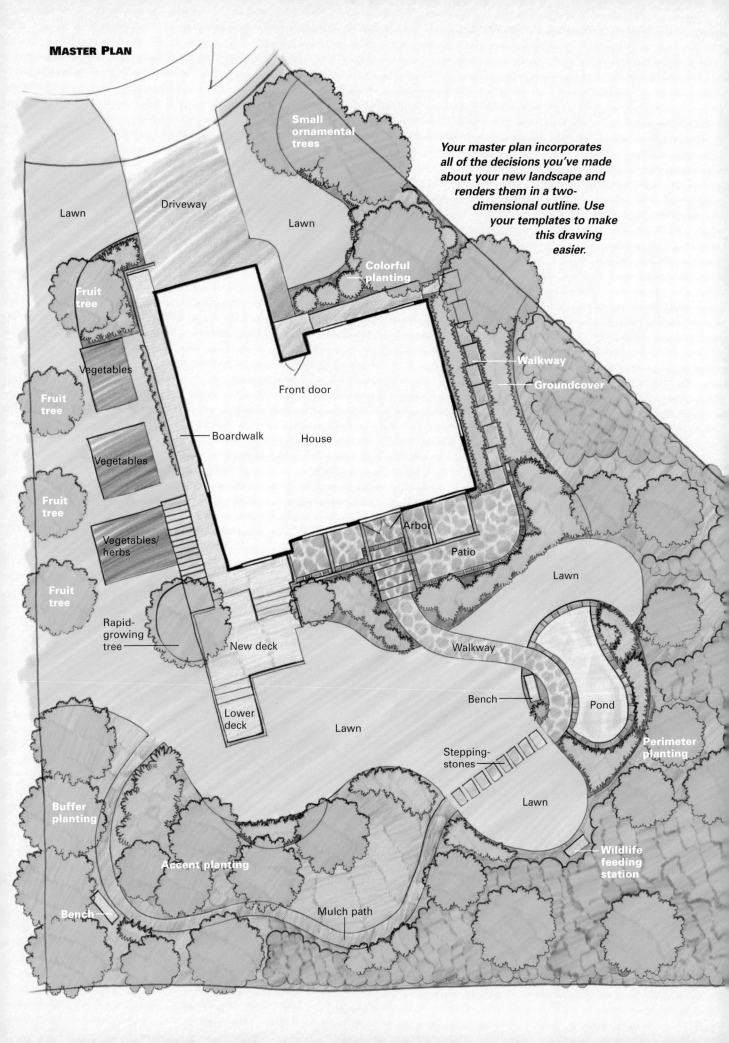

MASTER PLAN

Your master plan incorporates all of the decisions you've made about your new landscape and renders them in a two-dimensional outline. Use your templates to make this drawing easier.

Small ornamental trees

Lawn

Driveway

Lawn

Colorful planting

Fruit tree

Front door

Walkway

Groundcover

Vegetables

Fruit tree

Boardwalk

House

Vegetables

Fruit tree

Arbor

Patio

Vegetables/ herbs

Fruit tree

Rapid-growing tree

New deck

Lawn

Walkway

Bench

Pond

Lower deck

Lawn

Perimeter planting

Buffer planting

Stepping-stones

Accent planting

Lawn

Bench

Mulch path

Wildlife feeding station

BUILDING BASICS

With plans in hand, you're ready to build your new patio. In this chapter, you'll find instructions that will guide you through each step of the building process, from layout and groundbreaking to laying underground wiring.

Step by step, you'll learn how to build almost any kind of patio with almost any kind of material. And because the patio is often just the defining element of an overall patio project, we've included sections on building overheads, fences, and walls.

Before you start construction, schedule your material delivery. Arrange the delivery date so you have plenty of time to complete the site preparations. Then you can have the materials dropped close to the work area, eliminating having them on your driveway, only to have to move them to the construction zone later.

If you do need to store materials, keep them safe. Store bags of concrete mix where they won't get wet. Fence off a pile of flagstone or stacked lumber with yellow construction tape so children and visitors won't stumble into it. A brick or stone pallet can look like an inviting place for young children to play. Keep brick and stone on the pallets and don't cut the steel bands until you're ready to lay the material.

Consider the size of the project and recruit a crew of helpers if possible. This is especially important when pouring ready-mix concrete. Although you can take your time with any concrete you mix yourself, ready-mix won't wait. Once the truck arrives, you have to get the concrete into the forms quickly.

SAFETY FIRST

Construction tools cut, pound, and grind. Flesh doesn't stand up well to that kind of treatment, so be safety-conscious. Self-defense makes sense. We recommend the following:

■ Wear heavy-soled work boots with over-the-ankle support to protect you from wayward nails and ankle-twisting missteps.

■ Wear durable gloves and denim jeans or genuine construction togs, such as painter's pants, to protect your skin. Work clothes also have pockets to keep small tools at hand.

■ Wear safety goggles and ear protection when sawing, hammering, or using power tools.

■ Use a dust mask or OSHA-approved respirator to let you breathe comfortably when spraying or sawing.

■ Plug all tools into outlets that are protected by ground fault circuit interrupters (GFCIs).

■ Keep a first-aid kit handy for minor injuries.

■ Wear a tool belt. You won't misplace tools, and having them at hand saves time and energy.

■ Don't work with dull blades. They overwork the tool as well as the user, and they're dangerous.

■ Check before you dig. There's always a chance of running into utility lines if you haven't found out where they are first. Most utility companies will locate their lines free of charge.

Building a patio, even a small one, is a big job—and the job gets even bigger with large areas and ambitious designs. If you have any doubts about your ability to construct the patio yourself, find a contractor who's willing to let you carry out some of the work. You'll get a reduced price, access to top-quality tools, and advice. In addition, you'll learn new skills and will still be able to put your personal mark on your project.

RENTING TOOLS

It isn't necessary to have all the tools you will need already stashed in your toolbox. There are some tools you'll only use once or twice. The following make good candidates for renting.

■ Transit (for leveling the site)
■ Excavation equipment, such as a Bobcat, for large sites
■ Hammer drill
■ Power auger
■ Power tamper
■ Cement mixer
■ Reciprocating saw
■ Hydraulic jacks to hold framing in place during construction of an overhead structure

PREPARATION AND LAYOUT

If your yard has only a minor slope that will interfere with your patio location, adding a swale may be a sufficient remedy. Larger drainage problems may require a full-fledged drainage plan—and the help of a landscape professional. A grading plan, like the one shown above, indicates where soil has to be removed and how water will drain from the landscape.

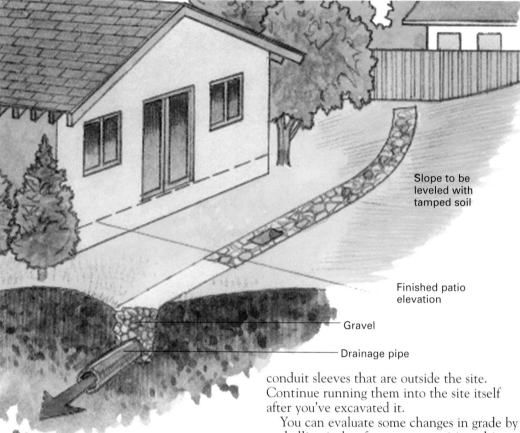

Slope to be leveled with tamped soil

Finished patio elevation

Gravel

Drainage pipe

No matter what size or style of patio you build, the first step is to prepare the site. Site preparation will vary from one project to another, but it generally includes two phases of work:
■ Removing debris, weeds and other unwanted vegetation, trees, and structures, such as old paving, posts, walls, and buildings.
■ Altering the landscape with grading.

GRADING

Making changes to the grade is often the first—and sometimes the only—step in preparing the site for a landscape project. If your patio site abuts a slope, you'll have to remove some—or all—of it to make it level. Even a perfectly flat site can often benefit from the addition of contours to the land.

Begin all the rough grading before laying out the site and minimize the amount of dirt you have to move by filling in low spots with the cut soil. This is the work that calls for heavy equipment. Leave the finish grading for last, which can be done with a garden rake.

After the rough grading is done, lay

conduit sleeves that are outside the site. Continue running them into the site itself after you've excavated it.

You can evaluate some changes in grade by eyeballing it, but for greater precision, drive stakes where you want the grade to change.

LAYING OUT THE SITE

The first step in laying out the site is to mark its perimeter. For very small jobs, you might be able to get by using an uncut sheet of plywood (see illustration, opposite page, top). But for larger sites, you'll need batter boards, mason's lines, and your dimensioned plan.

CALL IN THE PROS

Although you can do finish grading and many small excavations yourself, rough grading and major excavation call for earth-moving equipment. Costs include an hourly equipment fee plus an operator expense.

Even if you can do the work by hand, it may be more efficient to spend $500 to have it done all at once than to spend four weekends at hard labor. You'll free your time for things you can easily do yourself.

MAKING AND SETTING BATTER BOARDS

Batter boards are a homemade device that makes both layout and excavation more precise.

To make a set of batter boards (you'll need two sets for each corner, except where the patio abuts the house directly), cut scrap 2×4 lumber to 2-foot lengths, and point one end of each so you can drive them into the ground.

■ Fasten a 15- to 18-inch crosspiece to the 2-footers a couple of inches below the tops. The crosspiece will let you move the mason's lines so you can position them where you need them.

■ Set temporary corner stakes and drive the batter boards at right angles to each other, 2 to 4 feet beyond the proposed corners of your patio. Don't worry if they're not level; that comes later. Now you're ready for the mason's lines.

RUNNING MASON'S LINES

Tie one end of a mason's line to a nail driven roughly in the center of the crosspiece, run the line across to the opposite corner, and fasten it. Repeat the installation of the lines between the remaining batter boards. This is the outside edge of the patio. If your proposed edging is wide (timbers or concrete, for example), a parallel set of lines inside the

LAYING OUT A SMALL JOB

For small jobs on a flat surface, lay an uncut sheet of plywood to roughly establish square corners.

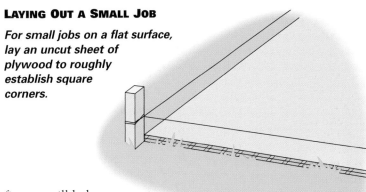

first set will help you mark the excavation width for the edging. Now you can level the lines.

■ Hang a line level (a small, lightweight plastic level with hooks at each end made especially for this purpose) in the middle of one of the mason's lines, and adjust the height of the line until the bubble in the level is centered between its marks.

■ Adjust the height of the line by driving in the batter boards or by repositioning the mason's line on the crosspiece.

■ Once you're confident that the first line is level, tighten the line at both ends so that it won't slip.

■ Repeat the leveling procedure until you have all lines level with each other.

To achieve slope for drainage (about 2 percent will do), lower the lines at the outside corners by 1 inch for every 4 linear feet. That may seem like undoing what you've already done, but the lines need to be level first so you have a point from which to start.

BATTER-BOARD LAYOUT

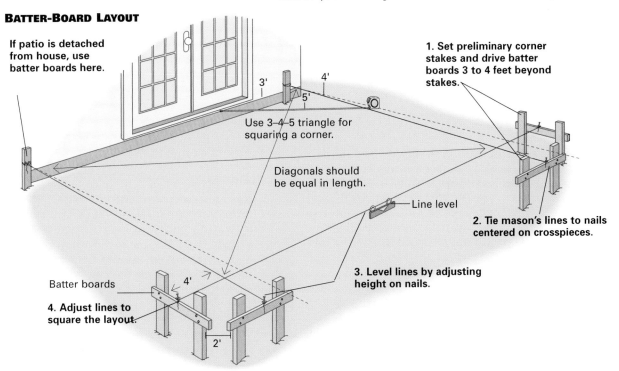

If patio is detached from house, use batter boards here.

3'   4'   5'

Use 3–4–5 triangle for squaring a corner.

Diagonals should be equal in length.

Line level

1. Set preliminary corner stakes and drive batter boards 3 to 4 feet beyond stakes.

2. Tie mason's lines to nails centered on crosspieces.

3. Level lines by adjusting height on nails.

Batter boards   4'

4. Adjust lines to square the layout.

2'

PREPARATION AND LAYOUT

continued

SQUARING THE CORNERS

The four lines of your layout (or three lines and the house line) should create a rectangle with square (90-degree) corners. There's a handy method for squaring layout corners called the 3-4-5 method. It's based on the geometric principle that when one side of a right triangle (one with a 90-degree angle) is 3 feet and the other side is 4, the hypotenuse (longest side) will be 5 feet exactly. Here's how to use the 3–4–5 method to check for square.

■ At the intersection of the lines on one corner, measure out 3 feet along one mason's line (or the house wall) and mark it with a piece of tape.

■ Then mark a point exactly 4 feet from the intersection along the other line.

■ Now measure the distance between your pieces of tape. If it is exactly 5 feet, the corner forms a 90-degree angle. If not, readjust the lines until the two markers are 5 feet apart. For large jobs, use multiples of 3, 4, and 5 feet, such as 6, 8, and 10; or 9, 12, and 15.

To double-check for square, measure both diagonals. Adjust the lines until the diagonals are equal and each side is the required length. When you're confident that the layout is square, cut notches in the crosspieces to mark the final location of the lines. That way you can take the lines down and retie them at the same point later.

MARKING THE EDGES

To mark the corners and edges of the site so you'll know exactly where to dig, suspend a plumb bob so that its line just touches the intersection of the layout lines. The point on the ground below the intersection of those lines will become the corner of the excavation.

■ Lower the plumb bob to the ground and have a helper mark the spot with a stake. If you're laying out the site yourself, let the plumb bob settle to the ground and let go of the line. Mark the point with a stake.

Drive a stake here and tie mason's lines between the stakes at ground level.

■ Plumb and stake each corner and tie a line at ground level tightly between them.

■ Repeat the procedure for the second set of lines (for the edging) if you've installed them.

■ Then mark the ground line with spray paint (get upside-down paint at your hardware store—it sprays when the can is inverted), or with powdered chalk from a squeeze bottle. The chalk comes in colors, so find one that stands out from the ground color. With the painted or chalked line on the ground, you have a clean edge to start your excavation.

BREAKING GROUND

Excavating the soil requires more than brute strength. There is some science to it. First remove the mason's lines from the batter boards to get them out of your way. If you're not installing forms, begin your excavation along the edges of the painted line. Forms will require some additional elbow room, so if you're using them, you'll have to dig out about a foot beyond the painted line.

■ Using a square shovel or spade, cut the sod along the painted outline of the patio. This chore becomes easier if you use the shovel to first cut the sod into strips about a foot wide.

To outline a curve, lay a hose in the desired shape and mark it with paint or chalk. Once you pull the hose up, you'll have a clean line.

ADJUST THE HEIGHT

All patio surfaces should be about an inch above grade to permit rain to flow off the surface. Subtract that amount from the depths of the material thickness and your patio surface will be slightly above soil level. A patio raised by this amount will also allow you to mow the edges without having to trim them separately.

You can remove the sod in squares or strips. Strips are better if you're not going to use the sod right away. Rolling the sod in strips will keep the roots moist.

■ Dig down 2 inches to preserve the roots. Push the shovel handle under the roots sharply to dislodge them. Roll the sod away from you as you go to keep a fresh edge continuously exposed. When you have each sod strip out, store it in the shade if you're not going to use it right away.
■ Use a rototiller set to the depth of the patio materials (see "Excavation Depths," below) to loosen the soil. Then excavate the trench for your edging so the edging will be at the height of the finished patio surface.
■ If you're using grid lines to help maintain your slope and depth, tie them now (see page 110 for more information). Otherwise, use a round-nose shovel to dig out the entire width between the painted lines, working from the center to the perimeter.
■ Dig out the soil to the depth equal to the combined thickness of all the materials, holding the shovel at a low angle to avoid digging too deep and removing the surface in small amounts. The excavation doesn't have to be perfect; bedding materials will even out variations.

If your patio will abut the house, snap a chalk line under the door to indicate the height of the patio surface on the house. It should be about an inch below the threshold unless you live in a climate with heavy snowfall.

EXCAVATION DEPTHS

The depth of your patio excavation will depend on the materials you use. Here's a guide to excavation depths for various materials.

BRICK OR STONE IN SAND: 8 to 9 inches (4 inches of gravel base, 2 inches of sand, and 2 to 3 inches of brick or stone). Brick- or stone-in-sand construction does not require a solid foundation. These materials are intended to heave with the earth in freezing weather and return to level when the frost is out of the ground. It is the moisture in the ground that expands when freezing, and the thick gravel base minimizes the heaving.

POURED CONCRETE: 8 to 10 inches (4 inches of gravel and 4 inches of concrete, with an additional 2 inches of optional sand between them).

MORTARED BRICK OR STONE: $10\frac{1}{2}$ to 12 inches (8 inches of gravel and concrete base, $\frac{1}{2}$- to 1-inch mortar bed, and 2 to 3 inches of brick or stone). In cold climates, some local codes require slabs for poured concrete and mortared patios to "float"—to permit the slab to heave in one piece. Excavate a trench 1 foot beyond the patio perimeter and 6 inches deeper than the patio excavation. You'll need to lay a gravel base in the trench the same depth as the footing. Dig out the turf about 6 inches beyond the lines to allow for forms.

LOOSE MATERIALS: 6 inches (2 inches of sand plus 4 inches of material).

PREPARATION AND LAYOUT
continued

EXCAVATING A PATIO SITE

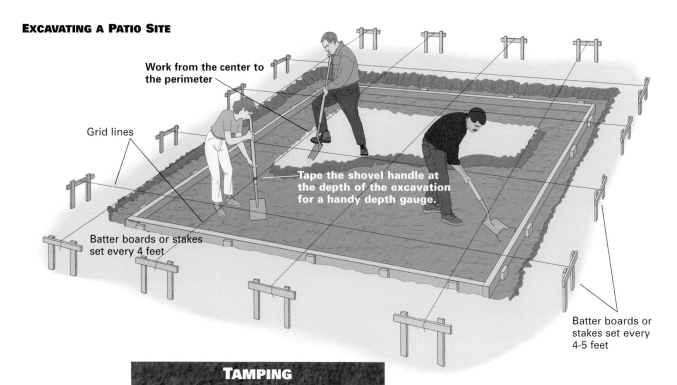

Work from the center to the perimeter

Grid lines

Tape the shovel handle at the depth of the excavation for a handy depth gauge.

Batter boards or stakes set every 4 feet

Batter boards or stakes set every 4-5 feet

TAMPING

Once you've excavated the site, you'll need to compact the soil to keep it from settling and to make a firm base for the bedding materials. Rent a power tamper for any area larger than 100 square feet; hand tamping is strenuous and produces inconsistent results on large areas. Moisten the soil before tamping it.

MAKING A SLOPE GAUGE

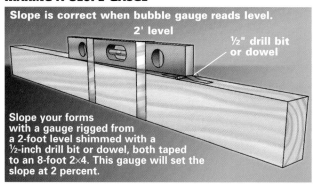

Slope is correct when bubble gauge reads level.

2' level

½" drill bit or dowel

Slope your forms with a gauge rigged from a 2-foot level shimmed with a ½-inch drill bit or dowel, both taped to an 8-foot 2×4. This gauge will set the slope at 2 percent.

GRID LINES

Grid lines help keep the slope of the excavation consistent across its surface. First, use a slope gauge (see "Making a Slope Gauge," at left) to slope your forms.

Set stakes or batter boards at 4- to 5-foot intervals outside the excavation line. Tie lines across the area at the same height above the forms. The grid lines will now follow the slope you've set on the forms.

If you are working on a small site, you can probably get by with the slope gauge, but using grid lines is more accurate, especially on patios larger than 10×10 feet.

EDGING

If you'll be pouring concrete, now's the time to install forms as illustrated at right. For other materials, this is usually the best opportunity to install the edging, as shown on the opposite page. Smooth edging surfaces will help you guide the screeding (leveling) of the base materials.

STAKING STRAIGHT FORMS

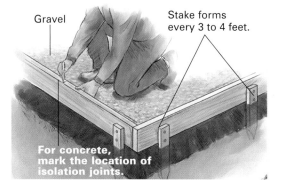

Gravel

Stake forms every 3 to 4 feet.

For concrete, mark the location of isolation joints.

STAKING CURVED FORMS

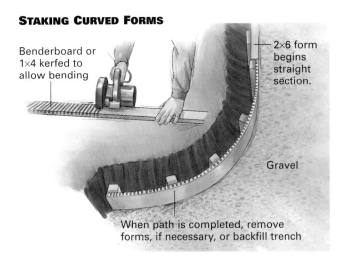

Benderboard or 1×4 kerfed to allow bending

2×6 form begins straight section.

Gravel

When path is completed, remove forms, if necessary, or backfill trench

INSTALLING PREFORMED EDGING

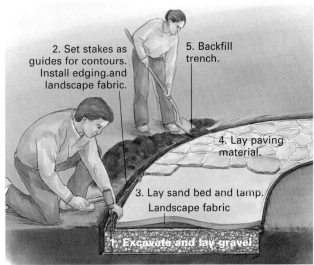

2. Set stakes as guides for contours. Install edging and landscape fabric.

5. Backfill trench.

4. Lay paving material.

3. Lay sand bed and tamp. Landscape fabric

1. Excavate and lay gravel.

INSTALLING TIMBER EDGING

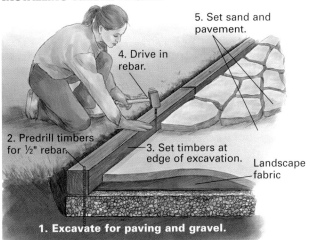

5. Set sand and pavement.

4. Drive in rebar.

2. Predrill timbers for ½" rebar.

3. Set timbers at edge of excavation.

Landscape fabric

1. Excavate for paving and gravel.

INSTALLING BRICK EDGING

6. Remove forms and backfill.

5. Set one or two rows of paving as you go.

4. Set brick edging.

2. Drive stakes every 3 to 4 feet and attach 2× forms.

Landscape fabric

3. Lay sand base and tamp.

1. Excavate and lay gravel base.

INSTALLING A CONCRETE CURB

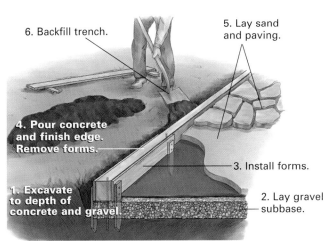

6. Backfill trench.

5. Lay sand and paving.

4. Pour concrete and finish edge. Remove forms.

3. Install forms.

1. Excavate to depth of concrete and gravel.

2. Lay gravel subbase.

INSTALLING FLAGSTONE EDGING

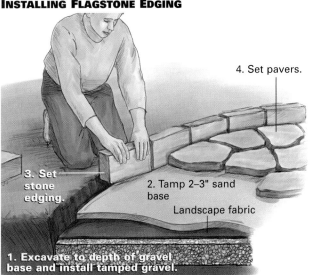

4. Set pavers.

3. Set stone edging.

2. Tamp 2–3" sand base

Landscape fabric

1. Excavate to depth of gravel base and install tamped gravel.

PREPARATION AND LAYOUT

continued

DRAINAGE

Now is the time to marshall your defenses against runoff and water damage that can't be fixed by grading alone—before you install bedding materials.

Drainage systems should appear on your dimensioned plan, but if you haven't yet included them, figure out now where any drainage pipes will exit—either into a lower spot on your yard, the storm sewer system (if allowed by local codes), or into one of the drainage receptacles shown on these pages. Then design the route from the source of the problem so you can get the water to its exit point.

If your patio will be near the end of a downspout, direct the downspout away from the house. Or tie it into an underground drainpipe. Here's how.
■ Dig a trench across the excavation and place flexible drainpipe in the trench.
■ Connect the downspout to the drainpipe.
■ Screen off the opening of the downspout (in the guttering) with wire mesh to keep debris from entering the system. Leaves stuck in the drainpipe under the patio may resist removal. Like the other options illustrated here, such drainage systems are virtually maintenance-free once they are installed.

INSTALLING A SURFACE DRAIN

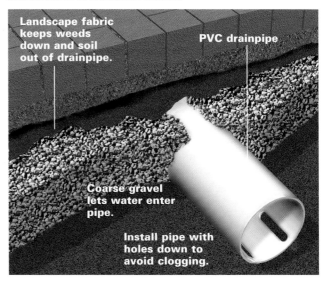

Landscape fabric keeps weeds down and soil out of drainpipe.

PVC drainpipe

Coarse gravel lets water enter pipe.

Install pipe with holes down to avoid clogging.

PATIO DRAINAGE: Dig drainage trenches either around the perimeter or under the surface. Subsurface trench depths will vary with the climate, so check with a landscape expert to get the right depth. Perimeter drains should be 4 inches deep and set in a concrete channel. In both cases, the trenches should slope 1 inch for every 4 feet. Line the recess of either kind with gravel and then install perforated drainpipe, keeping the slope consistent. Cover the pipe with more gravel, landscape fabric, and the patio bedding.

INSTALLING A PERIMETER DRAIN

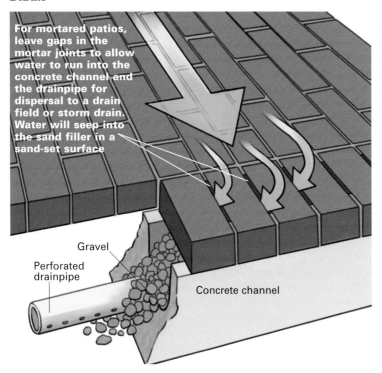

For mortared patios, leave gaps in the mortar joints to allow water to run into the concrete channel and the drainpipe for dispersal to a drain field or storm drain. Water will seep into the sand filler in a sand-set surface

Gravel

Perforated drainpipe

Concrete channel

DITCH YOUR DIFFERENCES

Drainage problems are often not restricted only to your yard. They will often cut across property lines and affect your entire neighborhood.

If there's a surface drainage problem in your landscape, make sure any ditches you create to solve your share of the problem don't make your neighbors' problems worse.

Arrange a meeting with all of the affected neighbors and an excavation contractor to see if an integrated solution can be found.

DRY WELL: A dry well is a large, gravel-filled hole located at a spot lower than the patio (but above the water table) and removed from the patio site. A dry well collects water and lets it slowly disperse into the surrounding soil. It must be connected to the site by drainpipe sloped 1 inch for every 4 feet. Dig a hole 3 feet deep and 2 to 4 feet wide. Fill it with coarse gravel; cover the gravel with landscape fabric, then topsoil and sod. (Landscape fabric keeps soil from washing into the gravel.)

DRY-WELL CROSS SECTION

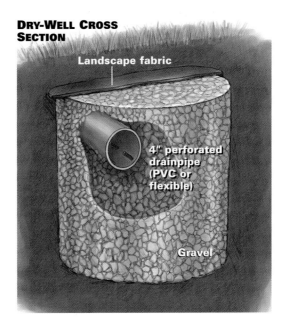

Landscape fabric

4" perforated drainpipe (PVC or flexible)

Gravel

OFF-SITE DRAINAGE TRENCH:

A typical drainage trench is 12 inches wide and as deep as needed to maintain a uniform slope of 1 inch per every 4 feet of horizontal run. Fill half of the trench with gravel, install perforated drainpipe (holes down), and then add more gravel. Cover the gravel with landscape fabric, soil, and sod. End the pipe in an unobtrusive area of your landscape.

CROSS SECTION OF AN OFF-SITE DRAINAGE TRENCH

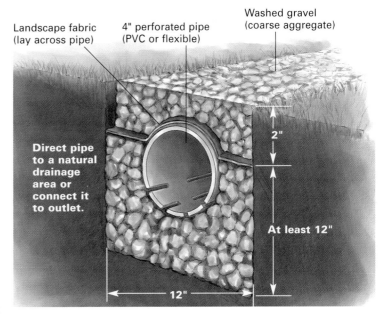

Landscape fabric (lay across pipe)

4" perforated pipe (PVC or flexible)

Washed gravel (coarse aggregate)

Direct pipe to a natural drainage area or connect it to outlet.

2"

At least 12"

12"

CATCH BASIN

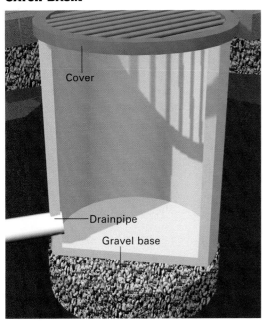

Cover

Drainpipe

Gravel base

CATCH BASIN: A catch basin is an open surface drain with a receptacle that holds water and disperses it through piping when it reaches a certain level. Dig a hole at the lowest point of the patio so the patio surface drains toward it. The hole should be wide enough to accommodate the prefab catch basin (available at garden centers) and deeper by 4 inches (for a gravel base). Dig a trench for the outlet pipe and slope the pipe to a distant dry well or, if codes permit, to the storm sewer system.

BUILDING A BRICK-IN-SAND PATIO

**CROSS SECTION OF
BRICK-IN-SAND PATIO**

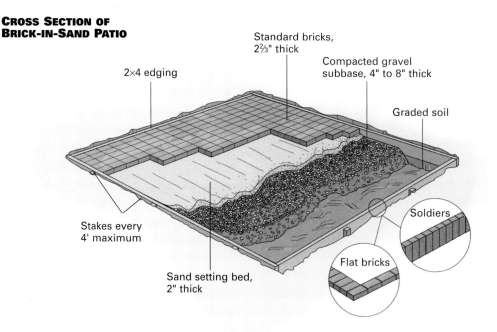

- 2×4 edging
- Standard bricks, 2⅔" thick
- Compacted gravel subbase, 4" to 8" thick
- Graded soil
- Stakes every 4' maximum
- Soldiers
- Flat bricks
- Sand setting bed, 2" thick

L aying brick in a smooth bed of sand is a fairly quick and easy way to install a patio. This installation allows you to work in stages, leaving the job partly finished and picking it up later—something you cannot do when pouring a concrete slab or installing a mortared patio. The keys to long-term success are a well-compacted base and a firm edging around the perimeter.

LAYOUT AND EXCAVATION

Before you lay out the site, calculate its dimensions so that you will minimize the number of cut brick. Divide the dimensions of the patio by the *actual* size of the brick you've chosen, including ⅛-inch gaps between each brick.

Then lay out and excavate the site, using the methods discussed on pages 106–110. The excavation should be deep enough for a 4-inch gravel base, a 2-inch sand bed, and the thickness of the brick (2 to 3 inches). Subtract 1 inch; you'll want the surface slightly higher than grade—the raised edge makes mowing easier. Allow for slope, moisten the soil and tamp it with a rented power tamper.

SITE SAFETY

Site preparation can leave an area temporarily hazardous. Take the following precautions.
■ Protect your trees: Use flagging tape to mark trees you want to keep. Siltation fences keep displaced soil from covering root zones.

■ Limit access: Designate and mark heavy equipment access points. Barricade driveways against equipment that can crack the concrete.
■ Keep it safe: Barricade holes (even shallow excavations) and make sure you remove tools at the end of each workday.

A WEIGHTY ISSUE

Before you drive the family car down to the home center to pick up brick for your patio, calculate their weight.

A single 2×4×8-inch brick weighs approximately 5 pounds. Each brick, laid flat, covers 4×8 inches, or 32 square inches, which is 0.22 square feet. There are 4.5 bricks per square foot, or 450 per 100 square feet.

At 5 pounds a brick, the weight of bricks for a small 10×10 patio (100 square feet) is about 2,250 pounds—more than a ton, and more than your car can carry.

A lift of bricks (the quantity in which they are shipped) contains 500 bricks. If you order a lift direct from the brick distributor, the shipping might be free. Call around to see.

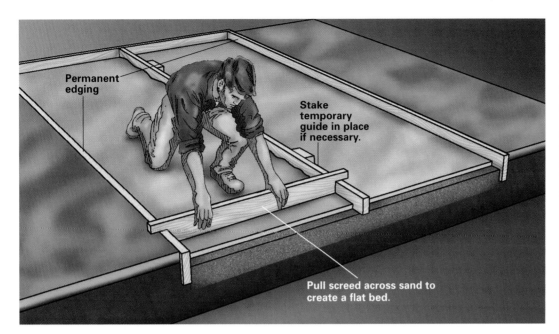

Permanent edging

Stake temporary guide in place if necessary.

Pull screed across sand to create a flat bed.

To screed small areas, set the screed board on the perimeter forms. If the patio site is wider than the screed, stake temporary guides within the surface areas of the patio.

The tamper is heavy, so enlist the aid of a helper. When you start the tamper, it may feel as if it's taking off. Once you've got the hang of it, make several passes. Fill in any depressions and compact the area again.

INSTALLING THE EDGING

Installation techniques for edging vary with the kind of edge you want to create.

■ **SOLDIERS AND SAILORS:** Soldiers are bricks set on end with the widest side facing up at surface level. Sailors have the narrow side facing up. Whichever you choose, set them in before you pour the gravel.

To install upright soldiers, dig an edging trench and add enough sand so you can set the bricks at the desired height. Use mason's line to keep them straight. Tap the bricks in with a hammer and board. Backfill the row with soil and tamp it lightly. After you install the patio surface, tamp the backfilled soil firmly, adding or subtracting soil as needed.

■ **BRICK OR STONE IN CONCRETE:** If the edging will be set in concrete, dig a trench wide enough for forms. Use staked 2× stock, with the top at the same level as the finished patio. Pour the concrete and let it cure for at least three days. Mortar the surface and install the edge material. Let the mortar cure for two days before removing the forms.

■ **TIMBER EDGING:** Dig the trench out from the perimeter and slightly wider than the timbers. Install the timbers, backfill behind them, and drive spikes into the ground though predrilled holes.

■ **PLASTIC EDGING:** Set rigid plastic edging in a trench and hold it in place with metal spikes. The top ridge of the edging should extend above the sand base by about half the thickness of the pavers.

If you're using edging that you will install after the paving is laid, install temporary screed guides (2× stock staked and even with the finished surface).

WORKING WITH BRICK

Compared to other paving materials, brick is relatively easy to cut, handle, and install. The work is even easier if you have the right tools. Some tools are available from a brick supplier; you should be able to find others you need at any large building-supply store.
■ To cut individual brick to a special size or shape, use a chisel called a brickset.
■ For driving the brickset, use a mason's hammer (the chiseled end is for trimming cuts).
■ For tapping bricks in sand or dry mortar without damaging them, use a rubber mallet.
■ To apply wet mortar to a brick surface, use a mason's trowel and use the handle to tap them in place.
■ To finish the surface of mortar joints, called striking, use a convex jointer or V-jointer.
■ Any time you cut brick, sharp fragments may break loose, so be sure to wear eye protection, gloves, and a dust mask if cutting or sawing.

BUILDING A BRICK-IN-SAND PATIO
continued

SETTING THE SUBBASE

Order the gravel and schedule its delivery so it can be dumped directly into the patio area. Gravel is heavy and very difficult to move around. To estimate how many cubic yards you will need, multiply the thickness in feet (for example, 4 inches equals 0.33 feet) times the width (in feet) times the length of the patio (in feet) and divide the total by 27 to get the volume in cubic yards.

■ Before you lay in gravel, set stakes at various locations in the bed, driving them in so the tops are 4 inches above the surface.

■ Shovel the gravel even with the stakes and rake it roughly level with a garden rake.

■ Set a long, straight 2×4 at an angle on the surface of the subbase to smooth it. Fill in low spots and rake away gravel from high spots until the surface is consistent over the entire site and slopes properly for drainage. When the surface of the subbase is uniform and meets the 4-inch marks on the stakes, compact the gravel with a tamper.

■ To prevent weeds and grass from growing through the subbase, lay down a layer of landscaping fabric before pouring the sand base. Overlap fabric joints by at least one foot to prevents sand from working down into the gravel.

LAYING THE SAND BASE

For the sand base, order unwashed coarse sand. It is less expensive than washed fine sand and works just as well.

Shovel the sand into the site and spread it evenly with a garden rake. At various locations, push a stake or rod—marked at 2 inches—into the sand. Push the sand into all the edges and corners until the surface is relatively uniform.

SCREEDING

Screeding is leveling. To make a screed, use a 2×4 or 2×6 long enough to span the patio and cut out the ends to produce "ears" that are a foot or more long. The cutouts should be wide enough to ride on

SCREEDING A LARGE PATIO

For a large patio, work in sections. Install a temporary screed guide. Rest the notched screed on the guide and on the edging to screed the first section.

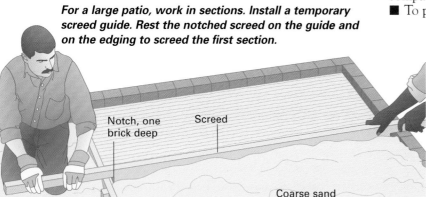

Notch, one brick deep

Screed

Temporary screed guide

Coarse sand

Install the pavers for the first section, using mason's line stretched between the edging and the temporary screed to act as a surface guide.

Mason's line pulled taut

Remove the temporary guide and screed the next section.

Screed

the edging or temporary guides and deep enough to level the sand at the thickness of your brick.

■ Pull the screed slowly across the entire surface of the sand base, working it from side to side as you pull it.

■ Soak the sand base thoroughly with a garden hose nozzle set to fine mist. Compact the wet sand with a tamper.

■ Fill in low spots with more sand; then wet and tamp again. Continue adding sand, tamping, and leveling with the screed board until the sand is uniformly 2 inches deep and the surface is consistent across the entire site.

SETTING BRICKS

Before you lay the brick, take a trial run. Lay out a small section, beginning in the corners and extending far enough to give you an idea of how often the pattern calls for cut brick.

Now remove the trial brick and start laying them in the corners—this time for real. If you use plastic edging, the outer row should fit snugly against it. For other edging, leave a ⅛-inch gap (use plastic spacers or plywood). Keep the lines straight by tying mason's line to bricks and stretching it across the surface.

■ Set bricks by pushing straight down— don't slide them—then tap them in place with a rubber mallet.

■ Lay out the pattern in all directions outward from the corner. Tap each brick into place with the mallet to make sure the surfaces are even.

■ Every three or four rows, lay a carpenter's level and sloping jig across the surface of the pavers to check your progress. (Cut a 2×4 to the angle of the slope and set the carpenter's level on it to make the level read accurately.)

If the surface is low in some places, remove the paver, add more sand, tamp, and replace the paver. If some spots are a bit high, adjust the paver height with a few taps from the mallet, or scrape out sand and replace the paver.

If you don't have one, rent a masonry saw to get professional-quality cut brick.

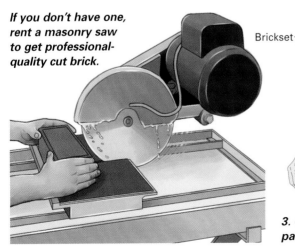

You may need to brush in sand and spray with water several times before the joints are completely filled.

FILLING THE GAPS

Sprinkle sand over the entire surface and sweep it back and forth—from all directions—into the joints with a push broom. When the joints are full, sweep the excess to one side and settle the sand with a fine mist from the garden hose. Continue sweeping sand and settling it until the joints are full. Then tamp the surface with a power tamper. You're not doing this just for aesthetics. The grains of sand act as tiny wedges to keep the brick from moving.

CUTTING BRICK

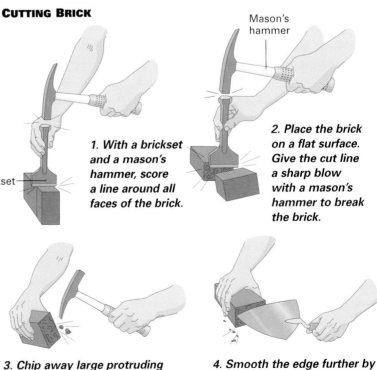

1. With a brickset and a mason's hammer, score a line around all faces of the brick.

Brickset

Mason's hammer

2. Place the brick on a flat surface. Give the cut line a sharp blow with a mason's hammer to break the brick.

3. Chip away large protruding particles with a mason's hammer.

4. Smooth the edge further by scraping with a pointed trowel.

SETTING BRICK ON A CONCRETE SLAB

Brick on mortar packs a double dose of patio building: You build one "patio"—the concrete slab—then add another—the brick surface.

If you already have a sturdy, level slab in place, you're halfway there. Laying brick on an old concrete patio, however, will raise its surface, so you will likely have to adjust the height of any door that opens onto your patio.

LAYING OUT THE SLAB

To lay out the excavation area for a new slab, start by making sure its measurements are equal to an even multiple of the dimensions of your brick pattern. Most paving brick is 4×8 inches, but some nominally sized 4×8 pavers are ½- to ⅜-inch less than the stated size.

■ Set out the brick pattern, spacing it for mortar joints. Measure the pattern and divide the slab measurements by the pattern dimensions. Adjust the final size of the slab so it will accommodate the pattern. That way you will minimize the number of bricks you have to cut—or eliminate cutting altogether.

■ Set temporary stakes at approximate corner locations. Using the techniques shown on page 107, lay out the site and square it with a 3-4-5 method. Drop a plumb bob at the intersection of the lines and drive stakes; these are the real corners. Run tight mason's lines at ground level for the excavation lines. Chalk or paint the ground line.

EXCAVATING

If your chalked or painted line represents the edge of the patio, including the edging, dig on that line. If the line represents the edge of the patio but not the edging, start digging about 12 inches outside it (you'll need the extra room to install forms), and excavate the site to a uniform sloped depth (see page 110).

SETTING FORMS

Drive 2×4 stakes at the corners and attach 2×8s for the forms. To keep the forms from bowing, drive 2×4 stakes outside the forms at 2-foot intervals. Attach the forms to the stakes with screws. Make sure the forms slope properly as you install them—measure down from the sloped mason's lines or grid lines. (See page 110 for more information.)

PREPARING THE BED

Next, pour in a 4-inch gravel base, shoveling it tight against the forms. Level the gravel with a screed (a 2×4 or 2×6 with the ends cut out so they ride along the surface of the forms). Add gravel to low spots and tamp it with a power tamper.

Lay in reinforcing wire mesh (use a gauge that is called 6×6 10/10) supported by and tied to dobies—small 2-inch-thick concrete (not brick) blocks that keep the wire mesh centered halfway through concrete when it's poured. Overlap the ends of the mesh by 4 inches and tie them with wire.

POURING THE SLAB

If you pour your own (easy enough on slabs 10×10 or smaller), make a runway for your wheelbarrow with 2×12s. If you use ready-mix, make sure the truck can get as close to the site as possible without damaging your driveway or lawn.

■ Mix bags of premix in a power mixer and pour it in wheelbarrow loads. Pour the concrete uniformly into the excavation, and work it up and down with a shovel to set it and release air bubbles. Drag a 2×4 (long enough to span the width) to level the concrete with the forms. Fill voids, and level again.

■ Roughen the surface of the wet concrete with a homemade scarifier—drive nails at 1-inch intervals into an 18-inch 2×2. The grooves made by the nails do not have to be deep—just enough to give the mortar a "tooth" to bind it to the surface. Then let the

BRICK IN MORTAR

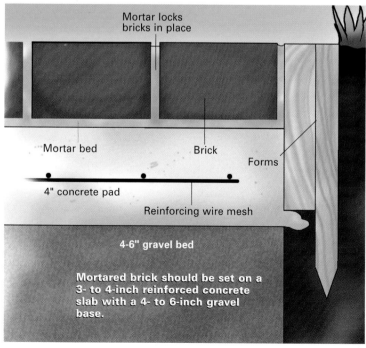

Mortar locks bricks in place

Mortar bed

Brick

Forms

4" concrete pad

Reinforcing wire mesh

4-6" gravel bed

Mortared brick should be set on a 3- to 4-inch reinforced concrete slab with a 4- to 6-inch gravel base.

concrete cure for three to seven days, keeping it moist with burlap (spray it occasionally), or cover it with plastic sheets.

LAYING THE BRICK

Before you start, reinstall mason's lines at the finished surface level of the patio. Then mix premixed mortar (type M is for outdoor use) in a mortar box or wheelbarrow. You'll know when you have the mix right when it hangs on the surface of a trowel turned on edge. Don't spread (or mix) more than you can handle in about an hour. On a hot day, mortar will start drying in as little as 15 minutes. Spread mortar in a ½-inch bed in 4×4-foot sections.

■ Start in a corner and work in square or triangular sections, depending on the pattern you have chosen. Push each brick straight down with a firm motion and tap it in place with a rubber mallet. Use ⅜- or ½-inch plywood spacers as you work—the same spacers you used when you calculated the pattern dimensions. Tie mason's lines to bricks and set them on line with your pattern to help keep the courses straight.

■ As you finish each section, lay a 2×4 on it. Pull out low pavers, remortar, and reset the brick. Tap down pavers that are high.

■ When you have laid the entire surface, let the mortar cure for three days; then pack the joints with grout. Use a pointed mason's trowel or, better yet, a grout bag. The bag has a pointed nozzle to squeeze the mortar into the joints—it's more precise and you'll make

SETTING BRICK IN A MORTAR BED

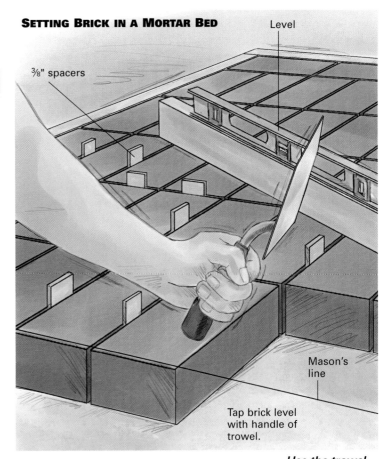

Level

⅜" spacers

Mason's line

Tap brick level with handle of trowel.

less mess. Clean spilled grout right away with a wet sponge. When the joints will hold a thumbprint, finish them with a jointing tool. Keep the surface moist for three or four days, so it cures slowly.

Use the trowel handle to tap bricks level into the mortar bed. Make sure the top of the surface is consistent— use a carpenter's level to check it every 6 to 8 square feet.

SETTING A MORTARED BRICK PATIO

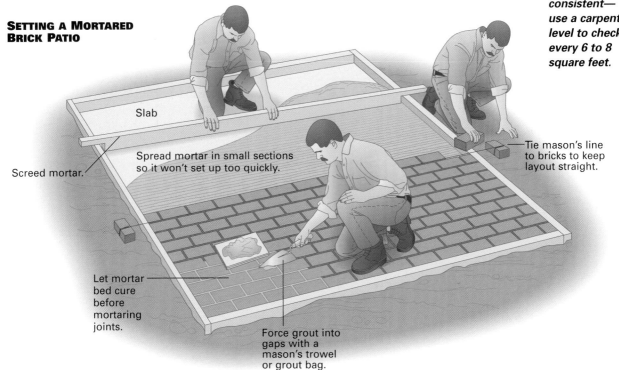

Slab

Spread mortar in small sections so it won't set up too quickly.

Screed mortar.

Tie mason's line to bricks to keep layout straight.

Let mortar bed cure before mortaring joints.

Force grout into gaps with a mason's trowel or grout bag.

FLAGSTONE PATIO

BUILDING A SAND-SET FLAGSTONE PATIO

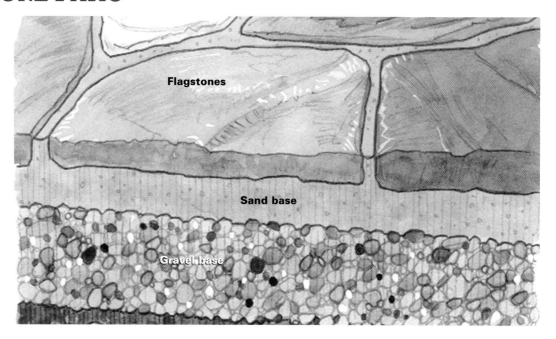

Flagstones

Sand base

Gravel base

The look of flagstone has a timeless appeal, and for good reason. Its rough-hewn surface brings a rustic charm to almost any landscape design.

Like brick, you can set flagstone on a sand base or mortar it to a concrete slab. Dry-set surfaces flex and fall back with changes in ground temperatures. Mortared surfaces are solid and need a concrete base to keep them from cracking. Both installations need a gravel subbase for support and drainage.

Installation techniques are substantially the same for both dry-set and mortared patios, as discussed below. What's different about setting flagstone is that you can't predict the pattern because its shape is irregular. Even cut flagstone is not uniformly modular, so you will have to experiment with your design before you actually set it.

To estimate the amount of stone required, figure a ton for every 120 square feet. Draw free-form designs on graph paper and count the number of whole squares to get the area. Order about 5 percent more for waste.

PREPARING THE SITE

Site layout for both a dry-set or mortared stone patio is the same. Because stone lends itself to free-flowing designs, you have more layout options than with regular materials.

RECTANGULAR DESIGNS: Unlike brick installations, stone patios do not have to precisely accommodate modular materials.

■ Figure the dimensions of your patio space—you won't need to make adjustments—but make sure your measurements include the width of your edging material, if any.
■ Drive temporary corner stakes and set batter boards at right angles 3 to 4 feet beyond the stakes.
■ Fasten mason's lines to the batter board crosspieces with nails (or tie them), square them with the 3-4-5 method (see page 107) and slope them for drainage (1 inch every 4 feet). Install a second set of lines to mark the interior of any edging material.
■ Mark the corners with a stake at the point

CUTTING FLAGSTONE

No matter what kind of layout or pattern you have chosen, you'll need to cut some of the flagstone, either to make them fit or to shape their contours.
Here are the basic tools you will need:
■ **Carpenter's pencil:** For marking cut lines on the stone.
■ **Brickset:** To score cut lines.
■ **Mason's hammer and small sledge:** For striking the brickset accurately and with enough force.
■ **Safety goggles:** Stone can shatter when it's cut. Wear a dust mask, too, if you're using a saw with a masonry blade.
For more information, see page 117.

under the intersecting lines where a plumb bob comes to rest. String mason's lines between the stakes at ground level and pull tight. The ground line marks where to dig. Chalk or paint along the ground line and pull it up.

CONTOURED DESIGNS: To make a free-flowing design or a rectangle combined with curves, stake out the patio's maximum length and width.
■ Lay rope within the limits defined by the stakes and experiment until you get the shape you want. Step back from time to time to evaluate the shape. When you're sure the contour is right, chalk or paint the rope outline.
■ Install batter boards as described above. In this case, you won't need the batter boards for squaring corners, but you will need them— or a slope gauge—for establishing an excavation that's sloped for correct drainage. For information about making a slope gauge, see page 110.

EXCAVATING

Excavation for both dry-set and mortared surfaces is the same, but each requires a different depth, and mortared stone will need forms and a concrete slab.

STONE-IN-SAND PATIOS require a depth of 8 to 9 inches (4-inch gravel base, 2-inch

BUILDING A MORTARED FLAGSTONE PATIO

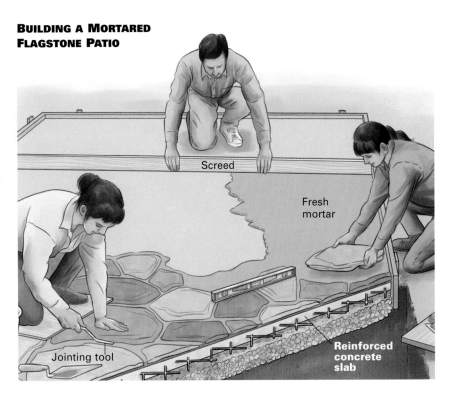

Screed

Fresh mortar

Jointing tool

Reinforced concrete slab

sand bed, plus 2 to 3 inches of stone thickness). Subtract 1 to 2 inches from this depth if you want the finished surface to be above grade. Excavate the site, as shown on pages 108–110, and check for slope as you go against perimeter and grid lines (see page 110). Moisten the soil and power tamp it.

MORTARED STONE excavations will need to be $10\frac{3}{4}$ to 12 inches deep (4-inch gravel base, 4-inch concrete pad, $\frac{3}{4}$- to 1-inch mortar bed and 2 to 3 inches of stone paving). Dig out the site with the proper slope, using mason's and grid lines for reference points. Moisten the soil and power tamp it.

SIZE, SHAPE, AND COLOR

Variety, a design strength of flagstone, also can be a weakness. Because flagstones range tremendously in size, you need to plan for sizes that will best fit the scale of your patio project. A variety of sizes will also add versatility to your design.

Shape is another factor that can work in your favor—or not, depending on the amount of time you're willing to spend finding stones that fit together well. In a carelessly chosen grouping, the stones will look as if they were placed by accident.

Finally, flagstones are available in several colors, sometimes within a single shipment from one supplier. If your design already uses variations in shape and texture, you may not want to add more contrast in color.

Lay out the shape of a curved flagstone patio design with a rope or hose. Step back and look at it from a variety of perspectives. Adjust it until you're happy with the shape; then mark the line with chalk or paint.

FLAGSTONE PATIO
continued

PREPARING AN EXCAVATION

Remove all sod and organic matter. Rake the area to level it, and tamp it firm. Then make forms for concrete or pour in sand for a sand-set base.

FORMS AND EDGING

Although flagstone patios can be edged with the same materials as brick, the irregularity of stone lends itself best to free-form designs with no edging or with hidden edging. Whatever your edging choice, installing it now will give you a consistent reference point for laying the surface level.

DRY-SET SURFACES: Use the methods described for edging a brick patio (see page 111), digging trenches for brick, timber, or plastic. You also can set temporary guides for screeding (staked 2× stock whose top edge is flush with the finished surface).

MORTARED-STONE SURFACES: Drive 2×4 stakes at the corners of the site and attach 2×8s to them with duplex nails or screws. To keep the forms from bowing, drive 2×4 stakes outside the forms and nail them also. Either use a slope gauge or measure down from the perimeter mason's lines so the forms conform to the slope for drainage.

PREPARING A CONCRETE SLAB

Hauling concrete is difficult—more so on uncovered turf. Make a runway from 2×12s so you can deliver the wheelbarrow to the site with less effort. Enlist the aid of helpers to move and settle the concrete in the forms.

MAKING A CONCRETE BASE

GRAVEL BED: Using the methods described on pages 107–110, thoroughly tamp and level a 4-inch gravel bed.

REINFORCEMENT: Lay in reinforcing wire mesh (ask for 6×6 10/10). The mesh will help keep the concrete slab from cracking. Overlap the joints in the mesh by 4 inches and tie them at the joints. Support the mesh and tie it to dobies (small 2-inch concrete blocks that center the mesh in the slab).

POURING THE SLAB: If your site is 10×10 feet or smaller, mix your own concrete from dry ingredients (see page 129). For larger sites, order ready-mix. Carry it to the site in wheelbarrow loads (a 2×10 runway will make this easier) and pour it to a 4-inch depth. Work a shovel up and down in the poured mix to fill recesses and remove air. Span the site with a 2×4 laid on the forms, and work the board back and forth to level the concrete. Roughen the surface with a scarifier (see page 118) or a notched trowel and let the concrete cure for three to seven days.

MAKING A DRY-SET BED

GRAVEL BASE: Drive stakes every 4 to 5 feet so the tops are 4 inches from the excavation surface. Shovel the gravel level with the stakes and spread it with a garden rake. Screed (see "Screeding," pages 116–117) the surface or level it with a 2×4, fill in low spots, and tamp with a power tamper. Lay landscape fabric to keep the weeds at bay.

SAND BED: Shovel sand into the site and spread it with a garden rake. Check for a 2-inch thickness and screed with a 2×6 long enough to span the site (or screed it in sections as shown on page 115). Cut out the ends of the screed so they ride on the edging or screed guides at a depth that will level the sand at 2 inches. Work the screed back and forth as you pull, moisten the sand, and tamp it. Add sand, moisten, and tamp until the bed is uniform.

TAKING A TEST DRIVE

No two flagstones are the same (not even those cut in rectangles), so you'll need to experiment with the pattern. This may take some time, but you'll be more satisfied with the results if you don't rush the process. You can do this before you excavate, but your dry

PREPARING A SAND BED FOR DRY-SET STONE

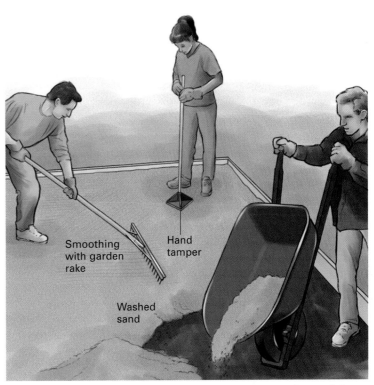

Smoothing with garden rake

Hand tamper

Washed sand

Pour in the sand, distribute it evenly with a garden rake, and then tamp it in place. The sand will need to shift a bit to accommodate the flagstones, so you don't need to get it perfect at this point. On small sites, you may be able to get by with a hand tamper; however, a rented power tamper is usually worth the expense.

run will be easier after excavation. Set stones on the surrounding ground so you can see the shapes and sizes. Then lay the pieces out in the bed, using the suggestions on page 124 as a guide. *Note: If you're working on a sand base, support your weight with 3×3 plywood platforms to keep from indenting and dislodging the sand.*
■ Don't treat the stones as individual pieces; see how they look in pairs and threes. Visualize sections, not puzzle pieces. Don't worry about getting the contours to match exactly; flagstones can be cut to fit. Use small stones as corner fillers.
■ Vary the size, shape, and color as you go. Variety can add spice to the "life" of your patio, too.
■ Keep the spacing as uniform as possible— ½ to ¾ inch for both dry-set and mortared surfaces. Use wider, consistent spacing for turf or planted joints.
■ Once the pattern is laid, stand back and look at it from different perspectives. Rearrange it if you don't like it; then leave the stones in place for the final bedding.

FLAGSTONE PATIO
continued

Experiment with laying the flagstones until you find a pattern with joint lines of fairly consistent width. Use a variety of sizes so you don't end up with a lot of little stones in one area.

Larger
flagstones
set pattern

Smaller
stones fill
gaps

Regardless of whether your patio is mortared or sand-set, when you lay the stones, use larger stones to set the general pattern. Use smaller stones to fill the gaps between the larger ones.

Before adding sand to the joints, place a long 2×4 at several angles across the surface, checking for high and low stones. Use a carpenter's level to check the slope. Pull up high stones, dig out sand to conform to the bottom of the stone, and reset. Add sand and place low stones. Then walk the surface and correct stones that "rock."

Sprinkle washed sand across the entire surface and sweep it into the joints with a push broom. When the joints are full, collect the excess and wet the sand with a fine mist. Continue adding sand and wetting it until the joints are full. Then sweep the surface clean.

To retain the pattern, lift the stones out in 3×3-foot sections—the size of an area you can finish in 10 to 15 minutes. Lay them on the grass next to the site in the same pattern. Mix enough type-M mortar (it's for outdoor use) for the section and spread it with a trowel on the surface of the concrete slab to 1-inch thickness.

Take the stones from the surrounding area and reset each one in the mortar bed, being careful to keep the joints at the original spacing. Push the stones down; don't slide them in place. Tap them with a rubber mallet. As you complete each section, lay a 2×4 across it. You are certain to have high and low stones. Fix them now—you won't be able to later. Pull out stones that are low, add mortar, and reset them. Tap down the high stones, and if necessary, lift them and scoop out just enough mortar to make them level. Then clean off any mortar spills with a wet broom and set the next and succeeding sections. Let the mortar cure three to four days, remove any temporary forms, and then fill the joints.

FILLING THE GAPS FOR PLANTS

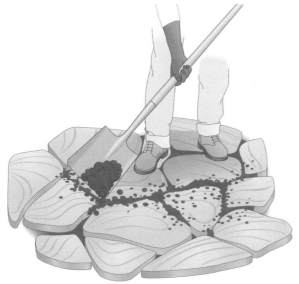

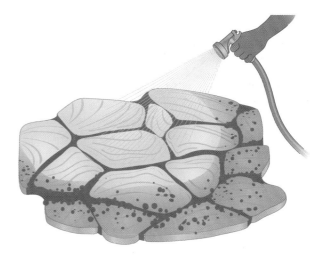

Plant seeds or plants and give them a head start with a fine spray from the hose.

Shovel loose soil into the gaps, filling the recesses between stones.

MORTARING STONE JOINTS

Mix mortar in a mortar box and fill the joints using a pointed trowel or mortar bag. The bag has a spout through which the mortar is squeezed into the joints—it's less messy and will reduce cleanup chores. Clean spilled mortar right away with a wet sponge. Wait until the mortar will hold a thumbprint and then finish the joints with a jointing tool. Cover the surface with plastic or burlap (you'll need to keep it wet) and let it cure for three to four days. Then install edging if you have not already done so.

CUTTING FLAGSTONE

1. Place an adjoining stone on top, and mark a cut line.

2. Score the cut line with a hammer and brickset. Tap repeatedly, moving the brickset a bit at a time along the line between each tap.

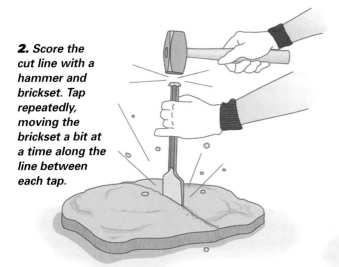

3. Set the stone on a pipe, place the brickset on the score, then break the stone with a single strong blow.

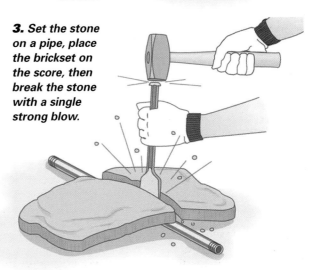

CONCRETE PATIO

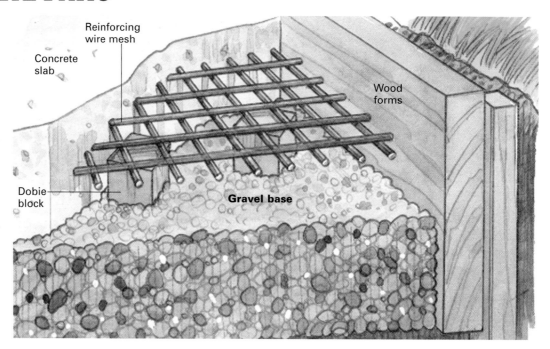

Reinforcing
wire mesh

Concrete
slab

Wood
forms

Dobie
block

Gravel base

To create a concrete slab that will stand up to the most severe weather, start with a gravel subbase. Add spacer blocks, called dobies, to support wire mesh in the middle of the poured concrete; then pour a 4-inch slab.

Concrete is one of the most versatile construction materials. When it's wet, it can assume almost any shape. When it's cured, it will stand up to hard use and extreme weather conditions. It accepts color and texture treatments and costs less than many other building materials.

Concrete has its drawbacks, however. Working with it requires strength and stamina; once you start a pour, you must finish it within a couple of hours, depending on weather conditions. (Get helpers, especially for any patio larger than 10×10.) Curing is not immediate—you will have to wait three to seven days before you can use your concrete patio. And once the concrete has cured, any mistakes made are permanent. The key to successful concrete work is careful preparation.

To estimate quantities, figure the volume of the area (see page 70). Figure twenty-five 80-pound bags of premix for every 50-square-foot section of a 4-inch slab. For any site that will take a cubic yard or more of concrete (or if you're not up to mixing), order ready-mix. The supplier will add ingredients to make it workable in most weather conditions.

WORKING WITH CONCRETE

Concrete work requires some tools and materials you may not own. Luckily, most are inexpensive to buy or rent. Here's what you need:
- 2× lumber for making forms.
- Round-nose and square shovels.
- Small sledge for driving form stakes and to consolidate concrete against forms.
- Carpenter's level to level forms and base material.
- Garden rake to smooth materials.
- Manual or power tamper for tamping soil and gravel.
- A clean wheelbarrow and a mason's hoe to mix concrete or mortar by hand. The wheelbarrow should have a steel body and a heavy-duty inflatable tire.
- A long, straight 2×4 (called a strike-off board or screed) to level the surface of poured concrete.
- A wooden float and a darby to finish the surface smoothly.
- Various mason's trowels for cutting and smoothing.
- Edging and jointing tools to create smooth edges and clean control joints.

Other items you'll need for concrete work are clean running water and plenty of physical endurance. The work is not complicated, but it requires speed, strength, and stamina. Line up a few volunteer helpers.

PLANNING

How thick to make the slab, as well as the amount and type of reinforcement to use, depends on its function. For patios and sidewalks, a 3-inch slab with no reinforcement is fine—although 3½ to 4 inches reinforced with 6-inch wire mesh is preferable. Let your local building codes be your guide.

Plan for drainage. If you don't want water to puddle on the slab, slope it 1 inch every 4 feet. To keep water from making small rivers at the edges of the patio, let the runoff pour into a mulched flower bed or

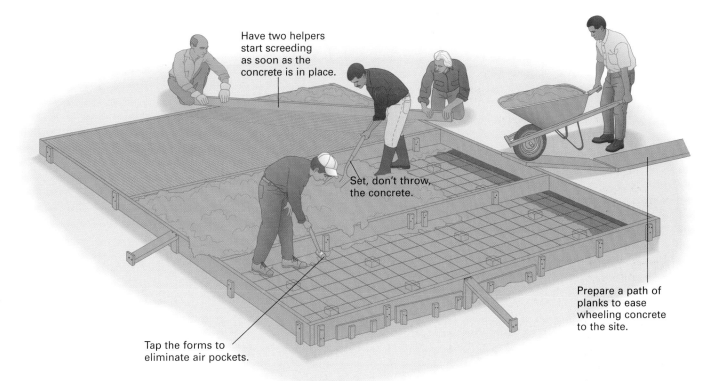

Have two helpers start screeding as soon as the concrete is in place.

Set, don't throw, the concrete.

Prepare a path of planks to ease wheeling concrete to the site.

Tap the forms to eliminate air pockets.

shrub border or dig a trench around the slab and fill it with gravel. For seriously wet sites, also embed a perforated drainpipe in the trench (see page 112–113). Crown the surface (make it a little higher in the center) so water flows away from the center and off all sides.

PREPARING THE SITE

After you have decided where to locate the patio, set temporary stakes at the corners. If the slab abuts the house, snap a chalk line to indicate its height on the foundation of the house—1 to 3 inches below the threshold to keep snow and rain out of the interior. Remember to include the thickness of any surface material if you're laying a slab base for mortared tile or other masonry.

Make batter boards and lay out the site and square the corners using the techniques shown on pages 106–107. If you are installing wide edging (timbers, concrete forms, or perpendicular flat brick), attach a second set of lines parallel to the first and separated by the width of the edging. Skip this step for narrow edging, and remember that the mason's lines represent the outside edge of the patio, including the edging. At each intersection, drop a plumb bob and mark the spot where it touches with a stake. Run a tight line between the stakes at ground level and mark it with chalk or spray paint.

Lower each line in the direction you want slope for drainage (1 inch for every 4 linear feet), or use a slope gauge as shown on page 110 when you install the forms.

EXCAVATING: Remove the mason's lines and remove the sod along the ground line. Then dig a 1-foot trench beyond the outside edge to allow room for the forms. Remove the sod and soil in the remaining area and install grid lines to make the depth uniformly sloped for drainage (see page 110). Moisten the soil and tamp it.

BUILDING FORMS: Wet concrete must be contained by forms—permanent or temporary—generally made of 2×8 stock. If the forms will be permanent, use redwood or cedar or pressure-treated lumber rated for ground contact. If possible, buy lumber that is long enough to span the entire excavation so you won't have to butt joints.

You can assemble the forms in the excavated site, but it's easier to do as much assembly as possible on the ground.

MAKING CURVED FORMS

Here's how to create curved forms.
KERFED WOOD: Make ½-inch cuts (at 1-inch intervals) in 8-inch-high pieces of ¾-inch stock. The board will bend at the kerfs (the cutouts) but will not break on gentle curves.
PLYWOOD: Cut strips of ¼-inch plywood.
SHEET METAL: Use 16-gauge sheet metal cut to 8-inch widths.

Drive stakes along the curve—inside and out—and fasten the forms to the exterior stakes. Remove the interior stakes before pouring.

CONCRETE PATIO
continued

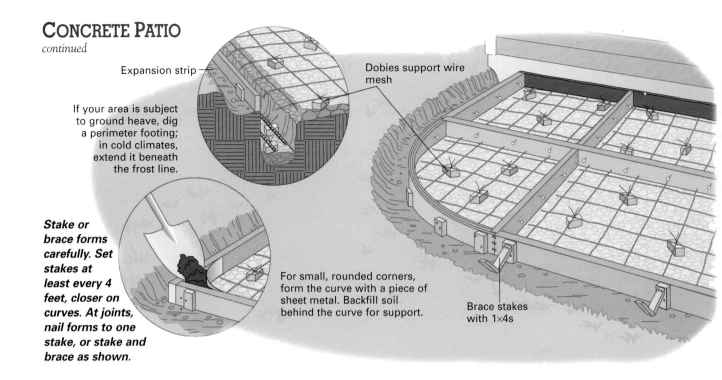

Expansion strip

If your area is subject to ground heave, dig a perimeter footing; in cold climates, extend it beneath the frost line.

Dobies support wire mesh

Stake or brace forms carefully. Set stakes at least every 4 feet, closer on curves. At joints, nail forms to one stake, or stake and brace as shown.

For small, rounded corners, form the curve with a piece of sheet metal. Backfill soil behind the curve for support.

Brace stakes with 1×4s

■ Attach 2×4 stakes (with deck screws) to the corners and at 2- to 4-foot intervals. Splice long sections with ½-inch plywood cleats screwed to the outside of the forms.
■ Set the stakes an inch lower than the top surface. The stakes will be hidden by landscaping later.
■ Align the inside edges of the forms directly under the perimeter mason's lines.
■ Make sure the forms follow the correct slope as you install them. Measure down from your grid lines or use a slope gauge.
■ If the forms are temporary, coat the inside edges with a commercial releasing agent so you can pull them away after the concrete has cured.
■ Cover the top edges of permanent forms with duct tape to protect them from concrete stains.

For slabs wider than 10 feet, install a temporary screed guide.

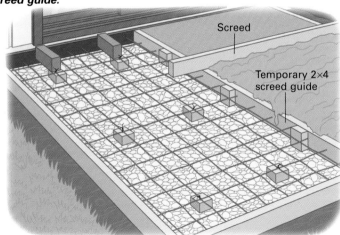

Screed

Temporary 2×4 screed guide

DIVIDER STRIPS

Divider strips section the surface. They are decorative, help keep the concrete from cracking, and divide the work into more manageable areas.

If your patio will be larger than 8×8, you will need divider strips—or you will need to cut control joints in the surface (see page 132). Install divider strips every 8 feet in each direction, using 2× stock staked at 2-foot intervals. Drive the stakes an inch below the strips so they will be covered by the pour. Divider strips are permanent; tape the top edges. After the concrete cures, seal redwood or cedar; pressure-treated wood won't need it.

PREPARING THE BASE

Spread a 4-inch base of gravel—crushed rock or class-5 pea gravel—on a firm soil base. Rake it evenly; then pack it with a power tamper or a plate compactor. A hand tamper is okay for small jobs, but you'll get a workout. Tamp until the surface is smooth, solid, and consistently 4 inches below the anticipated level of the finished slab surface.

For a stronger patio, reinforce the concrete with wire mesh (6×6 10/10). Lay the wire on 2-inch concrete dobies, tying it to the dobies, and overlap the ends by 4 inches. Cut the mesh with a hacksaw or wire cutters. Be cautious, however—the wire can spring back quickly, and it's very sharp.

MIXING CONCRETE

Depending on how much concrete you need, you have three choices for mixing it. In all cases, wear goggles, gloves, and a dust mask. Portland cement can cause severe burns. No matter how large your site is, wet down the gravel bed and the forms before pouring so they won't pull moisture from the mix.

SMALL SPOTS: For small areas, 10×10 or less, use premix in bags. Bagged pre-mix costs a few cents more per pound than separate dry ingredients but are worth the convenience, especially in small batches. There's no measuring—just add water and mix in a wheelbarrow or mortar box.

COMPACT PATIOS: For up to 10×10 patios, mix ingredients in a wheelbarrow or rented power mixer (see mix recipe below).
■ **Mixing in a wheelbarrow:** To mix concrete in a wheelbarrow, measure (in shovelfuls) the sand, aggregate, and cement. Mix the dry ingredients well with a hoe. Form a hollow in the middle and add water. Pull the dry ingredients into the center, working the mixture until it has an even consistency.
■ **Power mixing:** Power mixers are available in several sizes. A rental shop should be able to recommend one that's right for your project. Set the ingredients near the mixer so you won't have to carry them each time, and block the mixer wheels to keep it from abandoning your job.
■ Before starting, measure out the water; pour about 10 percent of it in the mixer. Start the mixer and add the dry ingredients.
■ Let the mixer run, adding water a little at a time until it reaches the right consistency. Tip the mixer to pour the concrete into a wheelbarrow, and roll it to the site.

Before pouring any mixture of your own, scoop out a small amount with a shovel and test it with a trowel. The concrete should hold its shape when sliced with the edge of the trowel but should be wet enough that you can smooth it out with the trowel's flat side.

BIG PATIOS: For areas larger than 100 square feet (anything that calls for a cubic yard of concrete or more), order ready-mix. But be aware that ready-mix requires some specific preparations.
■ Most concrete trucks are too large to drive to the patio site. You may need to pour the mixture from the truck into a wheelbarrow and roll it to the site on sturdy 2×12 runways. If you can get the truck to the site, make sure it won't damage driveway or lawn surfaces.
■ Some trucks with pumps, which deliver the

A wheelbarrow and bags of concrete mix are sufficient for small patios. For areas smaller than 100 square feet, buy the ingredients and rent a power mixer. For larger batches, rely on ready-mix.

mixture to remote sites. It may cost more, but it beats pushing a wheelbarrow.
■ More hands (and more wheelbarrows) make the work go faster. Have two or three helpers to spread the mixture in the forms and finish the surface. You'll also need someone to clear the chute after each load and one or two to push wheelbarrows.
■ Before the truck arrives, assign duties to each of your helpers— decide who will handle the truck arm, the wheelbarrows, the shovels and rakes, and the screed. The driver will run the mixer and control the chute, but that's about all. Some drivers may help, but check with the company first.
■ A fair amount of mix will run out of the chute after the flow has been stopped. Anticipate this overflow and signal the driver to stop the flow before the wheelbarrow gets too full.

DRY-MIX RECIPE

If you mix your own dry mix, here's a handy recipe.
■ 1 part portland cement
■ 2 parts sand
■ 3 parts gravel or aggregate
■ ½ part water
The moisture in the sand you buy and the atmospheric humidity will affect the amount of water you need to add to your concrete. The best way to test the sand is to squeeze a handful and then relax your hand. If the mix holds together without crumbling, add just ½ part water. If it crumbles or leaves your hand wet, adjust the amount of water as needed.

Combine the dry ingredients in a mortar box or wheelbarrow and stir in the water a little at a time. You want a consistency resembling a thick malted milk.

CONCRETE PATIO
continued

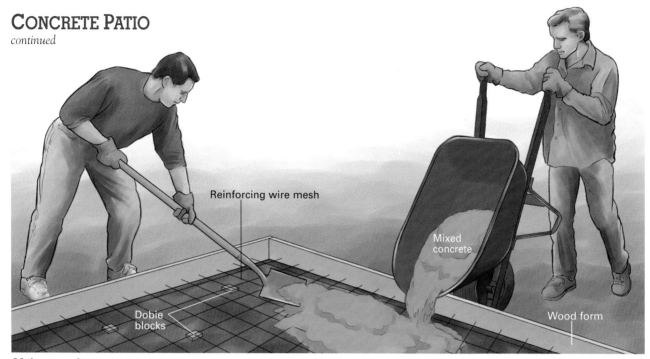

Reinforcing wire mesh

Mixed concrete

Dobie blocks

Wood form

Make sure the concrete is pushed into all the recesses around the forms and the dobies. Voids in the slab will weaken it and lead to cracks in your patio.

POURING CONCRETE

A concrete pour proceeds in a specific order. Once you get started, you and your crew will fall into a certain rhythm.

■ Start pouring in the corner farthest from the truck or mixing site.

■ Fill the excavation to the top of the forms and use a flat shovel or a hoe to distribute the mix and push it into the edges. Don't throw the mix—place it carefully to keep the aggregates from separating, which weakens the concrete.

■ Consolidate—or settle—the concrete by jabbing a shovel or 2×4 up and down in it. For maximum strength and durability, the mix must be dense but not packed.

■ Make sure the wire mesh or rebar remains centered between the gravel base and the finished surface. You may have to recenter it occasionally with a shovel or garden rake.

■ Add the next load of concrete as soon as you've spread the first one. Pour it where the first load ends—concrete needs a wet edge to bond. Be careful not to work the concrete too hard or to spread it too far; that can make the finished surface look uneven and could weaken it.

ADDITIVES

Engineers and chemists have developed ways to modify concrete to accelerate or retard setup time, prevent deterioration of a surface due to freezing and thawing, or make the mix workable in extreme heat or cold. Before ordering concrete, ask your supplier for advice on additives.

■ **AIR ENTRAINMENT:** This additive helps preserve concrete from freeze-thaw cycles in cold weather. Air-entrained concrete contains microscopic air cells, which help relieve internal pressures and prevent cracking. You can order air-entrained ready-mix, or you can add an air-entraining agent when mixing concrete in a mechanical mixer. But you can't mix it in by hand. Use only magnesium floats or darbies on air-entrained concrete—wood tears its surface.

■ **ACCELERATOR:** Accelerators make concrete set up faster on a cold day. They also reduce the risk of concrete freezing and cracking in cold weather. The accelerator of choice is calcium chloride.

■ **RETARDANT:** When the weather is hot and dry, use a retardant to slow the setup time.

■ **FIBERGLASS REINFORCEMENT:** Reinforcing additives may be available in your area, and for some projects, can take the place of steel reinforcement. Check with your local building department to see whether it is approved for your situation.

■ **WATER REDUCERS:** Sometimes called plasticizers, water reducers make concrete mix more workable and allow you to use 10 to 30 percent less water. Easy-to-work concrete results in less labor time on large jobs, and concrete made with less water is stronger.

SCREEDING

After filling the forms, you'll need to level the concrete with the top of the forms—a process called screeding, or striking off.

If the top of the finished surface will be flush with the forms, use a long, straight 2×4 as a screed; if the finished surface will be below the forms (for example, for tile or other mortared surfaces), cut out the ends of a 2×6 until it fits inside the forms at the bottom of the finished surface.

■ With one person at each end of the board, pull it along the forms with a side-to-side sawing motion. If there are humps in the surface after the first pass, screed again. Fill low spots with concrete; then screed again.

■ To finish, remove temporary guides, shovel concrete into the cavity they leave behind, and screed once more.

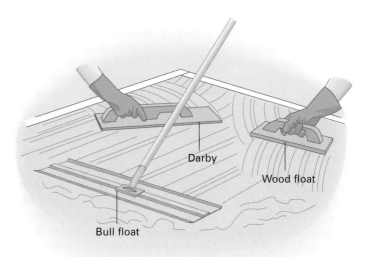

Start the smoothing process by floating the concrete with a darby, a wood float, or a bull float.

FLOATING

The next step, a preliminary smoothing called floating, pushes aggregates below the surface. Floating causes water to rise to the surface, but don't let this fool you into thinking that you have plenty of time to work. Float and edge each section before starting the next.

Avoid pouring new concrete against concrete that has already set up. This creates a cold joint, which fractures easily. While one or more people float a section, the finisher should be working right behind them.

Wooden floats are fine, but magnesium floats are smoother and easier to work with. Use a float that's big enough to cover the fresh concrete in the fewest passes.

■ For small areas that you can reach easily from the edge of the slab, use a hand float or a long darby, which extends your reach about 2 feet. Hold the darby flat as you move it across the surface, first in wide arcs. Then tilt it slightly and work in straight pulls.

■ For large areas, use a bull float—a smooth board or plate attached with a swivel joint to a long handle. Push the float away from you with the leading edge slightly raised so it doesn't dig in. Pull it back in the same manner. Overlap each pass until you have gone over the entire slab.

■ As soon as you have floated a section, separate the concrete from the forms by slipping a mason's trowel between the two and drawing it along the form. Cut in deeply if you will ultimately remove the forms, but slice down only an inch or so next to permanent forms.

Now is the time to apply custom finishes (see page 134). If you're not custom finishing, wait until the concrete sets up before you start the edging and final surface smoothing.

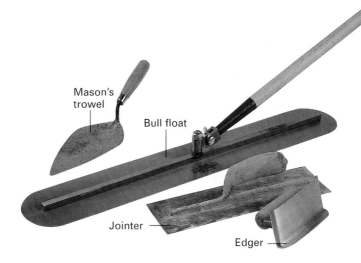

ARE YOU REALLY READY? A CHECKLIST

Readiness is the watchword when it comes to pouring concrete. Before the truck arrives, be entirely sure you have all your ducks in a row. Here's a basic list of tools and materials you will need. Your job may call for other items as well.

■ **TOOLS:** Hose, buckets, wheelbarrows, shovels, screed boards, hammers, wood or magnesium floats, darby and bull float (if needed), magnesium and steel trowels, edger, and jointer.

■ **MATERIALS:** Anchor bolts or post anchors (if needed) and wood planks to make a path or ramp for the wheelbarrows. All wire mesh and rebar should be in place before the pour.

■ **HELPERS:** At the very least, two. Unless you have experience, hire a concrete finisher. See that you and your helpers are clothed properly, with gloves and tight-fitting rubber boots for those who will wade into the wet concrete.

CONCRETE PATIO
continued

EDGING AND JOINTING

If you're going to leave the forms in as permanent edging, you can skip this step and go to the next. Unedged slabs, however, need to be rounded to improve their appearance and to minimize cracking or chipping.

Hold the edger flat on the concrete surface with its curved edge pressed against the form. Work it in short back-and-forth strokes, always tilting the leading edge up slightly and applying medium pressure. After finishing an edge, go over it again using long, smooth strokes.

CUTTING CONTROL JOINTS: After edging the slab, cut control joints into the surface of the concrete. (You can skip this step if you have installed permanent wood dividers.)

Concrete exposed to weather swells and shrinks with the seasons, resulting in irregular cracks in the slab. Control joints provide a place for the slab to crack where you want it to—along a straight line and under the joint so the crack isn't visible on the surface.

■ Slide the side of an edger in along a guide board (1× stock as long as the surface you're jointing), tipping up its leading edge slightly as you move it forward and back. The edger's curved lip creates a consistent rounded edge on the concrete. Don't try to cut a control joint without a guide; the joint will turn out sloppy looking. To make a guide, hold a

straight board across the top of the forms.
■ Make control joints about 20 percent as deep as the thickness of the concrete (¾ inch on a 4-inch slab). For patios, place control joints every 10 feet in both directions; for walks, at intervals equal to 1½ times their width (every 4½ feet for a 3-foot-wide walk).

You can also wait until the concrete has hardened but not cured (half a day is usually about right). Using a straight 2×4 as a guide, cut a line with a circular saw equipped with a masonry blade.

APPLYING THE FINAL FINISH

Depending on weather conditions, you may have as little as an hour (in hot, dry weather) or as much as half a day (in cool, humid weather) to smooth the slab surface to its final finish. Consider hiring a professional concrete finisher to help on large jobs. Smaller jobs offer a better opportunity to learn this skill yourself.

Finishing is performed with various tools and techniques, depending on the texture you want for the slab.
■ For a slightly rough texture, refloat the surface with a wood float.
■ Steel troweling creates a slick surface, like that on basement floors. Although it's not the best finish for an outdoor slab, troweling is the first step when creating some types of rough finishes.

To achieve a smooth steel-trowel finish, hand-trowel the surface two or three times. The concrete should be hard enough to support your weight on knee boards but fresh

To make a professional-looking rounded edge on your concrete patio, separate the concrete from the form by cutting between the two with a mason's trowel. Then round the edge with an edger.

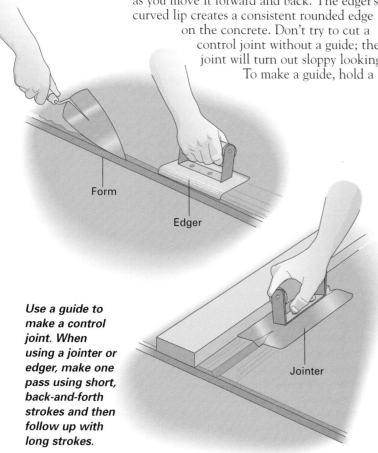

Form

Edger

Jointer

Use a guide to make a control joint. When using a jointer or edger, make one pass using short, back-and-forth strokes and then follow up with long strokes.

WHEN TO BEGIN THE FINAL FINISH

Wait until the sheen of water on the surface of the concrete disappears before you attempt the final finish. Step on it to make sure—your foot should leave no deeper than a quarter-inch impression. Evaporation can take minutes in hot, dry weather or more than an hour when it's damp and cool. Finishing while water remains on the surface results in concrete that is dusty or that spalls or has other problems after it has cured.

If you notice that the concrete is beginning to set up before the sheen has disappeared, sweep off the water with a push broom, soak it up with burlap, or drag the surface of the concrete with a length of hose. Whichever method you use, don't step on the wet concrete.

enough to produce a moistened paste as you work. Keep track of the concrete's wetness. If it gets too dry, it becomes unworkable. Overworking it when it is very wet can cause the top layer to flake off later.

■ Start troweling from the edge of the slab. Get into a comfortable position so you won't have to overreach. Do as much as you can from the lawn; then use a kneeling board to work in the middle.

■ Hold the steel trowel almost flat, with the leading edge raised slightly. Use long, sweeping arcs. Don't press hard. Overlap each succeeding arc by half the tool's length.

One finish that you begin by steel-troweling is brooming. It creates a patterned nonslip surface. Trowel the concrete; then drag a dampened broom across it in straight lines, curves, or waves. Soft brooms designed for this purpose produce a shallow pattern. Stiff-bristled brooms cut deeper. After grooming the surface, you may need to touch up the edges and control joints.

Plywood knee board

Keep your knees and toes from denting the wet concrete by supporting your weight on plywood sections. Use two boards or one board large enough to accommodate your knees and toes. Have a second set of boards handy so you can move around without stopping.

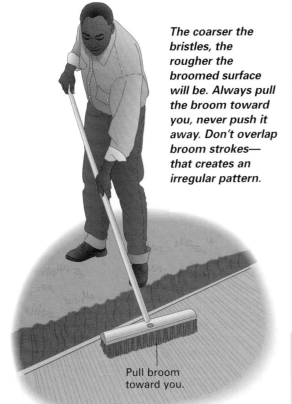

The coarser the bristles, the rougher the broomed surface will be. Always pull the broom toward you, never push it away. Don't overlap broom strokes—that creates an irregular pattern.

Pull broom toward you.

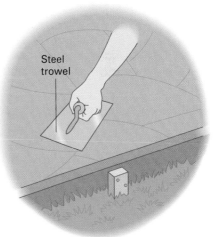

Steel trowel

For an extra-smooth surface, finish with a steel trowel.

POWER FINISHER

In hot weather, the concrete may harden faster than you can finish it by hand. The solution: Rent a power finisher, also known as a helicopter or whirlybird. This piece of equipment will allow you to produce a fairly smooth finish over large areas, even if you're not a skilled finisher. You'll still need to edge and joint the slab, and you might need to hand-finish small areas.

CONCRETE PATIO
continued

Floating, troweling, and brooming are only three of the many ways to produce decorative concrete surfaces. Here are some others.

SEEDED-AGGREGATE FINISH: Divide the project into manageable sections so the concrete mix doesn't harden before you can work in the stones. Pour the concrete so its surface is about ½ inch below the top of the forms; then screed, float, and finish it.

Sprinkle aggregate evenly over the slab. With a helper, press the aggregate into the concrete with long 2×6s or flat shovels. Embed the stones firmly so their tops are just visible. If necessary, go over them with a wood float to push them down more.

When the concrete has hardened enough to support your weight on knee boards, remove excess concrete around the stones with a stiff nylon brush or broom. Work carefully so you don't dislodge the stones. Remove the debris, spray a curing agent over the slab, and then cover it with a plastic sheet.

After the concrete cures for 24 hours, repeat the brooming followed by a fine spray of water from a garden hose to expose about half of each stone. The spray should be strong enough to wash away the concrete loosened by the broom but not dislodge the stones. Let the aggregate dry for a couple of hours; then hose off any film that develops on the stones. Again, cover the area with plastic so it can cure slowly. After curing, remove any haze on the aggregate with muriatic acid.

HAND-PATTERNED FINISH: Float the slab; then make geometric or random lines in the finished concrete with a joint-strike tool (see above). If you need to retrowel part of the surface, be sure to strike the lines again.

STAMPED FINISH: Use a steel or rubber stamping tool to produce patterns resembling brick, cobblestone, flagstone, and others.

First, measure the base of the stamp and adjust spacing so the pattern comes out evenly. Increase efficiency by using two stamps side by side. Set both stamps in place.

Joint-strike tool for hand-tooling

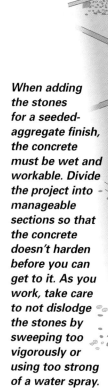

When adding the stones for a seeded-aggregate finish, the concrete must be wet and workable. Divide the project into manageable sections so that the concrete doesn't harden before you can get to it. As you work, take care to not dislodge the stones by sweeping too vigorously or using too strong of a water spray.

1. Spread aggregate.

2. Embed stones.

3. Smooth and settle stones with a wood float.

4. Sweep off excess concrete as the surface sets up.

5. Spray with a hose.

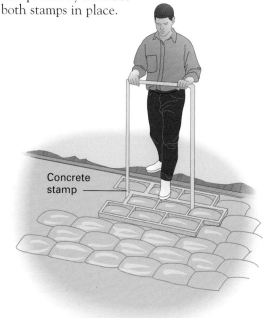

Concrete stamp

Create the effect of a stone walk by pressing a concrete stamp into the mix. Many patterns are available.

Stand on one and then step over to the other. The impressions should be about 1 inch deep. Smooth out the edges of the pattern with a joint-strike tool.

CURING CONCRETE

Although concrete will harden in a day, it doesn't reach adequate strength until it has cured for at least three to seven days. During this time, it must be protected from drying out too quickly. Concrete that dries too quickly will not be strong. You can help your slab cure properly with any of the following methods.

COVER IT: To prevent evaporation, cover the concrete with plastic. If the temperature is cool, use black plastic because it absorbs heat from the sun. Weight the edges of the plastic and any seams with small stones or boards to trap as much moisture as possible.

KEEP IT WET: If you are able to attend to your slab regularly, sprinkling it with water is better than covering it with plastic. Cover the slab with old blankets or burlap, and keep them wet. You can also wet the concrete directly. To avoid pitting the surface, wait until the concrete is fairly hard before spraying it.

USE A CURING AGENT: To facilitate curing, spray or roll a curing agent onto the slab. Clear or tinted white, these agents keep the concrete moist. Don't use a curing agent if you plan to cover your slab with tile, brick, stone, or flooring material. Mortar will not stick to the treated concrete.

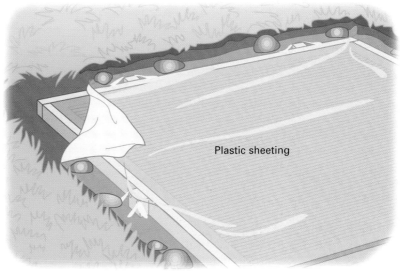

Plastic sheeting

Cover fresh concrete with plastic to stop evaporation while the concrete cures.

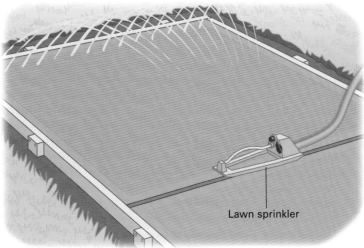

Lawn sprinkler

Watering the slab with a sprinkler or a hose as it cures is effective, as long as you are able to keep close tabs on things. Neither soak the slab nor let it dry out.

Straw

If there is a possibility of freezing weather, cover curing concrete with straw or insulating blankets. For cool but not freezing conditions, use black plastic.

COLORING CONCRETE

You can make a startling improvement in the looks of concrete by adding color. Use a coloring agent, which is available from most concrete suppliers. Mix the agent throughout the entire batch of concrete. Or pour uncolored concrete mix to within 1 inch of the top of the form; then mix pigment into the batch for the final layer.

TILE PATIO

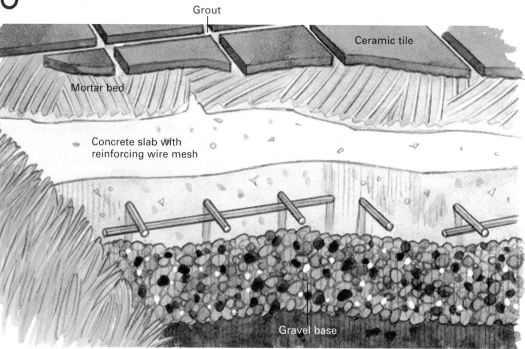

Grout

Ceramic tile

Mortar bed

Concrete slab with reinforcing wire mesh

Gravel base

Tile and grout are inflexible, and that makes them vulnerable to movement caused by temperature changes. To prevent tile and grout from cracking, reinforce the concrete slab with wire mesh and place control joints at 8-foot intervals in the concrete.

Tile can transform any patio into the most attractive area on your property. Depending on your choice of material, tile can look rugged or refined, and it will last for years if you install it properly on a stable foundation. The single most important requirement for a tile patio is a level and flat concrete slab.

PREPARING AN OLD SLAB

If you already have a concrete slab, it may be suitable for use as a tile base. Here's what to look for when you check its condition.

■ Dig down to see if the slab is 3 to 4 inches thick and rests on a 4-inch gravel base.

■ Look for cracks, severe chipping or sunken spots. If these are present, pull the old slab out and lay a new one.

■ Check for level. Tile needs a level surface with no more than ⅛-inch variance for every 10 feet. Lay a straight 2×4 across the surface of your existing slab.

■ Knock out high spots and minor flaking with a sledge and fill them and low spots with patching concrete

■ Cut control joints if necessary (see page 132) with a circular saw equipped with a masonry blade.

■ If the slab is intact and level, simply clean it with a solution of muriatic acid (1 part acid to 4 parts water). Then rinse it well and let it dry before applying the mortar.

PREPARING FOR A NEW SLAB

Before laying out your patio, plan its dimensions so that it will accommodate an even number of tiles or result in a pattern that requires minimum cutting.

■ Divide the patio dimensions by the measurements of your tile pattern (including grout joints) and adjust the patio size, if necessary. Then lay out the site with batter boards and mason's lines (see pages 107 for more information).

■ Level the lines; then slope them slightly for drainage (1 inch for every 4 feet). If your design includes wide edging, stake additional lines and level and slope them also.

■ Square the corners with the 3-4-5 method (see page 107 for more information) and drop a plumb bob to mark the corners. Tie lines at ground level between the corner stakes and mark them with chalk or spray paint.

■ Excavate the site to a depth that will accommodate the 4-inch gravel base, the 4-inch concrete slab, and the thickness of the mortar and tile. Subtract an inch or so from this depth to raise your patio slightly above ground.

■ Install forms (make them from 2× stock) attached to stakes driven in the ground. Next, pour in the gravel bed and screed it, using the forms as guides.

■ Tamp the gravel to a depth of 4 inches. Now you're ready for the pour.

POURING THE SLAB

For projects under 10 square feet, use premixed concrete. It comes in bags; all you have to do is add water. For sites up to 100 square feet, mix the dry ingredients yourself or order ready-mix. Ready-mix is a must for larger patios. Follow the steps below, reviewing pages 106–110, if you need additional information.

■ Pour the concrete level with the forms, work a shovel in it to remove air pockets, and use a long 2×4 to screed it level with the forms.

■ Finish the concrete with a wooden float but do not smooth it with a metal trowel— a slightly rough surface gives the mortar a tooth to bind it to the slab.

■ Let the concrete set up just until your footprint leaves a slight depression in the surface.

■ Do not round the edges—the tile will need support right up to the edge—but when the concrete sets (not cures), cut control joints with a jointer every 8 feet in both directions. Control joints give the concrete a place to crack under the surface without transferring the crack to the tile.

■ Then let the concrete cure (keep it moist by wetting it down or covering it with plastic) for three to seven days. Once it has cured, remove the forms and scrub the surface with water and a broom.

LAYING AN ISOLATION MEMBRANE

Isolation membranes help keep the tile and grout from cracking as the slab swells and contracts with changes in temperature. Many products require a two-part application. First, apply the adhesive with the notched side of a trowel to ensure a good bond. Then smooth on the membrane with the flat side of the trowel. Use long, sweeping strokes. Let the membrane cure completely.

TESTING THE LAYOUT

Test the layout before you start setting the tile. In general, you'll want many full tiles in the central part of the site (called the field) and as few cut tiles as possible on the edges.

Set tiles in place across the slab without any mortar, following these procedures.

■ Mark the center of the patio by snapping diagonal chalk lines from the corners.

■ Snap chalk lines also between the midpoints of each side.

■ Starting at the center point, lay tiles and spacers on both the horizontal and vertical

WORKING WITH TILE

If you haven't installed tile before, you might need to add a few tools to your toolbox. Don't compromise when buying tools—buy the best you can afford. Most tools for working with tile are inexpensive; you'll find them cheaper to buy than rent. One exception is a tile cutter, or wet saw, which you can rent from a tile supplier or a rental outlet. All in all, here's what you'll need.

■ A square-notched trowel for spreading mortar.

■ A rubber mallet for setting the tiles firmly in the mortar. A heavy mallet with a large face is more efficient and safer to use on large tiles.

■ A circular saw with a masonry blade, a snap cutter, or a wet saw, for cutting tiles. Ask your supplier for advice. You'll also need a pair of nippers.

■ A grout float for grouting the joints between tiles after the mortar has set.

■ A large clean sponge and clean water to wipe away excess mortar or grout before it dries.

Each project comes with its own requirements, which vary with the type of tile and the local climate. Ask your supplier for tiles that match the variations of your climate. Don't forget the spacers and backing strips for control joints.

axes, extending the tiles to all sides of the slab.

■ If one side ends with a full tile and the opposite side has only part of a tile, move the center point so both sides will have tiles of the same size (cut or uncut). Adjust the tiles on both axes.

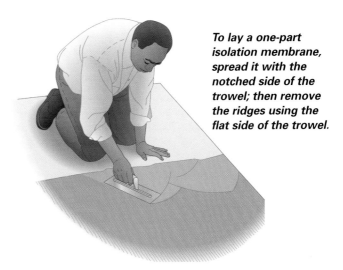

To lay a one-part isolation membrane, spread it with the notched side of the trowel; then remove the ridges using the flat side of the trowel.

TILE PATIO
continued

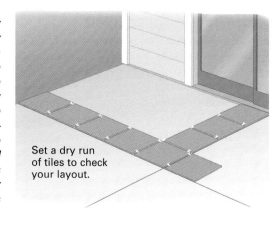

Draw perpendicular layout lines in the center of the slab and set the tiles in a dry run—complete with spacers— to make sure you will not end up with slivers or a row of cut tile that tapers along its length.

Set a dry run of tiles to check your layout.

■ When the layout best fits the dimensions of the slab, snap parallel reference lines every 2 feet. These lines will help keep the tile straight when you lay it.

■ Mark the locations of the control joints— you'll need to know where they are when you're setting the tile because you won't be applying mortar over them.

APPLYING MORTAR

Ideally, you should apply the mortar when the outside temperature is between 60° and 70° F. Don't work in direct sunlight—the mortar will set up too quickly.

Start with enough to lay just one or two tiles at first. As you get accustomed to the material, you'll develop a rhythm and gain some confidence. Then work in sections you can complete in 10 minutes.

■ Mix latex thin-set mortar in a 5-gallon bucket, following the manufacturer's directions. Mortar mixes much easier if you use a ½-inch drill with a mixing blade (most of them look like a miniature fan on a long shaft).

■ Let the mortar set for about 10 minutes; then mix it again.

■ Start at the center of the slab and spread a thin coat of mortar with the flat side of a ¼×¼-foot notched trowel. Lay the mortar right up to, but not covering, the layout and reference lines.

■ Then rake the mortar at a 45-degree angle with the notched side of the trowel, but don't scrape through to the slab. The grooves created by the notches give the mortar a place to expand and level under the bottom of the tile when pushed in place.

SETTING TILES

■ Drop each tile in place with a slight twist and tap it with a rubber mallet (or make a beater block from a short length of 2×4 covered with scrap carpet.) Set the beater block on the tile, carpet side down, and tap with a hammer. The block sets the tile and levels adjacent units. Use spacers to keep the tiles properly spaced for grouting.

■ As you press the tiles in place, the mortar should begin to squeeze up between them.

CUTTING TILE

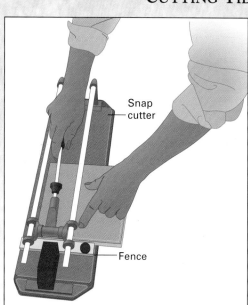

Use a snap cutter for straight cuts. Set the tile firmly against the fence; drag the cutting wheel across the tile in one smooth stroke to scribe a line on the tile. Push down on the handle to snap the cut along the line.

Snap cutter

Fence

You can have tiles cut by your supplier, but with the right tools, you can do it yourself. Rent the tools you need from your tile dealer or from most general rental centers. Here are some options.

■ If you expect to cut only a few tiles, rent a manual snap cutter. It's easy to use and the results will have you feeling like a real professional.

■ A power tile saw can save you hours of effort and piles of wasted material if your pattern calls for more than a few cuts.

■ You also can cut tile with a masonry blade attached to your circular saw. Always be sure the tile is clamped firmly in place.

■ If you do your own cutting, be sure to wear protection for your eyes, ears, and hands.

■ For cutting unusual angles or contours, score the tile with a glass cutter and snap away small pieces with a pair of tile nippers.

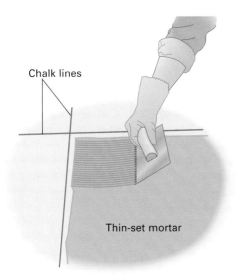

Chalk lines

Thin-set mortar

Using a notched trowel, spread thin-set mortar over a small area so that you will have time to lay all the tiles before the thin-set sets up. Avoid covering layout lines.

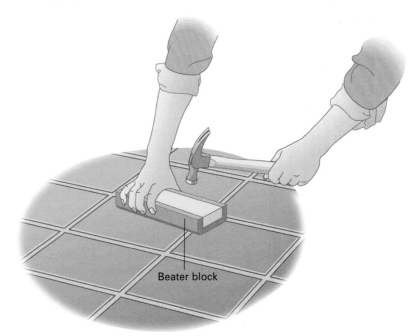

Beater block

Firmly embed the tile in the mortar by tapping it with a beater block and a hammer or rubber mallet. Make a block by stapling a piece of carpeting to a 2×4 scrap. This also ensures that adjacent units are at the same height.

If the mortar comes up more than half the thickness of the tile, you're using too much. Leave enough room for grout and for caulking the backing strips at the control joints.

■ Every now and then, pick up a set tile to make sure the mortar adheres evenly across its back. Modify your mortar-spreading techniques to apply more or less as necessary.

■ After completing each section, check your work for level with a straightedge. Quickly make any adjustments before the mortar sets. If a tile is too low, pull it up and apply mortar to the back and then reset it. If a tile is too high, scrape off excess mortar evenly and reset.

■ As you work, remove the spacers from tiles that have had a few minutes to set up. It's much easier to remove the spacers before the mortar has hardened completely.

■ Continue spreading mortar in both directions away from the intersection of the layout lines, taking care to leave yourself room to work. As you get closer to an edge, have the partial tiles ready so you can set them in place without searching for them or having to cut new ones.

Once you have set all the tiles, remove remaining spacers and check gaps between the tiles. With the tip of a masonry trowel, gently scrape out excess mortar. Press backing strips into the joints at the locations of the control joints in the slab (see page 140). Let the mortar set for at least a day before applying the grout.

WHEN TO SET CUT TILES

You can cut tiles for the edges and around obstructions as you go or wait until you have laid everything but the edges and then cut and set them all at once.

The latter technique will likely prove to be your best option. That way you have a firm, accurate surface on which to work. Cut all the tiles at once and lay them the second day.

USING A TILE SAW

If you have lots of straight cuts to make, rent a wet saw. Wear safety glasses and hearing protection. See that the blade is in good condition, and that the water bucket is full. Place the tile on the sliding table, and lock the fence to hold the tile in place. Turn the saw on, and make sure water is running onto the blade. Press down on the tile as you slide it thorough, taking care to keep your fingers out of the way. WHen the water runs out, refill the bucket; do not cut with the saw for even a few seconds unless water is running onto the blade.

TILE PATIO
continued

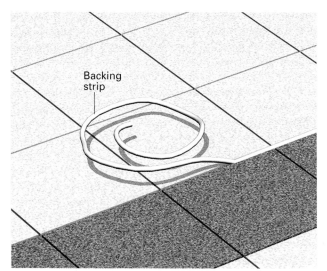

A large tile patio needs to flex in order to prevent cracking. Before grouting the tile, fit backing strips into the joints that will lie over the control joints in the slab. After grouting, remove the backing strips, and fill the control joints with silicone caulk that matches the grout.

Use sweeping, diagonal strokes—both to push the grout into the joints and to scrape away the excess. Look for a grout float with a smooth rubber face, backed by foam rubber; it will work better than one with a permeable, foam-rubber surface.

APPLYING GROUT

When the mortar is completely dry, prepare grout recommended for your tile. Follow the manufacturer's directions for mixing the grout, and keep it in a container you can seal. Grout used for exterior applications should contain latex, which is easy to clean up and needs little time to cure. If yours does not, ask your dealer if it's a type of grout to which you can add latex.

■ With a mason's trowel, scoop grout from the mixing container and place it on the tiles.

■ Holding a grout float at a 45-degree angle, push the float into the grout and spread it across the tiles with the trailing edge of the float.

■ Move the float at angles to the tile pattern so that the grout will fill and not pull out of the joints.

■ Spread grout in alternating directions to force out any air trapped in the joints.

■ When all the joints are full, clean off the grout float and use it to scrape excess grout from the tile surface. Be careful not to press the float into the joints—that will remove grout and undo all your hard work.

CLEANING UP

Check the manufacturer's directions for drying time before cleaning. This may be 15 minutes to an hour or more. You want the grout to dry until it won't dislodge when you remove the haze, but you don't want it to cure completely. If you wait too long, the cleanup will be much harder—cured grout is almost impossible to remove. Check the grout with the point of the mason's trowel to be sure it has hardened.

■ To remove grout haze, wipe the tile surface with a rough-textured, dry sponge and a clean, dry cloth.

■ Remove the backing strips from the joints over the control joints in the slab, and fill the empty joints between the tiles with caulk that matches the color of the grout.

■ Apply grout sealer to the finished joints. Take care not to get sealer on the tiles themselves. You may have to wait several days for the grout to fully cure before you apply sealer. Ask your dealer for the waiting period appropriate to your sealer.

■ Wipe away any extra sealer and buff the tile again after the sealer dries.

LAYING ADOBE TILE

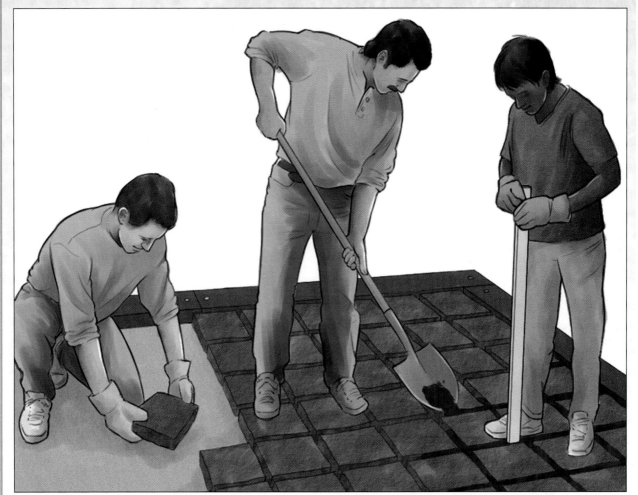

Adobe blocks are sun-dried and soft, and they may vary a bit in shape from one to the next. That's part of their charm, but it makes for a little extra work when laying them. Without lugs, you need to space the blocks by hand. Push down and turn each one as you set it. Add dirt fill or sand as soon as you can, and gently tamp the fill with a board. Use the tamping board gently to avoid moving the blocks.

Adobe blocks look comfortable and familiar, and they give your patio a casual air. Long associated with the Southwest, adobe block is gaining popularity as a paving material in other regions as well. That's because some manufacturers now add stabilizers, such as asphalt, that make the blocks more durable and less porous.

Traditional adobe (without asphalt) absorbs water easily and then breaks when it freezes, so it's poorly suited for use in northern climates. Even asphaltic adobe has geographic limits. If you live in a climate where winter temperatures freeze, some will crack when the moisture they absorb swells as it freezes. Check with your supplier to see if it is suitable for your patio.

■ Because adobe blocks are fragile, the foundation that supports them should be perfectly flat. Excavate the patio site to the thickness of the adobe blocks, plus a sand bed and gravel subbase deep enough to hold the blocks at ground level.

■ Adobe works with or without edging materials. If you want to contain the patio visually, use a border that complements the adobe. Pressure-treated landscape timbers are popular as edging for adobe because they share its rough and heavy look. Other options include loose fill, plantings, or adobe blocks of different sizes.
■ After concrete, adobe is the heaviest patio material most homeowners would want to handle. To prevent strain or injury while working with large pavers, have an assistant help you lift, place, and adjust the blocks.
■ Place blocks in a pattern that complements your property. If necessary, adobe blocks can be cut easily.
■ Once you have all the adobe blocks in place, fill in the joints with sand or mortar for easy maintenance. Tamp sand with the end of a board. You can even fill the joints with soil and plant them with light groundcover to give the entire patio an organic look. Use a piece of scrap lumber to tamp once again.

PAVER PATIO

Concrete pavers are available in several designs and colors. One of the most popular combines squares and octagons for a pattern of alternating shapes. The pavers are cast with lugs on the sides to create a small gap between each pair of adjoining blocks.

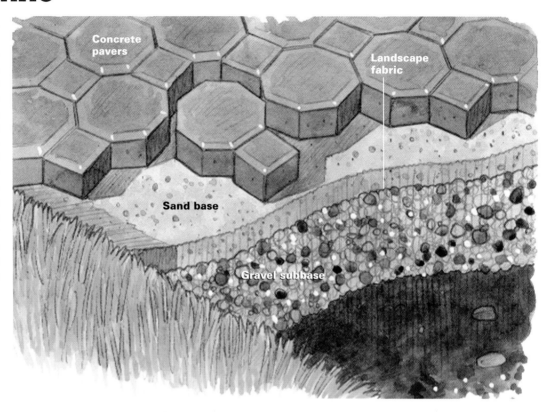

Concrete pavers combine the design versatility of tile with the easy installation of brick. They are made of cast concrete in sizes and patterns to fit any style or space and are designed to be set in a sand bed over a gravel base.

WORKING WITH CONCRETE PAVERS

You shouldn't need many specialized tools to lay concrete pavers, and the ones you do need are relatively inexpensive. Items you might need to buy include a masonry blade for cutting pavers with a circular saw, a mason's hammer, and a brickset (a cold chisel with a wide blade).

The only item you'll need to rent is a power tamper for compacting the subbase and for packing sand in the joints of the finished surface. A hand tamper will do for some small areas, but a power tamper will usually do a better and faster job.

■ For setting pavers without damaging them, use a rubber mallet.

■ To cut individual pavers to special sizes or shapes, use a circular saw with a masonry blade. Always wear eye and ear protection when cutting concrete pavers.

■ If you have more than a few pavers to cut, consider having your supplier cut them.

PLANNING THE LAYOUT

To make accurate estimates of how much material you will need, draw a trial layout on graph paper with ¼-inch increments.

Start with the outline of an approximate patio size and draw it to scale of ¼ inch = 1 inch. Then draw in your pattern to scale. Most patterns will lend themselves to sectioning. Figure how much area one section covers and the number of sections of the same size your patio dimensions will accommodate.

Adjust the final patio size so your patterns will be complete with minimal cutting. Then count the number of pavers in each section and multiply by the number of even sections to estimate material quantities.

Most suppliers will allow you to return unused materials, so buy 10 to 15 percent more than you expect to need. A leisurely return trip is more pleasant than interrupting your work because you ran out of materials.

CONSTRUCTION DETAILS

LAYING OUT THE SITE: Using the same methods discussed on pages 114–117 for a sand-based brick patio, lay out the site with batter boards and mason's lines. Square the corners, set corner stakes, and mark ground lines. Be sure to slope your mason's lines by 1 inch every 4 feet to achieve proper drainage.

EXCAVATION: Excavate the site to a uniformly sloped depth of 6 inches (4 inches for gravel and 2 inches for sand bedding) plus the thickness of the pavers. Measure the excavation depth from the sloped mason's and grid lines. Moisten the soil and tamp it with a power tamper.

EDGING: Precast concrete paver designs include individual units made for edging. Use them by themselves or combine them with other edging materials.

■ To create a border with contrasting materials, such as pressure-treated landscape timbers, place the edging materials in a trench on the outside of the patio area. Dig the trench to the depth of the edging material, plus several inches for a gravel base for drainage. Bricks used as a border would be similarly set or placed in a concrete bed for stability.

■ To make hidden edging that holds the pavers in place, set rigid plastic edging along the inside of the patio area. Hold the edging in place with metal spikes. The top ridge of the edging should extend above the sand base by half to three-quarters of the paver thickness. Backfill behind the edging with tamped soil and cover the top with soil so that it can't be seen.

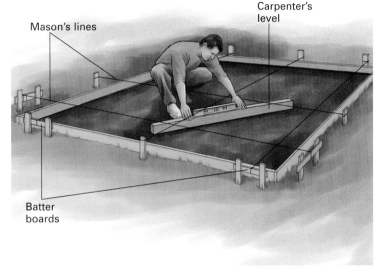

You can check the surface of a patio site for level most easily with a carpenter's level set on a long, straight 2×4. Remember to slope for drainage.

POURING THE SUBBASE: When you've completed the excavation and edging, drive several small stakes inside the excavation. Set the top of each stake at 4 inches above the excavated soil.

■ Pour gravel into the site—level with the stakes—and spread it evenly with a garden rake. Check the surface with a long, flat 2×4 to make sure it is uniform. Measure the surface from the mason's lines to make sure it's sloped correctly, or use a screed with cutouts riding on the edging surface.

When the subbase is level and consistent, compact the gravel with a tamper. Add landscaping fabric to prevent weeds from growing through.

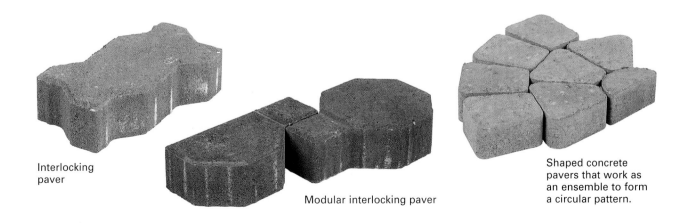

Interlocking paver

Modular interlocking paver

Shaped concrete pavers that work as an ensemble to form a circular pattern.

PAVER PATIO
continued

To create an even surface with a loose material like sand, lay PVC pipes on the surface before pouring in the sand. Add sand until it covers the pipes.

PVC pipes

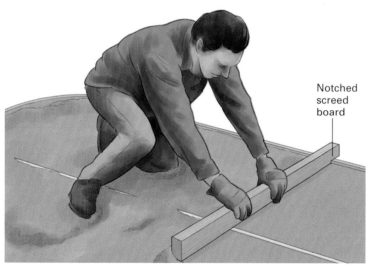

Notched screed board

Draw a screed board across the PVC pipes to level the surface. Because the sand bed will probably be lower than any edging materials, notch one end of the screed board accordingly.

Concrete is especially hard, so use a specialty tool designed for the purpose if you need to cut any pavers. You can rent a tub saw from rental shops, tile stores, or concrete contractors.

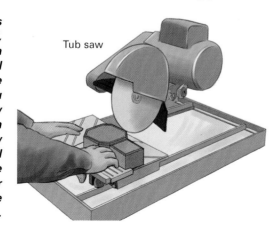

Tub saw

CREATING THE BASE: Shovel clean sand on top of the gravel and spread it with a garden rake. Push the sand gently into the edges and corners, taking care not to disrupt the landscaping fabric or subbase.

■ Check the bedding for slope and consistency, and adjust the surface as needed. To get the sand base at a consistent level, you can mark a piece of PVC pipe at 2 inches and push it in the sand or lay lengths of 2-inch PVC pipe about every 3 to 4 feet.

■ Make a screed with cutouts that will ride on the edging at the thickness of your pavers (or directly on top of the PVC pipe). Screed the sand, working the board back and forth across the surface as you pull.

■ Soak the sand base using a garden hose with a sprayer attachment set to fine mist.

■ Compact the wet sand with a power tamper.

■ Fill low spots and indentations with added sand, and tamp flat again.

■ Continue adding sand and tamping until the base is consistent across the entire site. Pull out the PVC pipes, if you've used them. Fill in the recesses left by the pipes and tamp again.

CUTTING PAVERS: Although you can reduce the amount of cut pavers by making your design come out in even sizes, cutting at least some pavers is probably unavoidable. Concrete pavers are hard—as hard as tile and almost as thick as brick, so they're difficult to cut. You can break pavers with a baby sledge and a bricklayer's chisel, but you're not likely to get clean edges. To make your cuts clean, rent a tile saw that handles concrete, or use a masonry blade on a circular saw (be sure to clamp the paver tightly and wear safety goggles and ear protection).

SETTING THE PAVERS: Starting in a corner, lay the first few pavers in place. If you are using rigid plastic edging, the pavers should fit snugly against it. For other edging, leave a space for sand. With a rubber mallet, tap each paver on the top to set it in the sand base, and on the side to make sure it fits well against its neighboring paver.

■ Most pavers are cast with spacing lugs; push the pavers tightly against each other. If your pavers don't have lugs, use ⅛-inch scrap plywood to space them.

■ As you lay more pavers, work in two directions to keep your design from shifting to either side. To check your progress, look at the pattern after setting every few pavers, and test the surface with a carpenter's level or a straight 2×4.

■ If the surface has low spots (it's almost impossible to avoid them), remove a few

No matter how carefully you prepare the sand bed, some pavers will need a little help before they line up just right. If a paver rides a bit too high, tap it with a rubber mallet. If that isn't enough, take the paver out and remove a small amount of sand before replacing it. You also may need to add sand to fill low spots.

CASTING YOUR OWN PAVERS

Casting your own pavers takes time, but you can create exactly the look you want, especially if your design calls for 12- to 18-inch pavers. Make forms of 1×4 lumber with plywood bottoms to cast loose pavers, or dig shallow recesses in the ground to cast them in place for a path.

    Experiment with different colors, shapes, and textures. To fit the average person's walking stride, set the finished pavers with the centers about 18 inches apart.

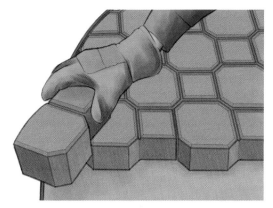

Place cut pavers in the same order as the main pattern. If you wait until all the uncut pavers are in place, you may have trouble getting the others to fit.

pavers, add sand, and replace the pavers. High spots can sometimes be fixed with a few taps from the mallet. Make adjustments as you work; you won't want to start over.

■ After you pave every few square feet, stretch a mason's line across the surface to make sure the layout is straight.

■ After you pave more than half the patio in any direction, and before you reach the opposite side, measure the remaining distance. Then measure the paved section to see how the remaining pavers will fit. If the distance can't be filled with whole pavers, you may prefer to move the edging on the far side instead of cutting an entire course of pavers.

FINISHING THE JOINTS: Cover all the pavers with fine sand and spread it with a push broom. Sweep from all directions to pack sand well into the joints.

■ When the joints are full, sweep the remaining sand from the patio, being careful not to sweep it out of the joints. Wet the surface with water and tamp it with a power tamper. Let it dry, and check the joints to make sure they are all filled. Add sand to any joints that need more, sweep the area clean, and soak it again.

Once you have all the pavers in place, spread a layer of clean, dry sand over the surface. (Get washed sand from a building-supply store; it's often sold as play sand for children's sandboxes.) Sweep sand into the joints from several directions, collect the excess, and wet the surface with a garden hose. Continue adding sand and spraying until the joints are full.

MAKING PATHS AND WALKS

A walk is usually easier to build than a patio because you can reach its entire surface from outside the forms. The techniques for building a path or walk are the same as for a patio, but expect differences when laying out the walk and building forms.

Because they receive only foot traffic, concrete sidewalks are often just 3 inches thick. In areas without frost heave, you may be able to pour them directly on the ground without a gravel base, but check with your building department to see if local codes permit such installations.

HOW WIDE?

Two people can walk together comfortably on a 4-foot-wide walk and can easily pass each other on a 3-foot-wide walk. A person in a wheelchair needs a 40-inch-wide walk, and a person using a walker needs one at least 27 inches wide.

If you're planning to lay brick or other modular material, make the width an even multiple of its dimensions so you won't have to cut odd-size pieces. Add ⅛ to ½ inch per course to your planned width to allow for sand or mortar joints, and add the width of your forms.

Use mason's line and stakes to establish the perimeter of the excavation for your path.

LAYOUT

Layout procedures will vary slightly depending on whether your walk is straight or curved.

STRAIGHT WALK: Stretch two parallel mason's lines between stakes driven into the ground, making sure the walk is square with the house or other predominant features in the landscape.

CURVED WALK: Lay two hoses to outline the the desired shape.
■ Measure between them every foot or so to ensure that each side conforms to the other.
■ Pour flour, sand, or chalk over the lengths of hose; then remove the hoses to leave an outline of the walk's edges on the ground.

BUILDING THE PATH

The surface of the walk should be slightly higher (½ to 1 inch) than ground level and slightly sloped so water won't puddle. Excavate the walk the same as you would for a patio of the same materials (see pages 106–110). Then construct the walk in the same order as you would a patio.
■ Set forms or edging. Some materials, such as flagstone, won't require edgings.
■ Install subbase and base materials.
■ Install surface materials.

EXCAVATING FOOTINGS

MIXING MATERIALS

Add interest to your path or wall by combining materials. Combine loose materials with stepping-stones—either natural stones such as flagstone or manufactured concrete rounds. Concrete rounds come in many sizes and colors; you can even make your own. An aggregate stone surface will complement your path better than stones with smooth surfaces. Place the stones about 2 feet apart.

As an alternative to stepping-stones, cut wood rounds from a weather-resistant species, such as redwood or cedar, or any durable wood species, such as oak. If you use wood rounds from your local lumber mill, apply three coats of clear wood sealer to all surfaces.

The steps for laying a dry-brick path include excavation, installing permanent edging, placing the sand base, laying the brick, and sweeping sand into the joints. The permanent edging can be redwood, cedar, or mortared brick or stone. Drive the edging stakes below the surface of the turf and cover them with soil. Edging holds the bricks in place; sand in the joints stabilizes them.

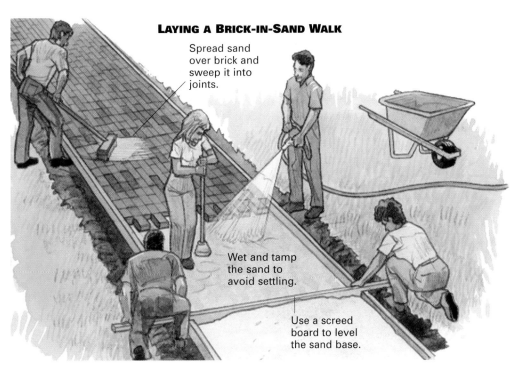

LAYING A BRICK-IN-SAND WALK

Spread sand over brick and sweep it into joints.

Wet and tamp the sand to avoid settling.

Use a screed board to level the sand base.

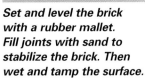

Set and level the brick with a rubber mallet. Fill joints with sand to stabilize the brick. Then wet and tamp the surface.

Set the width of a brick path to include any permanent edging. That way you'll minimize cutting brick. Use a mason's line as a guide to level the brick as you set them.

MAKING A SOFT PATH

Low-cost natural, durable, and attractive materials—pea gravel, crushed rock, wood chips or other organic material—can produce a walkway that is every bit as appealing as more expensive alternatives.

To create a path with natural loose materials, lay it out and excavate to a depth of 8 to 9 inches. Lay in timber forms or other edging if the path will run through a lawn. The edging will keep the path materials from migrating into the grassy area. If the path runs through a woodland area, you won't need the edging, but you can include it if it suits your design. Pour in a gravel base and then 2 inches of sand and tamp it. Put landscape fabric over the sand to prevent weed growth. Then spread and level the stones or wood chips.

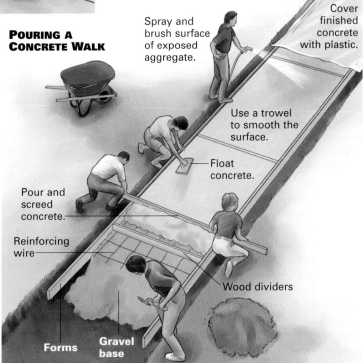

POURING A CONCRETE WALK

Spray and brush surface of exposed aggregate.

Cover finished concrete with plastic.

Use a trowel to smooth the surface.

Float concrete.

Pour and screed concrete.

Reinforcing wire

Wood dividers

Forms

Gravel base

Build a concrete walk with the same techniques you would use for a concrete patio. Make sure to let the concrete cure for three to seven days before using it.

DESIGNING STEPS AND STAIRS

Transitional stairs or steps are sometimes needed in a patio project. Stairs between two patio levels carved into a hillside can lie on a natural slope. Stairs that need to bridge abrupt level changes, such as a patio floor to a doorway in the house, need to be built up from a level surface. Design your steps as an integral part of the patio and pick materials that complement its style.

climb will feel gentle and you may be able to reduce the overall number of steps. Let each tread overhang the riser below by about 1 inch. This overhang is the architectural detail that signals that a step is ahead.

RISE AND RUN

Whether you're building steps into a hillside or against a vertical surface, you need to calculate the total run—the horizontal length from the front edge of the bottom step to the back edge of the top step, not including any landings. You also need to measure the total rise—the perpendicular distance from the base of the stairway to the top step. This exercise results in dimensions for the tread and risers.

Here's how to compute them.

■ Drive stakes at the top and

MEASURING THE RISE AND RUN (LONG SLOPE)

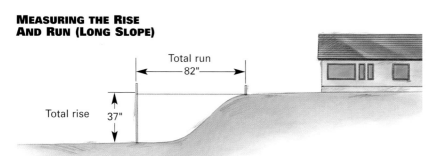

Total run 82"

Total rise 37"

EASY ASCENT

Most landscape steps should be gradual— short risers with deep treads are preferred. (Tread refers to the part of the step on which you place your feet. Risers separate one tread from the other.) To climb extremely steep slopes —10 percent or more—construct a series of steps with landings at least 30 inches deep. If you slope each landing a little, the

MEASURING THE RISE AND RUN (SHORT SLOPE)

Total run

Total rise

COMFORTABLE TREAD/RISE RATIOS

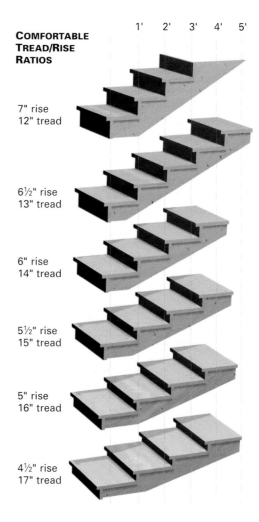

1' 2' 3' 4' 5'

7" rise
12" tread

6½" rise
13" tread

6" rise
14" tread

5½" rise
15" tread

5" rise
16" tread

4½" rise
17" tread

bottom of the slope. Stretch mason's line from the top stake (tying it at ground level) to the bottom stake, keeping the line level across the span.

■ Measure the horizontal distance between the stakes (opposite page). This is the total run of the steps.

■ Measure the distance from the ground to the line on the bottom stake. This is the total *rise*.

■ Calculate the unit rise. Divide the total rise by 6 inches—the standard comfortable height for outdoor steps. Round the result to the nearest whole number. This is the number of 6-inch risers needed for the slope.

In the example, divide the total 37-inch rise by 6, which results in 6.1 risers. Round that up to 7.

Now divide the rise again by the number of steps (7), which in this example results in a riser height of about 5¼ inches—a little lower than the ideal 6 inches. (It's better to be a little low than too high.)

■ Calculate the unit run next. To figure the unit run, divide the total run by the number of steps from the first calculation.

In the example, divide the total 82-inch run by 7, resulting in tread of about 11¾ inches. You can adjust both figures slightly to assure a comfortable climb (see "Trip-Proof Steps," below).

In the example, you could safely install 6-inch risers and 13-inch treads or 5-inch risers with 15-inch treads, making small adjustments in the path to keep the steps equal and at the correct height.

TYPICAL STEP CONSTRUCTION

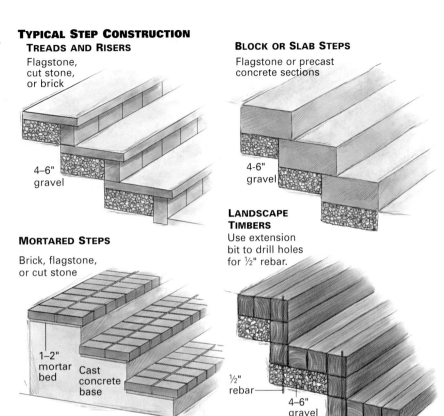

TREADS AND RISERS

Flagstone, cut stone, or brick

4–6" gravel

BLOCK OR SLAB STEPS

Flagstone or precast concrete sections

4-6" gravel

MORTARED STEPS

Brick, flagstone, or cut stone

1–2" mortar bed   Cast concrete base

LANDSCAPE TIMBERS

Use extension bit to drill holes for ½" rebar.

½" rebar

4–6" gravel

Tread surface can be any material; loose material should be set below rear surface of tread and edged on the sides.

TRIP-PROOF STEPS

Outdoor steps will be comfortable to climb if twice the riser height plus the tread depth equals a number from 25 to 27. That works out to a tread depth of 13 to 15 inches for a standard 6-inch rise (2×6 = 12, 12+13 = 25, 12+15 = 27). After you complete your preliminary calculations, adjust the rise and run of your stairs to comply with the formula. Using this formula will virtually guarantee safe and comfortable landscape stairs.

BUILDING STEPS

Building steps in your landscape will require the same general methods used in construction of the patio—layout, excavation, and installation of the base materials.

All step materials require a stable gravel base for support and drainage. Mortared steps call for a concrete base, which in turn, means you have to build forms. The illustrations above will give you a general idea of how to build your steps. For more detailed instructions, see the specific sections in the following pages.

SELECTING STONES FOR STEPS

If you are building flagstone steps, use stones from 2 to 4 inches thick. Flagstone steps are considerably heavy. To make your stair-building efforts less strenuous, have these large stones delivered at the top of the site, not the bottom.

You will begin installing them at the bottom, but sliding them down the slope is much easier than hauling them to the top.

Avoid tearing up the turf by laying an 8-foot sheet of plywood next to the site and pushing or pulling the stones in place.

BUILDING WOOD STAIRS

Stairs let you connect different parts of your landscape with one another. A simple flight of steps can help you expand the useful area of your patio, provide additional places for guests to sit, and can act as a decorative extension of your patio design.

PRESCRIPTION FOR STAIRS

Build stairs anyplace in your landscape where you have more than a 1-foot rise from one surface to another. Most stairs should be at least 36 inches wide and the tread depth and rise will depend on the location (see "Rise and Run," page 148). Wider stairs require a center stringer.

If your stairway will rise more than 8 feet, add a landing. Two short flights of steps look better and provide an easier climb than one long flight. Whether you build one short flight or multiple stairways, all stairs should have the same unit rise and run. (See pages 148–149 for calculating the rise and run.)

All wooden stairs have these parts:
Treads: The surface you walk on.
Stringers: The part that supports the treads. Stringers can be closed (with treads set on stair cleats inside the stringers) or open (with treads set on cutout notches).
Risers: An optional enclosure for the back of each step.

Unless you are constructing wood steps from one level of a patio to another or steps that terminate on a patio, you will need to install a landing pad at the bottom.

CHOOSING LUMBER

Choose clear, straight boards for the stringers, at least 2 feet longer than the total run of the stairs; this allows you to cut the ends where they attach at the top and to the landing. Stringers for one or two steps can be 2×10s; use 2×12s if more than two steps.

MARKING STRINGERS

The procedure for marking closed and open stringers is the same.
■ With your carpenter's square and a tape or stair gauge, mark the unit rise on the short arm of a carpenter's square and the unit run on the long arm.
■ Set the carpenter's square on the top of the stringer with the crown side up and draw light pencil lines for the unit rise and run.
■ Move the square down for each step. Mark the bottom step 1½ inches shorter than the others to allow for the thickness of the tread.

CUTTING AN OPEN STRINGER: To make an open stringer (with treads resting on the top of cutout notches), do the following:
■ Cut on your marks with a circular saw, stopping just short of the corners.
■ Finish each cut with a handsaw to keep the stringer from becoming weak at the corners.
■ Test your stringer by holding it in place; then use the first stringer as a template for marking the other.
■ Apply sealer to all newly cut surfaces.

MAKING A CLOSED STRINGER: To make a closed stringer (with treads supported by cleats on the inside), do the following:

STEP-BY-STEP ANATOMY

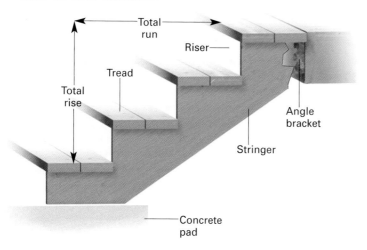

Total run

Riser

Tread

Total rise

Angle bracket

Stringer

Concrete pad

MAKING A LANDING

When you calculate the total rise and run for your stairway, include the height of your landing. A landing can be a poured concrete slab, densely packed gravel, or footings under the stringers. Local building codes may affect your choice of materials, so check before you build.

The landing doesn't need to extend below the frost line, but it must support the stringers and keep them off the ground. Pour the landing slab along with the deck footings or after the deck is finished.

■ Cut only the top and bottom edges.
■ At the lines, attach stair cleats with
1¼-inch decking screws driven through
pilot holes.
■ If you plan to use straight stringers on the
sides and a notched stringer in the middle of
your stairway, cut the middle one first and use
it to mark the locations for the cleats on the
two side stringers.

BUILDING THE LANDING PAD

The bottom of the stairway should rest on a
firm, slightly sloped concrete or masonry
surface about an inch above grade.
    To make a concrete pad, first mark its
location.
■ Set the stringers in place and mark the
ground where the stringers rest.
■ Mark a perimeter about 2 inches wider
than the foot of the stringer.
■ Dig out 8 inches of soil and install
2×8 forms staked with 2×4s.
■ Add 4 inches of gravel, tamp it, lay in
reinforcing wire mesh, and pour the concrete.
■ Drag a straight board over the forms to
level the concrete.
■ Trowel it smooth and let it cure.
    You also can set bricks or pavers
in sand or tamp gravel or stone
inside timber edgings.

ASSEMBLING THE STAIRS

Before assembling the stairs, you must
install posts if you use them to support
a handrail.
■ Tack the stringers at the top and mark
the ground for the posthole locations.
■ Take the stringers down and dig holes at
least 3 feet deep, or to the level specified by
local codes.

EASY SPEED AND ACCURACY

Stair gauges can speed up
your measuring and
marking jobs. Stair gauges,
available at building-
supply stores, are small,
hexagonal brass blocks
with set screws. They
fasten on the sides of a
carpenter's square to
provide consistent
measurements from one
step to the next.

■ Attach the stringers to the the framing.
    Follow the next steps regardless of whether
you've installed posts.
■ Square the stringers.
■ Plumb and attach the posts.
■ Measure the distance between the stringers
and cut treads to fit.
■ Attach the treads (notched around the
posts if necessary), and fill any postholes
with concrete.
■ Fasten treads to the notches or stair cleats
with galvanized ring- or spiral-shank nails or
with decking screws.

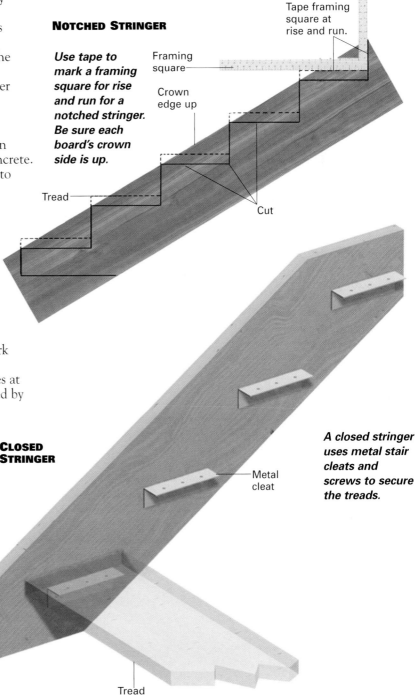

NOTCHED STRINGER

*Use tape to
mark a framing
square for rise
and run for a
notched stringer.
Be sure each
board's crown
side is up.*

Tape framing
square at
rise and run.

Framing
square

Crown
edge up

Tread

Cut

CLOSED STRINGER

Metal
cleat

Tread

*A closed stringer
uses metal stair
cleats and
screws to secure
the treads.*

BUILDING CONCRETE STEPS

Concrete steps provide one of the easiest solutions to changes in grade. You can buy precast steps—generally with 6- to 7¼-inch risers and 11- to 60-inch runs—but building your own is more fun. Here's how. Design their dimensions as you would any steps or stairs (see page 148).

BUILDING FORMS

For steps between fixed heights, cut the form from a sheet of ¾-inch plywood. (You may need two sheets for a large stairway.)

■ Using a framing square and the techniques discussed on page 150, draw the steps on the plywood (see below), sloping the upper landing so that water drains away from the structure. If the steps will be paved with a mortared surface, subtract the thickness of both the paving and bedding material from the height of the first riser only. *Note: All of the other steps should be the height you computed earlier. Keep in mind that the finished surface of the steps will be higher than the tread line on the form.*

■ Draw light lines for each step. Then draw darker lines, angling the risers back 1 inch and raising the backs of the treads ¼ inch per foot.

■ Cut the plywood sheet and set it in place to make sure you drew the layout correctly. If it's OK, use this form as a template to mark and cut a sheet for the other side of the stairs. Set the two forms in place and support them

HILLSIDE-STAIRS FOOTINGS

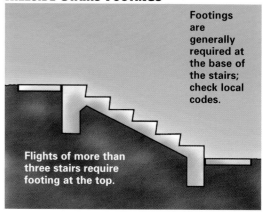

Footings are generally required at the base of the stairs; check local codes.

Flights of more than three stairs require footing at the top.

with stakes and braces made of 2×4s (see the illustrations on opposite page). Check for square and plumb as you assemble the form.

■ To make risers, rip-cut 2×8s to the calculated riser height and bevel their bottom edge at 30 degrees to leave a space so you can slip a trowel under the form as you finish the step below.

EXCAVATING THE SITE

Excavate the site 6 inches below grade and a foot wider and longer than the finished steps. If drainage is poor, excavate an additional 4 inches and add a gravel base.

HILLSIDE STAIRS: Prop the side forms in place and roughly square them.

■ Drive 24-inch 2×4 stakes every 2 feet along one side board.

■ After plumbing the board and checking

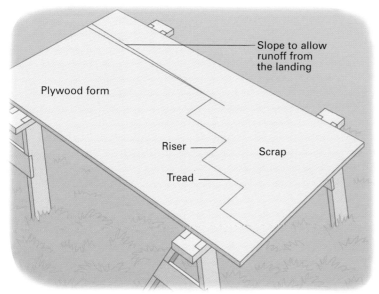

Slope to allow runoff from the landing

Plywood form

Riser

Scrap

Tread

Carefully plan your stair layout. You may need fewer or more steps than you had anticipated; if so, measure again and refigure the dimensions.

STEPS FOR A SLOPING YARD

For landscape steps, use this technique. Dig two 3- to 4-inch-deep trenches in the slope, as far apart as the width of the steps. Set 2×12s on edge in the trenches. Ensure that they are parallel; then stake them in place.

Excavate a series of stepped platforms between the forms. These don't have to conform to the finished steps; they provide a place for a 4-inch layer of concrete.

Use plywood for the forms. First, mark the point where the steps and the finished surface of the walk leading up to them will meet. Next, using a level, draw the risers and treads, starting at this bottom step and working up. Make light, erasable lines and experiment before coming up with identical, easy-to-climb steps.

the slope of the treads (1/4-inch drop per foot), fasten the side to the stakes with two-headed nails or drywall screws.

■ Position the other side of the form and stake it in place.

■ Attach boards to the top and bottom of the side forms, and stake them in place.

■ Place riser boards with the beveled edge facing down and out, and nail them to the side boards.

■ Brace the center of the risers with a long 2×6 set on edge. Attach it to the risers with 2×4 cleats angled so they won't interfere with the treads.

■ Stake the bottom of this brace firmly.

■ If the stairway is long, stake the top, too.

STAIRS AGAINST A STRUCTURE:

Assemble the form by attaching the risers to the sides. Do not put a back on this form. Set the form against the wall.

■ Square and plumb the form, making sure it's level from side to side and has a 1/4-inch drop per foot on the treads and the landing.

■ There will be tremendous pressure on this form from the weight of the concrete. Stake it all around with 2×4s attached with two-headed nails, and brace the stakes. The bigger and taller the stairway, the greater the number of stakes and braces.

■ Make sure there is no space where the form meets the wall. Use silicone caulk or isolation joint material to help close small gaps.

■ Brace the center of the risers with a 2×4 or a 2×6 set on edge and attached to the risers with angled 2×4 cleats. Firmly stake the bottom of this brace.

■ Paint the wall inside the form with mastic to serve as an isolation joint.

POURING AND FINISHING

■ Coat the forms with a releasing agent.

■ Pack gravel into the base of the form. To cut down on the amount of concrete needed, fill the forms with rubble, such as broken pieces of concrete. Leave enough room that the concrete is at least 4 inches thick at all points.

■ Reinforce the steps with wire mesh.

■ If the steps attach to a house, drill holes in the foundation and insert rebar.

■ Starting at the bottom step and working up, spade concrete around the edges first and then fill the center.

■ Pour the concrete flush with the tops of the forms, screed it level, smooth with a float, and broom-texture the surface.

■ Remove forms when the concrete sets.

■ Use a step trowel to finish inside corners, and an edger and a steel trowel for the rest.

HILLSIDE-STAIRS FRAMEWORK

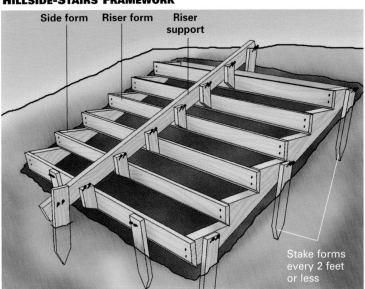

Adequate bracing is essential to maintaining square forms.

BUILDING STEPS AGAINST A STRUCTURE

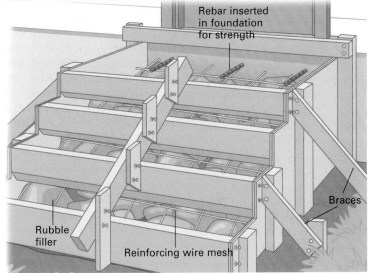

Keep forms upright and plumb with 2×4 stakes and braces. Attach the riser forms to both of the side forms and to step braces to prevent the concrete from deforming the forms.

FINISHING STEPS

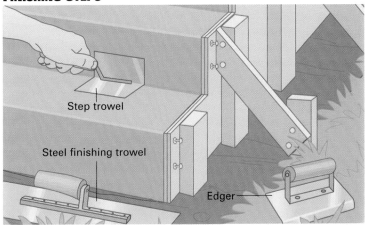

Finish the inside corner of the step with a step trowel. Rounding the outside edges of the step with an edger prevents chipping.

RETAINING WALLS

Retaining walls can cut into slopes, freeing space otherwise unsuitable for a patio. Concrete block, brick, timber, natural stone, or precast decorative units are all suitable materials.

Because they must hold back the pressure of the earth and water behind them, retaining walls must be designed with special considerations. First and foremost, they must allow a passage for water to drain out and away from them.

Dry-stacked materials must be built so that each course staggers backward into the slope. Staggering adds strength and will keep the wall from bowing or collapsing.

BRICK WALL

Lay a brick wall on a concrete footing. Note the line stretched between wood corner blocks as a guide to keep the courses straight. Walls more than a foot high require a double thickness of bricks.

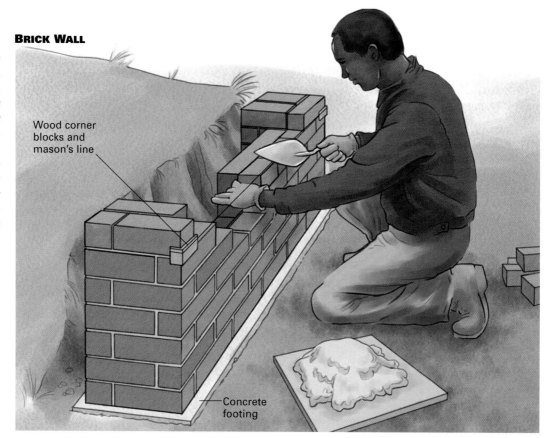

Wood corner blocks and mason's line

Concrete footing

DRAINING A RETAINING WALL

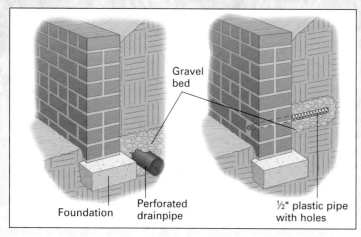

Gravel bed

Foundation

Perforated drainpipe

½" plastic pipe with holes

Without adequate drainage, water pressure can build up behind a retaining wall and crack it. Dig a trench at least 8 inches deep and wide behind the foundation (far left). Shovel gravel into it, making one end higher than the other. Lay perforated drainpipe, holes facing down, on the gravel. The slope of the gravel directs water away from the wall.

Another solution is to place ½-inch perforated plastic pipe every 4 feet along the wall in the first above-grade course (left). Cut an inch off adjacent bricks to fit the pipe. Build up mortar under the pipe at the back of the wall so the pipe tilts up into the backfill. Surround the pipe with a few inches of gravel as you backfill.

MORTARED STONE

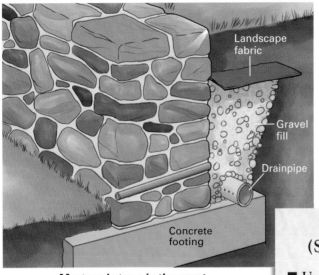

Mortared stone is the most permanent material to use for a retaining wall. Pour a concrete footing as the base. A large drainpipe carries away most rain water, and small drainpipes—called weep holes—let excess water pass from the other side.

Make a batter guide from a board cut to the height of the wall and then cut at an angle along its length. Taper the guide 1 inch for every 2 feet of wall height. Tape a carpenter's level to its straight side and use it to check the wall as you build it. When the level's bubble is centered, the angle is correct.

STONE TIPS (SO YOUR WALL WON'T)

■ Use large flat stones for the base, which will be slightly wider than the top.

■ Set base stones in two parallel rows. Twist and shift each one, and remove or add gravel until it sits solidly.

■ For all courses, use stones that are more flat than round.

■ Sort the stones into piles by size so you can quickly find the size you need.

DRY-STACKED STONE

To keep the weight of water runoff from destroying your dry-stacked retaining wall, install a drainage system. Lay perforated drainpipe in gravel so it can carry water away to a dry well or another area that will soak up the runoff. Add more gravel and then the landscaping fabric. As you build up, fill the area behind the wall with gravel, and finish off the top with soil and sod or plantings.

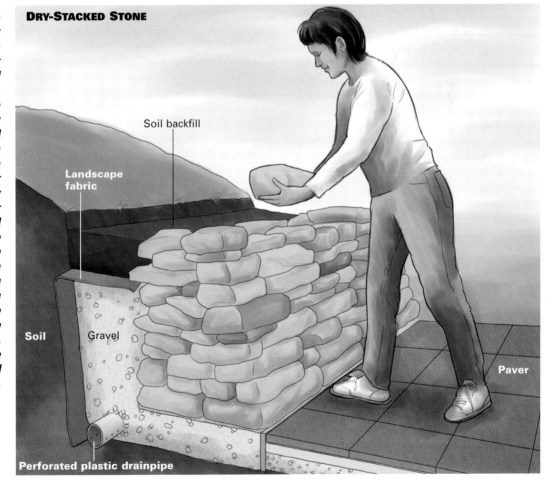

RETAINING WALLS
continued

LAYING CONCRETE BLOCK

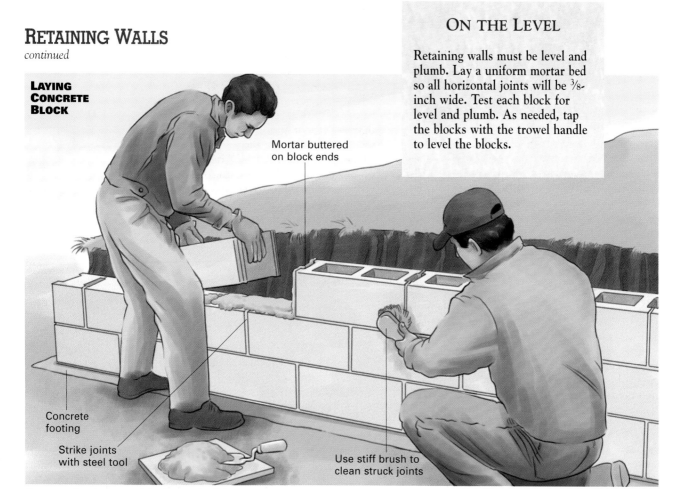

Mortar buttered on block ends

ON THE LEVEL

Retaining walls must be level and plumb. Lay a uniform mortar bed so all horizontal joints will be ⅜-inch wide. Test each block for level and plumb. As needed, tap the blocks with the trowel handle to level the blocks.

Concrete footing

Strike joints with steel tool

Use stiff brush to clean struck joints

Lay out the concrete blocks so the joints are staggered, as shown. For greater strength on high walls, use reinforcing wire mesh in mortar between joints and fill the cores of the blocks with mortar.

PRECAST BLOCK

GREEN WALLS

Use blocks cast in the shape of oversized flowerpots to construct planted, or "green" walls. Simply remove soil to position and level the blocks and fill the planting area with the soil. Stairstep your design up the slope face and plant flowers or groundcover.

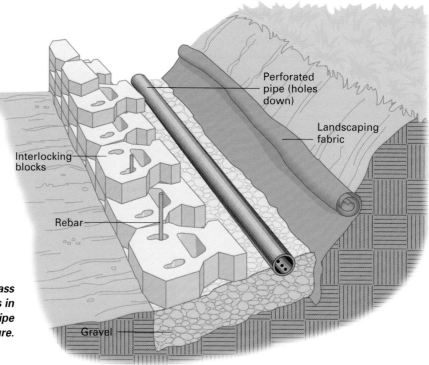

Perforated pipe (holes down)

Landscaping fabric

Interlocking blocks

Rebar

Gravel

Sections of rebar or fiberglass anchoring pins help hold the blocks in place. Gravel and perforated pipe prevent damage from water pressure.

INTERLOCKING BLOCK

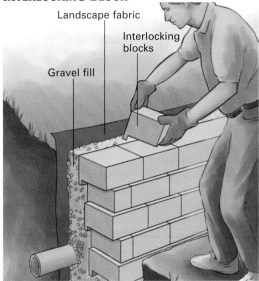

Landscape fabric

Interlocking blocks

Gravel fill

Some concrete blocks are self-battering—made with a ridge along the lower back edge that hooks against the block below it. These ridges also set each succeeding course back from the one below it. Interlocking blocks work best for walls that are no more than a few feet tall.

MAINTAINING TIMBERS

Termites and carpenter ants will consume a lightly treated timber wall. Buy .40-grade treated timbers for protection against the bugs. Check the wall periodically for signs of insect infestation and use an aerosol insecticide to keep insects away. When the wall darkens with mildew and dirt, use a deck cleaner to clean it. Once a year, use a sprayer to apply a clear wood sealer to exposed wood.

DEADMEN

If you're building a retaining wall more than 2 feet high, strengthen it with deadmen—perpendicular timbers attached to parallel timbers set in trenches in the slope.

Dig the trenches at the third or fourth course and about 6 feet back into the slope—at a depth that will make them even with the course they attach to.

Cut and lay 6-foot-long timbers in the trenches. Fasten the deadmen to the wall and rear timbers with 12-inch spikes or rebar driven through them.

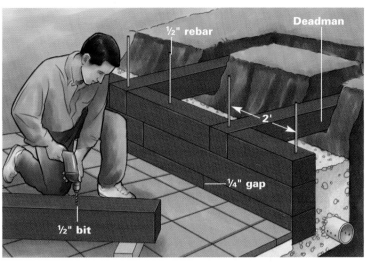

½" rebar

Deadman

2'

¼" gap

½" bit

TIMBER WALLS
The first course of timbers will be at least partially below grade. Be sure it rests on a thick bed of gravel so water can drain away. Install perforated drainpipe to carry away additional runoff.

POURED CONCRETE WALLS

A poured-concrete retaining wall requires forming and placing a large amount of concrete, so consider hiring a contractor to build it.

The process involves inserting rebar horizontally in the concrete footing; it will help support the heavy wall. Other rebar are bent at a 90-degree angle and wired in place before the footing is poured. Then the vertical rebar are wired to horizontal rebar every 12 inches from the footing to the top of the wall. Forms are assembled at the front and back sides of the wall, and concrete is poured into the forms. When the concrete wall has cured, the forms are removed and gravel is filled into the space between the wall and the earth slope. A perforated drainpipe laid near the footing provides drainage behind

the wall. The top foot of the wall is backfilled with soil.

Note that the footing is stabilized by earth fill on the front face and by the weight of gravel and earth on the back side of the wall.

If the wall is more than 3 feet high, the concrete forms need to

be set so the base of the wall is thicker than the top and the face of the wall slants back toward the sloped soil.

DECORATIVE WALLS

Laying stones of irregular size will result in mortar joints that are not uniform or straight. Use mason's line as a guide to keep the wall plumb. At its base, the mortar bed atop the footings must be thick enough to fill the joints between stones. Use small stones to fill gaps and reduce the size of the mortar joints.

MORTARED STONE

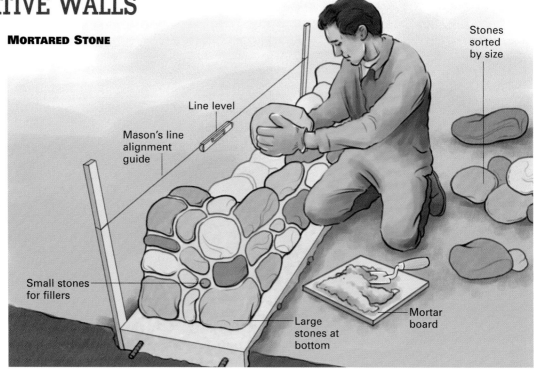

Line level

Mason's line alignment guide

Stones sorted by size

Small stones for fillers

Large stones at bottom

Mortar board

Wonderfully versatile, decorative walls do far more than add colorful accents between your property lines. They define spaces, separating one from another. They impart a sense of permanence to the landscape, blocking erosion of the soil and standing firm against future whims of nature's design. They corral pets and help keep out strays, frame things you want to showcase and hide things you don't want to see. They can lift vines to new heights and knock down high winds. Time only enhances their beauty and your reputation for having had the foresight to build them well.

DRY-STACKED STONE

For stability in a dry stone wall, keep the batter sharp and lay bond stones every three or four courses.

Cap stone

Bond stone

Batter guide

Tamped gravel in trench at least 12" deep

MORTARED BRICK

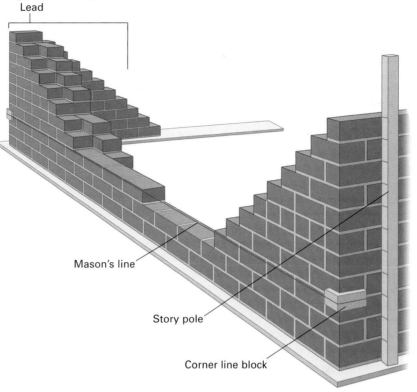

For walls 8 feet long or more, build leads in each corner, as shown. By building leads, you will have neat corners and even courses. Leads provide a place to set the line blocks so that instead of checking each brick with a level, you simply line it up with the mason's line.

GREAT WALL OPTIONS

Don't build a plain old wall if you want something more attractive. Enhance your wall with special features. For example, a brick or stone wall can incorporate a planter or enclose a waterfall that spills into a pool.

For flowers or groundcovers, such as ivy, interrupt dry stone or timber at random with exposed soil. To include a fountain or waterfall, buy a low-voltage electric pump at your home or garden center.

Spice up your design with unique brick patterns. Dry-lay the pattern first and be sure any divisions are multiples of the brick dimensions.

STONE WALL COST CONTROL

You can cut your costs by filling the core of the wall with less attractive stones than those used on the wall's face.

To avoid wasting mortar, adjust batch sizes to the amount you can use in two hours. When laying a stone wall, the consistency of the mortar must be thick enough to support the weight of the stones without displacing the mortar.

STUCCO ON A BLOCK WALL

Basic concrete block has an industrial appearance, but that can be remedied with stucco. First coat the blocks with a latex bonding agent. Then apply the stucco coats of the desired color.

MORTARED CONCRETE BLOCK

A block wall calls for many of the techniques that apply to a brick wall. Chalk a layout line; then lay the first course in a 1-inch mortar bed. Build leads and string mason's line to maintain even courses.

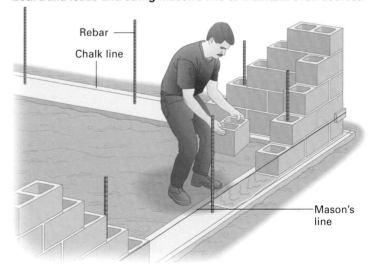

POSTS, PIERS, AND FOOTINGS

Much of the privacy, shade, and ambience of patios comes from arbors, fences, and other structures that rely on posts for support. You have two techniques to anchor posts. Either bury part of the post in the ground, or fasten it above ground to a concrete pier or footing. Most fences are built with posts set in the ground. In packed soil, set the post in an earth and gravel base. In sandy, loose, or moist soil, set the posts in concrete.

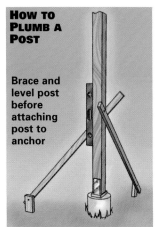

HOW TO PLUMB A POST

Brace and level post before attaching post to anchor

LAYING OUT THE SITE

Using batter boards and mason's line, lay out the perimeter of your fence or other structure and square the corners with the 3-4-5 method. (See page 107 for more information.)

Many structures have posts spaced 8 feet apart; your design may require different spacing. Lumber is sold in even-numbered increments, so space posts in even multiples of feet to avoid waste.

Factory-made fence panels require precise post placement. Lay the panels on the ground or mark and dig postholes as you go.

POSTS

SINKING POSTS: Using a posthole digger, dig a hole that is three times as wide as the post and half its exposed length.
- Shovel in 4 inches of gravel and set the post.
- Plumb the post and brace it.
- Then shovel in 2 more inches of gravel.
- Complete the earth and gravel installation or fill the hole with concrete.

SETTING POSTS: Cut dadoed or mortised joints after the posts are set. With other styles, let the height run wild and cut the post-tops along the entire line later. Here's what to do.
- Divide the actual size of your posts by 2 (a 6×6, for example, measures 5½ inches thick)

DEPTH AND DIAMETERS

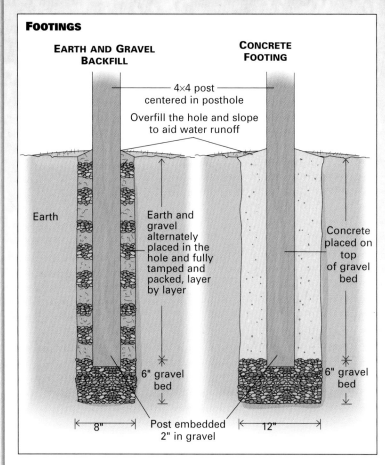

FOOTINGS

EARTH AND GRAVEL BACKFILL

CONCRETE FOOTING

4×4 post centered in posthole

Overfill the hole and slope to aid water runoff

Earth

Earth and gravel alternately placed in the hole and fully tamped and packed, layer by layer

Concrete placed on top of gravel bed

6" gravel bed

6" gravel bed

8"

12"

Post embedded 2" in gravel

Here are some guidelines for posthole dimensions. Consult your local building department for information specific to your area.

Posthole-depth terminal posts. As a general rule, one-third of the total post length should be below ground (at a minimum depth of 24 inches) and two-thirds above ground. Thus, a 6-foot terminal post should be 9 feet long and set in a 3-foot posthole. Line posts can be set slightly less deep. Line posts for a 6-foot fence can be 8 feet long and set in 2-foot holes. Local codes may require depths below the frost line.

Posthole diameter. The minimum diameter of the posthole depends on the footing.
- Earth and gravel. Make your posthole diameter at least twice the width of the post. A 4×4 requires an 8-inch diameter, a 6×6, a 12-inch diameter.
- Concrete footings. Make the posthole diameter at least three times the width of the post. A 4×4 post requires a hole 12 inches in diameter; a 6×6 requires one 18 inches in diameter.

and move your mason's lines this distance away from their original position. This new position will place the lines in the plane of the outside post faces, as shown at right.

■ Stand an end post in its hole and twist its base into the gravel bed about 2 inches. On two adjacent sides and about two-thirds up the post, pivot 1×4 braces on a single two-headed nail (its two heads make removal easy). Then plumb the post on two adjacent faces with a 4-foot carpenter's level or post level, keeping the post face just touching the mason's line. Stake the braces securely, attaching them to the post with a couple of box nails or screws. Repeat the process for the other end posts.

■ To help keep the intermediate posts straight, stretch another line between the end posts about 18 inches below their tops. Then set, align, and brace each successive intermediate post.

■ When all the posts are braced, shovel in the footing filler, either alternate layers of earth and gravel or concrete. Double-check each post for alignment and plumb. If you've installed concrete footings and you plan to fasten the rails and infill with screws, you can cut the posts and build the rest of your fence or overhead after the concrete sets. If you're going to nail your fence frame, wait until the concrete cures—about three to seven days. In either case, leave the braces in place.

CUTTING POSTS: If you've set the posts with their heights wild, now's the time to cut them to length.

■ Measure one end post from the ground to the post height and mark it. If the grade is level, snap a level chalk line from that point to the other end post. That will mark all posts at the same height. If you're building a contoured fence, measure the same distance up the other end post and snap the chalk line between them. Make sure all posts are marked and resnap the line if necessary.

■ Carry the marks around each post with a try square. If you're building a contoured fence, you will cut at an angle—carry the marks across the downslope and upslope faces first; then connect these lines on the fourth side.

■ Cut each post to height with a handsaw or a reciprocating saw. You'll be on a ladder, so be careful. Above all, be patient. If you use a circular saw, start with it and finish the cut with a handsaw. Sharp blades make the job faster and safer.

ALIGNING AND BRACING POSTS

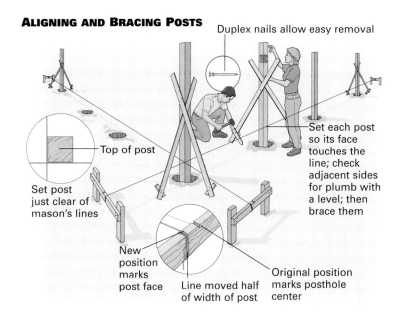

Duplex nails allow easy removal

Set each post so its face touches the line; check adjacent sides for plumb with a level; then brace them

Top of post

Set post just clear of mason's lines

New position marks post face

Line moved half of width of post

Original position marks posthole center

MARKING POSTS FOR CUTTING

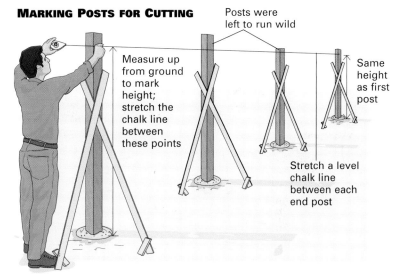

Posts were left to run wild

Measure up from ground to mark height; stretch the chalk line between these points

Same height as first post

Stretch a level chalk line between each end post

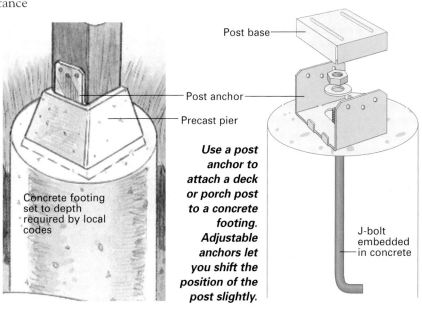

Post base

Post anchor

Precast pier

Concrete footing set to depth required by local codes

Use a post anchor to attach a deck or porch post to a concrete footing. Adjustable anchors let you shift the position of the post slightly.

J-bolt embedded in concrete

BASIC FENCE BUILDING

Most fences are made with 4×4 posts sunk into the ground, with two or three horizontal 2×4 rails that support vertical or horizontal boards or panels (often called the infill). Use materials that will resist rotting: pressure-treated lumber or naturally resistant species such as redwood, cedar, or cypress. Even if painted, untreated pine and fir will not outlast pressure-treated wood.

LAYING OUT AND SETTING POSTS: Using the procedures discussed on pages 160-161, lay out the site, set the posts, and cut them. If your fence runs down a slope, refer to the illustrations below and cut the posts for a stepped or a sloped fence.

FRAMING THE INFILL: Before adding rails and infill, cut the posts. Stretch a taut line from one end or corner post to the other. If the ground is fairly level, or if you want the fence to follow the slope, attach the line at both ends the same height from the ground (you can use a water level to make sure the height is the same). Mark all the posts at the line and cut them with a circular saw.

If you want a fence that steps down, use the same method to establish height, but install fence sections that are plumb. Then cut the posts.

■ **Installing rails:** Cut 2×4 rails to span the outside faces of the posts or to fit snugly between them. For inside rails, hold the rail in place and mark it. Attach the rails with rail hangers, or predrill pilot holes for galvanized nails or screws.

■ **Cutting and attaching infill:** Cut the infill lumber at the same time, and make a spacing jig to speed installation. If the infill stock is wider than 2 inches, attach it with two nails or screws at each joint.

■ **Adding a kickboard:** To keep the dog in the yard, add a kickboard at the bottom—extending almost to the ground. If your pet likes to dig under the fence, install a pressure-treated board in a trench dug several inches into the ground.

STEPPED FENCE

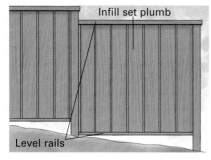

Install plumb posts on a sloped site as you would on a level site. For a stepped fence (left), attach level rails and then cut the posts. For a sloped fence (right), cut the posts and install the rails so they follow the slope of the ground. Install the infill plumb in both cases.

SLOPED FENCE

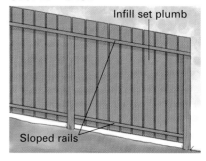

When the posts are set and cut, measure for inside rails. Use scrap pieces of wood to keep the bottom rail about 6 inches above the ground until you toenail it with 8d galvanized nails or use 2½-inch deck screws.

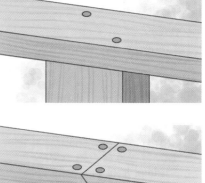

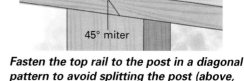

Fasten the top rail to the post in a diagonal pattern to avoid splitting the post (above, top). Miter adjoining pieces (above).

INFILL INSTALLATION TIPS

SPACING THE INFILL

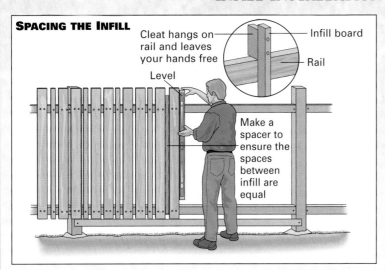

Cleat hangs on rail and leaves your hands free

Infill board

Rail

Level

Make a spacer to ensure the spaces between infill are equal

CUTTING ANGLED INFILL

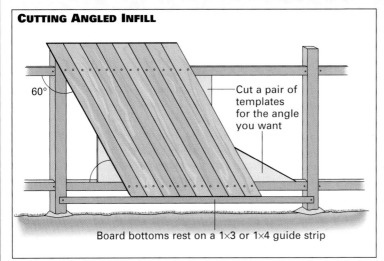

60°

Cut a pair of templates for the angle you want

Board bottoms rest on a 1×3 or 1×4 guide strip

INSTALLING A KICKBOARD

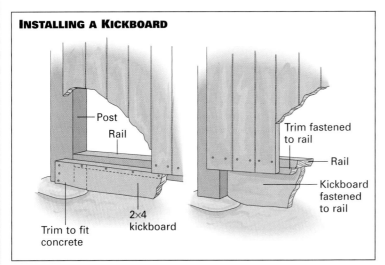

Post

Rail

Trim to fit concrete

2×4 kickboard

Trim fastened to rail

Rail

Kickboard fastened to rail

Whether your fence incorporates surface-mounted or inset infill, these tips will make fence building easier and result in a sturdier, better-looking job.

■ Don't scrimp on fasteners—either in quality or quantity. Galvanized or treated nails or screws cost slightly more but will last longer and stain the fence less than plain steel. Stainless-steel fasteners are the best choice. In addition to their own weight, fences have to carry extra loads imposed by rain, snow, wind, and climbing kids. Much of this stress falls on the fasteners—use plenty of them.

■ Hang boards plumb. Check the infill as you go—every few feet at least—with a 4-foot level (smaller levels may not be as accurate). If the infill has gotten out of plumb, disassemble your work and correct it.

■ Equalize the spaces between pieces of infill. Make them regular with a cleated spacer; it will save you from measuring for each piece. Hang the cleat on the top rail so you can free both hands to hold the infill as you fasten it.

■ Keep angled infill even. Use a bevel square or make templates to properly position angled infill onto the frame.

■ Make bottom edges flush and smooth. Use guide boards to help place the infill (tack a 1×3 or 1×4 to the surface of the posts), unless your design intentionally calls for random lengths. Reposition the guide as you work your way down the line.

■ To finish a wild-top edge, chalk a line at the cutting height. Then tack a 1×3 or 1×4 guide so a circular saw's soleplate can ride on it. Set the blade deep enough to cut through the infill, but no deeper. Rest the saw on the cutting guide and cut the entire top of the fence in one pass.

■ Install kickboards. Kickboards will close the gap under the bottom rail, providing a more finished look, and will keep animals from crawling under the fence. They also keep flat rails from sagging. Overlay them on the posts or inset them under the bottom rail; trim with a 1×2 if you want. Because it touches the earth and is subject to rot, the kickboard should be made of pressure-treated lumber, heartwood, or a decay-resistant species such as cedar or cypress.

BUILDING A FRIENDLY FENCE

This decorative lattice fence panel with its windowed basket enhances privacy and camouflages unpleasant views. Still, it admits sunlight and breezes.

The instructions assume you are building the fence from scratch, but you could install the window in an existing fence. If your posts are no more than 4 feet apart, remove the fencing between two posts and cut a lattice panel to fit.

BEFORE YOU BEGIN

For a friendly-yet-private screen, cut a window in a lattice panel to accommodate a hanging basket. Make just one panel for a small privacy screen. Or build an entire lattice fence, putting window panels near seating areas.

■ Buy prefabricated lattice panels to harmonize with the rest of your landscaping. We use square lattice, but diagonal lattice is OK and more commonly available.
■ Most manufactured lattice is only ½ inch thick. Consider building your own from ¾ inch stock; it's sturdier and longer lasting.
■ Use weather-resistant, pressure-treated lattice and lumber or dark-colored heartwood of redwood or cedar to resist rot.
■ When buying the posts, factor in the depth of the postholes. If the holes will be 3 feet deep and the fence 6 feet high, for instance, you need 9-foot posts, so buy 10-footers.
■ Prime, stain, or apply water-repellent sealer to all pieces after cutting them. Give the fence a second coat after it's assembled.
■ Use double-dipped deck screws or hot-dipped galvanized nails to avoid rust streaks.

BUILDING THE FENCE

Building this fence is a relatively easy project and the result is very elegant. Simply follow these instructions:

LAYING OUT THE SITE: If the posts are not already in place, stake the layout and stretch mason's line between them to mark the location for new posts.
■ Dig postholes no more than 4 feet apart and to a depth required by local codes.

PREPARING POSTHOLES: Shovel a few inches of gravel into the bottom of each posthole, and insert the posts.
■ Use a post level to check for plumb, and temporarily brace the posts.

SETTING THE POSTS: Fill the holes with earth and gravel or concrete (see page 160).
■ **Earth and gravel setting:** Fill the hole about ¼ full, then tamp the soil repeatedly with a 2×2 until it is firm.
Add more soil, tamp, and repeat until the hole is filled. Mound the soil above grade and slope it so rainwater runs away from the post; then tamp the top firm with a 4×4.
■ **Concrete setting:** Be sure to crown the top an inch above grade and slope it downward so rainwater runs off.
■ **Both settings:** Mark the post height by drawing a line all the way around with a square. Cut off the tops of the posts with a circular saw.

BUILDING THE FRAME: Lay a 2×4 flat on top of the posts; attach it by driving two 3-inch deck screws or 16d galvanized nails into each joint.
■ Cut another 2×4 to fit snugly between the posts and 3 inches above the ground. To install it, drill angled pilot holes and drive nails or screws through the 2×4 and into the post.
■ Measure the distance between 2×4s to ensure they are parallel.

INSTALLING THE NAILERS: Cut rear 1×2 nailers to run along the back edge of the posts and 2×4s. They should be as long as the opening between the 2×4s.
- Attach the nailers to the inside of the posts, wide side facing the post, with 1⅝-inch deck screws every foot or so.

FITTING THE PANEL: Measure the opening between the posts and the 2×4s.
- Lay a lattice panel on sawhorses and mark it for cutting, checking that it is symmetrical.
- Cut with a circular saw, and test to see that the panel fits in the opening.

MAKING THE CUTOUT: Use a framing square and a straight board to mark the cutout in the lattice. The size of the cutout depends on the size of the basket. Plan on a 20×30-inch opening for a 12-inch basket.
- Make sure the cutout is centered exactly in the panel; then cut it out with a circular saw.
- Place the lattice panel in the opening, pressing it against the rear nailers.
- Cut 1×2 front nailers, and use them to sandwich the lattice panel tight.
- Attach the front nailers the same way.

FRAMING THE CUTOUT: Frame the cutout with pieces of 1×2. Cut front and rear frame pieces to fit, so they just cover up the cut ends of the lattice.
- While a helper holds two framing pieces so they sandwich the lattice, drill pilot holes through the rear framing piece and lattice and partway through the front framing piece wherever the frame and lattice cross.
- Drive 2-inch screws through each pilot hole. (You may need

shorter or longer screws, depending on the lattice thickness.)

FINISHING: Reapply the finish to the entire structure.

HANGING THE BASKET:
- Drill a pilot hole in the rear of the top 2×4, centered above the opening; screw in a threaded eye hook.
- Hang the basket from the eye hook.

MATERIALS

- Lattice panel
- Lumber: 4×4 posts, 1×2s for nailers and framing, 2×4s
- Deck screws or galvanized nails
- Concrete
- Eye hook
- Planter basket
- Tape measure
- Posthole digger
- Post level
- Circular saw
- Drill
- Hammer
- Framing square
- Sawhorse

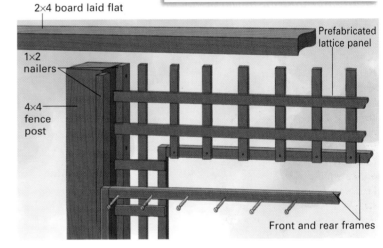

2×4 board laid flat

Prefabricated lattice panel

1×2 nailers

4×4 fence post

Front and rear frames

Hang the plant from the 2×4, not the lattice.

Lattice rests on the bottom ledger board.

After cutting the lattice, sandwich it between 1×2 nailers attached to the fence posts (above). Build two 1×2 frames for the front and rear of the opening, and screw them to the ends of the cut lattice. Top the structure with a 2×4 laid flat over the posts.

Support the lattice on 2×4s while cutting the opening.

BUILDING A PRETTY ARBOR

Frame a private dining nook with this elegant arbor. The materials are inexpensive and its construction requires only basic do-it-yourself skills.

With cooling shade and greenery, this handsome, vine-covered arbor adds to the beauty and comfort of a patio. The lower rafters should span no more than 80 inches from beam to beam. For increased shade, top the arbor with lattice or 1×2s spaced 1½ inches apart. For less shade, space the rafters farther apart.

MATERIALS

- Lumber: 6×6 posts, 2×10s, and 2×2s
- Concrete mix
- Deck screws
- Tape measure
- Posthole digger
- Carpenter's level
- Shovel
- Backsaw
- Miter saw
- Circular saw
- Clamps
- Drill
- Saber saw
- Chisel
- Hammer

GROUNDWORK

For a freestanding arbor, sink support posts at least 3 feet into the ground. That means, for example, a 9-foot-tall arbor needs 12-foot posts.

Laying out the site for your arbor relies on the same techniques as laying out any rectangular structure. For more background, see pages 106–107. Then lay out the arbor site using the techniques shown on page 185 and square it with the 3-4-5 method.

POSTS: Using a clamshell posthole digger or auger, dig the postholes at least 30 inches deep. If you live in an area with freezing winters, the posts will rise and fall an inch or so as the ground freezes and thaws, unless you dig the holes below your frost line. Frost heave poses a problem, especially if the arbor is attached to another structure.

- Shovel several inches of gravel into the bottom of each hole, and insert the posts. (You will cut them to height later.)
- Brace the posts temporarily but firmly so they are plumb (perfectly vertical). For braces, use 3- to 4-foot 2×4s or 2×6s at the bottom, and 1×4 or 2×4 angle braces that are anchored to stakes driven into the ground (see illustration on the opposite page). Getting the posts both plumb and placed the correct distance apart may require shifting and reshifting. (If you are off by an inch, it won't be visible.)
- Combine water and bagged concrete mix and fill the postholes. Work the mix up and down with a stout stick to remove all air pockets. Overfill each hole so that rainwater will run away from the post.

FRAMING

The frame supporting the arbor roof consists of doubled 2×10 beams. Collar pieces add a decorative touch and help mark the position of the beams.

COLLARS: Measure and mark the arbor height on one of the posts; then measure down 9½ inches.

- At this point, draw a line around the post using a small square.
- Miter the 2×2 collar pieces and attach them to the post aligned with the lines you drew. Drill pilot holes and attach each collar piece with two 1⅝-inch deck screws.
- With a helper, place a level on top of a long, straight board (as long as the arbor); then set one end of the board on top of the 2×2 collar. Mark the collar height on the other posts. Install all other collars.

CUTTING THE POSTS: Set a short scrap piece of 2×10 on top of each collar piece; draw post cutoff lines. Cut the posts with a reciprocating saw.

BEAMS: Measure the distances between the posts at the top, and miter-cut 2×10s for the outer beam pieces. (It's OK to bend the posts an inch or two if they are not equidistant.)

- Working with a helper, place each beam piece on top of the collar pieces at either end, and attach them by driving three 3-inch deck screws into each joint.
- Measure and cut the inside beams and laminate them to the outside beams with polyurethane glue and 1¼-inch deck screws driven every foot.

THE ROOF

The arbor roof consists of notched 2×10 lower rafters set perpendicular to the upper rafters.

CUTTING THE RAFTERS: Cut all the 2×10 rafters to length. The lower rafters are 2 to 3 feet longer than the arbor's width, and the upper rafters are 2 to 3 feet longer than its length.
■ On a copier, enlarge the pattern illustration below until it measures 9½ inches high. Use it as a pattern for the rafter ends. Cut one rafter end with a saber saw, and use it as a template to mark the others. Also at this time, cut the decorative ends, which slip over the arbor frame.

NOTCHING THE RAFTERS: Cut the notches as shown. For the lower rafters and decorative ends, notch the bottom of each end so the rafters will fit over the beams. On top, cut a notch for the upper rafters to fit into. Cut notches on the bottom of the upper rafters for every lower rafter. Place all rafter notches an equal distance apart.
To mark the notches, clamp the upper rafters and all the lower rafters together, and mark their top or bottom edges all at once.
■ Cut the notches first with a circular saw and then a saber saw. Clean the corners with a handsaw and chisel. As you work, check to see that the notched rafters will fit tightly together.

SETTING THE RAFTERS: With a helper, set the lower rafters on top of the beams, spacing them evenly.

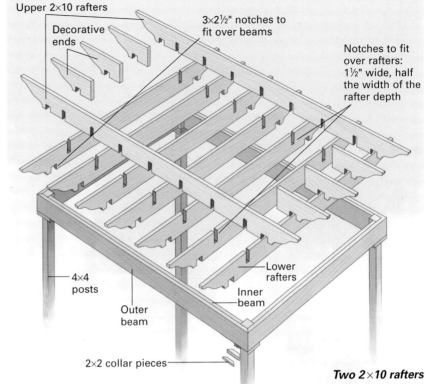

Upper 2×10 rafters
Decorative ends
3×2½" notches to fit over beams
Notches to fit over rafters: 1½" wide, half the width of the rafter depth
4×4 posts
Outer beam
Lower rafters
Inner beam
2×2 collar pieces

■ Slip the upper rafters onto the lowers, fitting the pieces together jigsaw-like. This requires jiggling and tapping with a hammer.
■ Once all the pieces are put together, drill angled pilot holes and drive 3-inch deck screws everywhere a rafter rests on a beam.
■ If the structure wobbles, stabilize it with angle braces as shown (bottom, right).

APPLYING THE FINISH:
■ Apply two or more coats of stain, finish, or paint to the arbor.

Two 2×10 rafters span the arbor in one direction. To help stabilize the arbor, two others run perpendicularly to this row, slipping into notches near the scalloped end of the bottom rafters. Between these two upper rafters, a series of short, notched, decorative ends balance the design.

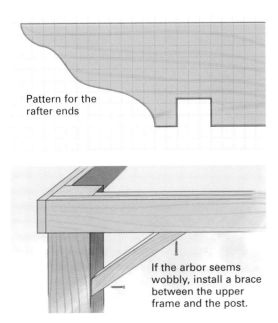

Pattern for the rafter ends

If the arbor seems wobbly, install a brace between the upper frame and the post.

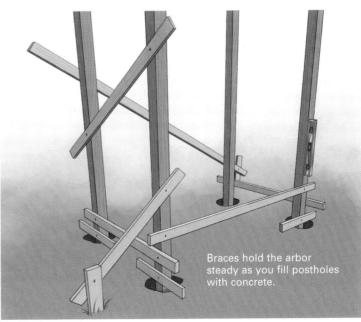

Braces hold the arbor steady as you fill postholes with concrete.

LIGHTING

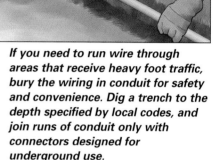

If you need to run wire through areas that receive heavy foot traffic, bury the wiring in conduit for safety and convenience. Dig a trench to the depth specified by local codes, and join runs of conduit only with connectors designed for underground use.

Low-voltage lights are available in styles that range from Victorian revival to high-tech. Most are designed for use in the ground; many also can be mounted on deck railings, under stairs, or along fences. Halogen bulbs cost more initially, but they are less expensive to operate.

Adding lights to a patio takes planning, but it's not difficult. Choose the system you prefer—either line-voltage or low-voltage systems—review the installation guidelines, and prepare to enjoy your patio day and night.

LINE-VOLTAGE LIGHTING

A line-voltage system uses the 120-volt AC power in your house. Working with line voltage is easy enough for homeowners with experience doing their own electrical work. Most outdoor line-voltage wiring requires approval from a building inspector, however.

LAYOUT: Using wooden stakes, mark the location of lights, switches, junction boxes, and receptacles.
■ Tie colored lines between the stakes to show where to dig trenches for wiring.
■ Run the line to the power source.

CONDUIT: Cut away the sod for wiring trenches. Then cut conduit to length and lay sections in place. Attach fittings as you work.
■ Avoid making sharp bends in the conduit. The wire inside should be able to slide through it smoothly.
■ Wherever the conduit will attach to a junction box or fixture, mount the junction box securely—to the side of the house, for example. Attach fittings to the conduit.

WIRING: Using a tool called a fish tape, pull wire through the conduit to each box and receptacle. Pull out several inches of wire at each location for making the connections.
■ Run wire from the beginning of the circuit to the house wiring. Leave it unconnected at this time.
■ If you're uncomfortable finishing the wiring yourself, have an electrician complete the job. Otherwise, wire the switches first, followed by the junction boxes, receptacles, and fixtures.
■ Make sure all outdoor circuits have GFCI protection, and use waterproof gaskets on all exposed components. Point the open ends of all wire connectors downward so they don't collect water.

FINAL CONNECTIONS: Turn off the power at the main service panel. With all other parts of the system wired, connect it to the circuit you have chosen. Turn the power on.
■ Turn on each fixture to test the bulbs, and replace the ones that don't work. If any fixtures are not getting power, turn off the electricity at the main service panel and check the fixtures with a multitester. When all the fixtures work, adjust the lights at night to create the look you want.

CLEANUP: When you are satisfied with the placement of your outdoor lighting, fill in the trenches and cover them with sod. Secure any conduit and wires that extend above ground.

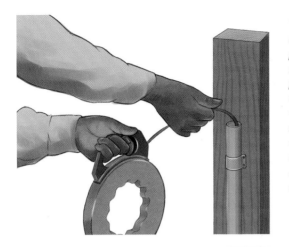

When the conduit is in place, you may have trouble pushing wire through it. To work around bends and over long distances, use a fish tape and pulling lubricant.

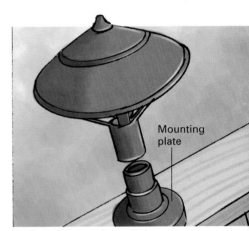

Link the fixtures to the electrical supply lines with wire connectors. Turn on the power at the source to test the bulbs.

INSTALLING A LOW-VOLTAGE SYSTEM

Low voltage is safe, easy to install, and inexpensive to operate. The easiest way to install a low-voltage system is to buy a low-voltage lighting kit, which includes cable, lights, and a transformer that lowers voltage so it is safe to the touch. Purchase a kit with a timer or a photovoltaic switch to turn the lights on automatically when it gets dark.

■ Mount the transformer near an outdoor receptacle where it won't be damaged.

■ Lay out the light fixtures and poke the mounting stakes into the ground. Dig a shallow trench for the cable, lay it in, and cover it. Plug in the transformer.

■ If you want to place lights on a railing or a fence, run the cable where it is out of the way, and fasten it with cable staples about every foot, so it won't dangle. Use mounting plates that are designed for installing light fixtures on a horizontal surface.

■ Connect the parts of a low-voltage system to the transformer, and then plug it in. Check each connection in the circuit to be sure everything is finished. Then turn the power back on.

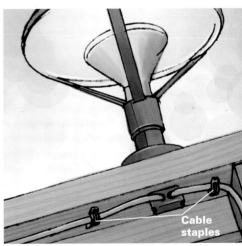

To install low-voltage lights on a railing, purchase a kit with mounting plates. Drill the hole; then install the plate with the screws provided.

Mounting plate

GFCI outdoor receptacle

Low-voltage system transformer

Low-voltage lighting is inexpensive and easy to install. Different systems will cast light on almost any outdoor area or feature. After you've laid out and installed the fixtures, run the cable in a shallow trench.

Cable staples

Run low-voltage cable alongside posts and under rails, or wherever it will be least visible. Fasten it with round-top cable staples (standard square-top staples may cut the cable).

BUILDING A FOUNTAIN

This do-it-yourself fountain can add a splash to any patio.

Complete this quick fountain project in an afternoon. Inexpensive and easy to assemble, the fountain brings the cooling sound of water to your patio.

STEP 1: Locate the fountain within reach of a garden hose and an outdoor electrical outlet. That will show it to its best advantage; it will be the focal point of your patio. If the outlet isn't protected, have a GFCI outlet installed. For safety, install metal conduit or PVC pipe between the outlet and the fountain to run the electrical cord through.

STEP 2: Dig a hole for the bucket. The bucket should fit snugly with its lip rising just above the surface of the soil. Cut a ½-inch-wide slit in the lip of the bucket with a handsaw for the pump's cord to pass through. Wipe the bucket clean.

STEP 3: Mark the center of the saucer on its back by measuring across the saucer horizontally and vertically, drawing a light line along the ruler. The center of the saucer is located where the lines cross. Drill a hole for the tubing to go through at this point using a ¾-inch masonry bit. Next, drill several drainage holes around the saucer. If drainage holes in the pots are too small for the tubing to pass through, enlarge them with the drill and masonry bit. Also, drill additional drainage holes in the pots.

STEP 4: Rinse pots, saucer, and rock to remove dust that might clog the pump. Set the pump on a brick

MATERIALS

- 5-gallon bucket
- Submersible pump
- Flexible water garden tubing long enough to run from the pump to the fountain
- Fountain nozzle
- River rocks
- 12–14" saucer
- 12–14" pot
- 10–12" pot
- 6" pot
- Metal conduit wide enough to admit pump plug
- Drill with ¾" masonry bit
- Shovel
- Knife or handsaw

SELECTING A PUMP

Submersible pumps come in various sizes for pumping different amounts of water. The size of pump you choose depends on how much water your water feature holds. Most small fountains and ponds require the simplest submersible pump, designed to recirculate 50 gallons or less. Larger ponds with waterfalls necessitate heftier pumps. Most pumps run economically, costing pennies per day, and require little maintenance.

in the bucket, threading its electrical cord through the slit.

STEP 5: Thread the flexible tubing through the saucer, leaving just enough tubing underneath to reach the pump. Attach the tubing to the pump. Fill the bucket with water and place the inverted saucer on top of it.

STEP 6: Thread tubing through the center hole of the largest pot. Set the pot on the saucer and fill it with river rock. The rock holds the tube upright. Thread the remaining tubing through the drainage hole of the top pot; then set it on the river rock.

STEP 7: Pull the remaining tubing up (don't stretch it) and fill around it with river rock. Cut the tubing so that the fountain spout is even with the rim of the pot. Attach the fountain nozzle to the end of the tubing.

STEP 8: Wipe dust from the fountain; then turn on the pump. Because soil around the fountain may become damp, plant this area with water-loving plants.

NOTES:
- All pot dimensions refer to diameter.
- Always wear eye protection when drilling.
- If there is a chance of a small child pulling the fountain over, use PVC pipe instead of flexible tubing. Anchor the fountain with bricks in the bucket. Always supervise children near water features.
- In cold climates, store your fountain indoors to prevent the pots from cracking. Store the pump submerged in water so its seals won't dry out and shrink over the winter.

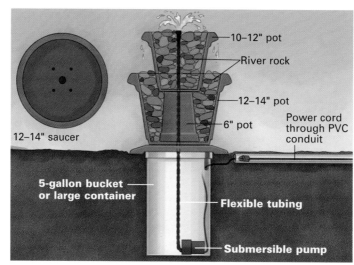

10–12" pot
River rock
12–14" pot
6" pot
Power cord through PVC conduit
12–14" saucer
5-gallon bucket or large container
Flexible tubing
Submersible pump

PONDS

Ponds can make a big splash next to or as part of your patio. A garden pond also adds sparkle to your overall landscape, showcases goldfish and aquatic plants, and lures birds and other wildlife to your yard. Having a pond near your patio can be soothing, fascinating, and fun.

MATERIALS: Flexible pond liners have revolutionized the use of water in home landscaping. The liner is a low-cost, easy-to-install, custom-fit alternative to concrete or molded forms. Molded fiberglass ponds come in many sizes and shapes, but expect to pay extra for fanciful custom designs.

LAYOUT AND EXCAVATION: Outline the pond shape on the lawn with a garden hose.
■ With the hose in place, remove the sod within and excavate to a depth of 9 inches, sloping the sides at about a 20-degree angle. Leave a ledge—a shelf for aquatic plants—then dig again to a total pond depth of 18 inches. Slope this final excavation also. Your garden-supply center can help you select attractive plants for the ledge.

LEVELING THE EDGE: Level the edge of the pool along its entire perimeter.
■ Center a post in the excavation area and extend a leveled 1×4 from the post to the edge. Mark a horizontal line where the 1×4 intersects the grade.
■ Dig to this depth around the perimeter of the pond, repositioning the board as you go. Your edging should be at least 2 inches above the patio or lawn grade to prevent any runoff from contaminating pond water.

LINING THE POOL: Line the pool bottom with damp sand and spread the liner over the excavation. Press the liner down and add 4 to 6 inches of water. The weight of the water will form the liner to the pool.
■ Adjust the liner to prevent wrinkles, and fill in increments, adjusting as you go.
■ Fill the pond, lay flagstone or pavers on the pond edge, and cut away the excess liner.
■ Install a GFCI outlet to provide power to a submersible pump, which circulates and aerates the water.

A vinyl liner keeps this pond full and clear; use rocks or patio blocks to conceal the edges. Rigid plastic pools in various sizes and shapes are available at most garden centers.

INSTALLING A POND LINER

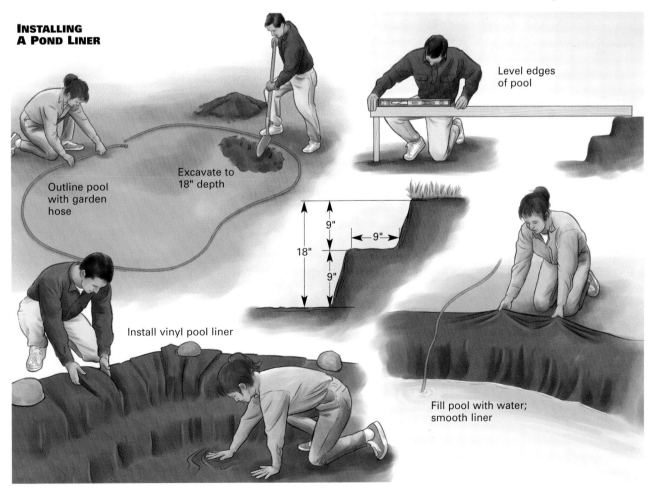

Outline pool with garden hose

Excavate to 18" depth

Level edges of pool

18"
9"
9"
9"

Install vinyl pool liner

Fill pool with water; smooth liner

BUILDING FLOWER BEDS

If your soil quality is poor around your patio, consider building the soil up to form a raised bed. As little as 4 to 6 inches of rich soil will support many kinds of annuals. Mound soil slightly so water will drain toward the sides. To contain soil, frame beds with materials that match the shape of your bed.

The best flower bed plan will fail without proper soil. Soil provides all plants with water and nutrients; soil anchors plant roots. The attention you give soil in this planning stage will pay you back with years of healthy plants and flowers.

Few sites are blessed with the rich, well-drained garden loam recommended in most planting directions. But you can modify almost any kind of soil to grow the plants in your plan, as long as your climate suits them.

MAKING GOOD SOIL

A good soil for planting has topsoil that is several inches deep. It's reasonably fertile, has a good balance of sand, silt, and clay particles, and has just the right amount of air space between those particles to promote balanced drainage and water retention.

Good soil must also have acceptable pH—a measure of its acid and alkaline properties. The most accurate way to find out your soil's pH is to have samples of it tested by a laboratory. State agricultural colleges and local soil conservation offices usually do soil testing for a nominal charge; many county extension offices also offer the service. If soil testing isn't available in your area, check the Yellow Pages under "Laboratories." Or you can also easily test your own soil with an inexpensive kit from a garden center.

SOIL AMENDMENTS

No matter what soil problems you start with, from heavy clay that drains too slowly to light sandy soil that drains too quickly, the best thing you can do is to amend it by adding lots of organic matter. As it decomposes, it creates humus—a soft, dark substance that improves drainage, structure, microbial activity, aeration, and other soil properties. Aged manure, ground bark, and straw are common organic amendments. Agricultural by-products such as peanut hulls, cocoa bean hulls, or ground corncobs are also excellent and inexpensive; check to see what is available in your area. A quick method of amending your soil is to purchase and import topsoil. If your topsoil is shallow, this may be the best solution.

PREPARING BEDS

Some of your flower bed plantings will require bed preparation. Determine the size you want the beds to be, and then measure and stake them before preparing the soil. If you would like to create a free-form bed, you can define the shape with a garden hose (see page 171).

SOIL PREPARATION FOR LAWNS

You can start a new lawn from seed, sod, sprigs, or plugs. Sod is the best choice if you're in a hurry; seed is cheaper, less labor-intensive, and offers the greatest choice of turfgrass varieties; plugs are the only choice for some turfgrasses. No matter how you plant, lawns won't grow well unless the soil beneath them is reasonably healthy.

Improving the soil for lawn growth is as important as for any other planting. Take time to test the soil, and be sure to specify that the test is for a lawn. Amend the soil as needed; if your soil doesn't need amending, broadcast a starter fertilizer over the area, about 50 pounds of a 5-10-5 fertilizer per 1,000 square feet.

If your soil is more than 60 percent clay or 70 percent sand, work in at least a 2-inch layer of organic matter or a 3-inch layer of topsoil that is high in organic matter.

Till to a depth of 6 inches, or on larger lawns, make one or two passes with a tractor-mounted disk. Then broadcast starter fertilizer and rake the surface smooth. The soil will be soft after this procedure; rent a roller and fill it one-third to one-half full with water and roll the soil. Don't wait long to plant after rolling.

If you are working in an area where an old, undesirable lawn must be removed, rent a sod stripper—a machine about the size of a lawn mower—to take off the existing vegetation. (Consider hiring someone to complete this step.) In either case, be prepared to lose some of your topsoil along with the sod. Then prepare the soil as outlined above.

When preparing the soil for the beds, you can use the traditional dig-and-till method or the much simpler method of creating raised beds.

DIGGING AND TILLING

Digging and tilling is a traditional option. Turning the soil to the depth of a spade or fork (single digging) is uncomplicated but labor-intensive. Here's how:

■ First, clean off any debris that can be removed from the planting area.

■ Spread amendments and fertilizer and till them into the soil with a shovel, spade, or fork. Turn the soil over to bury the weeds and grass. Dig one row at a time. Forks are effective in light soil; spades work best in clay or uncultivated soil.

To double-dig a bed, here's how.

■ Dig a spade-deep trench about 2 feet wide and cart the soil to the far end of the bed.

■ Now dig the trench another spade depth. If the soil at the bottom of the trench is reasonably good, loosen or turn it with a spade or garden fork to the full depth of the blade or tines; then mix in the amendments thoroughly. If the soil at the bottom is rocky or compacted, remove it, pick out rocks or roots, mix in amendments, and then return it to the trench.

■ Dig the next trench, but turn the topsoil into the previous trench. Inverting the layers would bring poorer subsoil to the surface.

If your soil is reasonably fertile and free of rocks and tree roots, rototilling is easier. You can rent a walk-behind rototiller at any garden or rental shop. If the soil is hard or dry, it may be necessary to make several passes with the tiller, with each pass tilling a couple of inches deeper than the one before. Make these successive passes at right angles to one another. Do corners by hand.

After tilling, use a cultivator to smooth the surface. For a seedbed with more finely textured soil, use a garden rake. Bury hard clods and rocks below tilling depth at the end of the planting bed.

NO-TILL BED PREPARATION

Here's an easier method for preparing small beds for perennials, annuals, and groundcovers—even shrubs. It accomplishes all requirements of soil texture, fertility, and pH and requires no tilling. In effect, you're making your own soil. Here's how to build an easy bed right on top of your lawn.

■ Start with a base of sandy loam (purchase it at building supply stores), 8 to 12 inches deep. Unless the garden site is extremely weedy, underlying grass need not be removed.

■ Add a thick (6- to 12-inch) layer of compost or aged manure, mounding it smoothly. There is no need to till the beds.

■ Simply prepare each planting hole individually, mixing the loam and compost or manure before placing each new plant.

Cow manure or compost is a better top dressing and mulch choice than peat, which is extremely difficult to rewet when dry. A thick blanket of manure conserves moisture, helps keep beds weed-free, and looks tidy. Over time, earthworms will incorporate the loam and manure, so you'll need to replace it annually.

A NO-TILL BED

3 to 4" of limestone chips or decomposed granite

6 to 12" of composted manure

Existing undisturbed soil

Landscape fabric weed barrier

Bed built atop existing lawn

PREPARING BEDS THE EASY WAY

Step 1: Start by laying weed-barrier cloth along the paths. Spread sandy loam 8 to 12 inches deep on top of bed area.

Step 2: Add a 6- to 8-inch layer of compost or aged manure, mounding it smoothly. No need to till.

Step 3: Cover the edges of the weed-barrier cloth with soil; then cover the path with gravel to hold cloth in place.

PATIO PLANS

This chapter features plans for 12 patios in a range of styles from walk-out installations that extend the use and style of an interior room to detached patios that can be located away from the house or used to expand your current outdoor living space. Each plan includes a list of materials.

You'll find simple designs that fit level landscapes and more complex two-level installations that not only accommodate, but also take advantage of sloping terrain. Some plans combine the best features of attached and detached patios: Part of the patio is close to the convenience of the house; the other part provides access to a desirable place away from the house. Walkways link the patio functionally and aesthetically.

If you need more information about any aspect of the construction of a plan, brush up your skills with the techniques illustrated in the previous chapter. Specific applications and variations are given with each patio plan. Complete directions for building benches, overheads, and a reflecting pool are supplied too, so you'll be able to achieve the look you want.

Even if you're drawn to a particular patio as you leaf through this section, read all the plans before making a final decision. A combination of features from different plans might best suit your specific location.

This site needed a design that would fit both the upper and lower planes of the slightly sloping yard. The deck provides a floor-level outdoor sitting area, and the ground-level patio expands the space without requiring expensive grading.

HOW TO ADAPT A PLAN TO YOUR HOUSE

You can adapt any plan in this chapter by changing the paving material, altering the walls, steps, ponds, and overheads or modifying the overall size or shape. You may also have to change the construction of the patio, depending on your local building codes and soil conditions.

ALTERING SIZE

The dimensions of most of the patios described in this chapter are based on a multiple of a 3×5-foot rectangle and measure 18×30 feet. Using a 3×5 proportion to size a patio gives it a pleasing dimension. To make your patio larger or smaller, increase or decrease it by multiples of 3 and 5—to 21×35 or 15×25, for example. If you can't get the exact proportions, try to come as close as possible, both for aesthetics and to create an area that's easy to use.

Changes in the perimeter measurements often have a great impact on the overall size and utility of the patio. A small change can mean a big difference in usable surface and in the amount of material needed to pave it.

Don't make your patio too small. Patios should be no smaller than 12×20 feet or its equivalent area (240 square feet), unless it is intended for a very limited or highly specialized function. For example, a small patio outside a bedroom might be ideal for breakfast or sunbathing. The same size patio would be too small outside the family room.

Although an 18×30-foot patio may seem large, especially when compared to the size of most indoor rooms, it produces a comfortable amount of outdoor living space. It is large enough to accommodate the broader scope of outdoor activities while allowing several different uses at the same time. It is also large enough to hold outdoor furniture.

CHANGING SHAPES

Patios are typically rectangular but that configuration is not mandatory. Choose any shape that fits your overall landscape design.

RECTANGULAR VARIATIONS: Start with the easiest modification—a variation of the rectangle. For example, wrapping a deck around a corner of the house or adding an extension will change the shape from a rectangle to an L. Add a broad walkway and it becomes a U, Z, or a T.
■ Think of each leg of an L, Z, or T as a separate section divided from the others by control joints, permanent forms, or edging.

FREE-FORM VARIATIONS: Even free-form shapes can take their cue from the rectangle.
■ Bend the perimeter of the patio so it curves and follows the lines of a landscaping feature, such as a creek bed.
■ Round corners with a curve or angle them.
■ Whatever the shape, always maintain a usable area of 240 square feet. A 240-square-foot circle, for example, has a diameter of 17 feet, 6 inches. A patio twice that size has a diameter of 24 feet, 9 inches.

CHANGING FOOTINGS

Local climate and soil conditions can affect the depth and style of post and stair footings, as well as their need for reinforcement. Be sure to follow local codes. Consult your county or municipal building office.

NEW CONSTRUCTION ON AN OLD PATIO: If you're adding a new structure to an old slab, you may not have to dig new footings. Be sure of three things:
■ That the slab is constructed properly.
■ That it's in good condition.
■ That it's thick enough to bear the load of any overhead you plan to add.

If your existing patio passes muster and if your plan conforms to local building codes, you can mount the posts for an overhead in galvanized post anchors fastened directly to the concrete slab.

BUILDING ON FILLED LAND: For structures built on filled land, you may have to dig exceptionally deep footings and reinforce them with rebar, especially if your plans call for overheads. Filled land settles over time, so stairs and overhead structures attached to a house must be stabilized with footings that reach below the frost line and into undisturbed subsoil.

CALCULATING MATERIALS

If you change a patio plan in this chapter, you'll need to recalculate the materials.

LUMBER: Adjustments for the lumber and fasteners are straightforward. Remember that dimensioned lumber is sold in even-numbered lengths. If your alterations result in an 11-foot length, you'll need a 12-foot board.

FILLERS AND CONCRETE: Materials such as crushed rock, gravel, concrete, and sand are sold by volume, and changes will require a bit of calculation. See "Estimating Materials,"

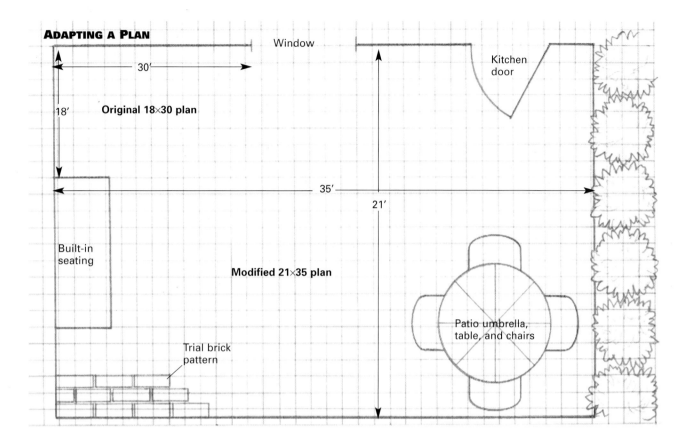

ADAPTING A PLAN

Window

30'

Original 18×30 plan

18'

Kitchen door

35'

21'

Built-in seating

Modified 21×35 plan

Trial brick pattern

Patio umbrella, table, and chairs

page 70, if you need to brush up on the math. Many suppliers can help you calculate your material requirements.

OTHER MATERIALS: Materials such as reinforcing wire mesh, pavers, and bricks are sold by the square foot or the equivalent. A 540-square-foot patio needing reinforcing mesh would require 540 square feet of mesh.

Determining how many bricks or pavers are required depends on the size of the materials you select. If, for example, it takes 5 pavers to cover a square foot, multiply the area by 5. For example, 540 sq. ft. × 5 = 2,700 pavers.

If a paver covers more than a square foot, it's simpler to divide the area of the patio by the area covered by the paver. For example, one 18-inch square paver covers 2¼ square feet. Divide the patio area by 2.25, and it looks like this: 540 sq. ft. ÷ 2.25 = 240 pavers.

Adjusting the size or shape of a patio plan calls for some thinking on paper. With a bird's-eye view of the alterations—carefully drawn to scale—you can experiment with ideas without getting bogged down in detail.

WALK-OUT PATIO

You'll find this basic ground-level patio easy to construct, and its simplicity makes it adaptable to any size yard, any style house, and most budgets. If you're looking for a plan that serves as the basis for a more complex installation, this one is perfect. Add overheads, planters, or other features as dictated by your overall design.

CONSTRUCTION HIGHLIGHTS

A one-level concrete slab located directly outside the room that it serves creates a simple transition between the indoors and the outdoors. Finish the surface by coloring the concrete or stamping it. You can also use the slab as a base for mortared paving, such as brick or flagstone.

Based on an 18×30-foot rectangle, the patio's leading edges are curved to add interest and to conform to the flow of the surrounding yard. Design your plan to follow the contours of flower beds or add tight, looped curves to create pockets for flowers and shrubs. The basic design is so versatile that its dimensions and materials can be easily adapted to individual situations.

LAY OUT THE SITE

■ Set the corner stakes for an 18×30-foot rectangular patio. Lay out the site with batter boards and square the corners. (See page 107).
■ Establish the curved edges inside or outside the perimeter with a garden hose.
■ Mark the curves on the ground with powdered chalk or paint; then remove the hose.

OVERHEAD VIEW

30'

18'

EXCAVATE

■ You can build this patio on compacted earth if local codes allow; but for added stability, you should include a gravel base for improved drainage. Dig out the area to the depth that will accommodate a 4- to 6-inch gravel base and the paving materials you have chosen (see "Excavation Depths," page 109).
■ Slope for surface drainage. Surface drainage is another factor that must be taken into account when excavating. A patio should slope away from the house at a rate of 1 inch per 4 linear feet and so should the floor of the excavation. Use a slope gauge or slope the layout lines and put up grid lines if necessary. Measure down from the lines to keep the slope consistent (see page 110).

MAKE THE FORMS

■ Build 2×4 forms and stake them to the straight edges of the site.
■ Make the curve from kerfed 1× stock or benderboard ripped into 3½-inch strips. Drive stakes along the layout line at intervals of 2 feet or less. Bend the hardboard along the stakes, and screw the form in place (see page 111).

POUR THE PATIO

Install reinforcing wire mesh cut to fit the forms and pour the concrete using the techniques shown on pages 126–135. Have a crew on hand to help with the pour.
■ To keep the slab from cracking, cut control joints after an initial floating. Cut them in both directions every eight feet.

MATERIALS LIST

Element	Quantity*	Material
4-6" base	10 cu. yd.	crushed rock or pea gravel
reinforcement	540 sq. ft.	wire mesh 6×6 10/10
control	30 ft.	expansion joint
4" slab	7 cu. yd. (varies)	ready-mix concrete

Quantities will vary with site conditions.

FLAGSTONE PATIO WITH PERGOLA

This patio is a simple walk-out structure paved with flagstones and shaded with a pergola—a useful addition for a site that receives too much sun and requires afternoon shade. Compare this plan with the patio illustrated on the previous pages and notice how much the paving material affects the look and ambience of a simple design.

CONSTRUCTION HIGHLIGHTS

Although a flagstone patio has a more interesting surface texture than an unadorned concrete slab, its construction will prove more labor-intensive, time-consuming, and costly. In effect, you have to build two patios, first installing the slab; then mortaring the flagstone on the surface. Once you've laid the foundation (see pages 120–123), lay out the stones in a pattern that is aesthetically pleasing and trim the stones to fit before laying a mortar bed and setting them (see page 124).

The pergola is integral to this patio. Carefully plan the patio and the pergola as a unit before beginning construction. Size the roof so that it covers the door between the house and patio, and projects over at least one-third the surface of the patio. See page 41 for alternative rafter angles and slat designs that control the amount of shade cast on the patio. Once you've picked the size and location of the pergola, pour the footings for it before you pour the concrete patio base.

LAYING OUT THE SITE

■ Set the corner stakes for an 18×30-foot rectangular patio. Lay out the site with batter boards and square the corners (see page 107).

EXCAVATING

■ Excavate deep enough to accommodate all the layers of the finished patio: a 4- to 6-inch gravel subbase, a 4-inch-thick concrete slab, a ½-inch-thick mortar bed, and 1- to 2-inch-thick flagstones. See pages 120-121 for more information on layout techniques.
■ Slope for surface drainage—1 inch per 4 linear feet. Use a slope gauge or slope the layout lines and put up grid lines if necessary. Measure down from the lines to keep the slope consistent (see page 107).

PERGOLA FOOTINGS

■ Start by marking the exact locations of the posts on the ground. Make the footings at least 18 inches in diameter and 6 inches deep, or the depth recommended by local codes.
■ Pour piers in fiber form tubes with an 8- to 10-inch diameter and set post anchors in the concrete.
■ Install flexible expansion joint material around the base of the piers.

MAKING THE FORMS

■ Build 2×4 forms and stake them as illustrated on page 110. Wet concrete is remarkably heavy—stake the forms securely.

POURING THE PATIO

■ Install reinforcing wire mesh cut to fit the forms and pour the site using the techniques shown on pages 106–111. Order the ready-mix and have a crew on hand to help with the pour.
■ After an initial floating, cut control joints in both directions.
■ Let the finished slab cure for three to five days.

MATERIALS LIST

Element	Quantity*	Material	Length
18×30 PATIO			
	10 cu. yd.	crushed rock or pea gravel	
	30'	expansion joint	
	540 sq. ft.	reinforcing wire mesh 6×6-10/10	
	7 cu. yd. (varies)	ready-mix concrete	
	540 sq. ft.	paving flagstone, irregular shapes, 2" thick	
9×12 PERGOLA			
Framing**			
Posts	2	4×4s	10'
Built-up beams	2	2×6s	16'
Ledger	1	2×6	16'
Rafters	17	2×4s	10'
Knee braces	2	2×6s	8'
Fasteners			
	2	galvanized post anchors	
	15	galvanized joist hangers	
	19	⅜×6" lag screws, washers	
	4	½×6" carriage bolts, washers, nuts	
	2 lbs.	16d hot-dipped galvanized joist-hanger nails	
	1 lb.	8d hot-dipped galvanized common nails	

*All quantities may vary with site conditions.

**Use rot-/insect-resistant lumber.

OVERHEAD VIEW

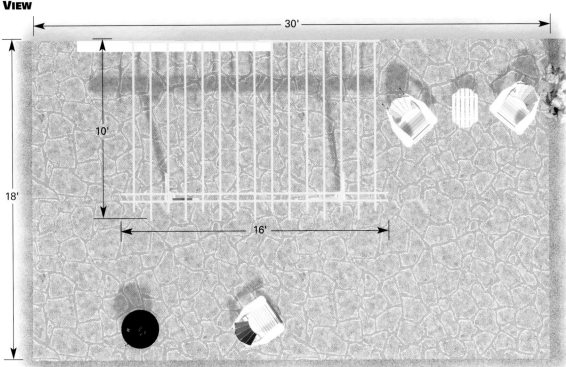

FLAGSTONE PATIO WITH PERGOLA

continued

INSTALLING THE FLAGSTONE

Make a dry layout of the flagstone pattern, fitting them together with joints that are as close as possible to ½ inch wide. Trim and cut the stones as necessary, so that adjoining stones have similar contours (see page 125).

■ Set the stones off to the side of the site, keeping them in the pattern in which you have arranged them. Then add forms for the mortar bed, if necessary, and trowel on a small section of mortar on the pad. Pull a screed board across the forms to level them.

■ Set the stones in place and level them as illustrated on page 121. Once the first section is in place, move on to the next section of the patio, mortaring and laying stones as you go.

■ Let the mortar bed set for 24 hours; then add mortar to fill the joints with a mortar bag. When this mortar has set up sufficiently, finish the joints with a pointing tool.

BUILDING THE PERGOLA

Like any outdoor structure constructed from wood, build this one with rot-/insect-resistant lumber, such as the heartwood of redwood, cedar, or cypress, or from pressure-treated lumber. If you use pressure-treated wood, cutting it will expose surfaces that have not been treated. Coat the cut surfaces with a preservative.

ATTACHING THE LEDGER: The pergola roof is supported on one end by posts and a beam. The other end is fastened to a ledger bolted to the house framing. The installation differs slightly, depending on whether you are working on a one- or two-story house.

■ **One-story house:** Find the studs in the wall and position the bolts to go into them. The illustration below shows how to attach the ledger to a one-story house.

LEDGER DETAIL

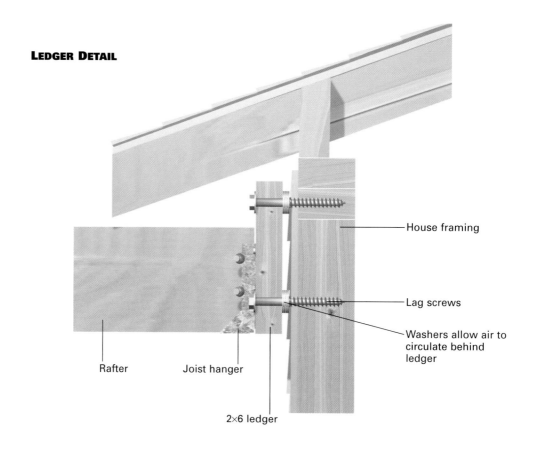

House framing

Lag screws

Washers allow air to circulate behind ledger

Rafter

Joist hanger

2×6 ledger

■ **Two-story house:** Determine the floor level of the second floor, measure down 2½ inches and draw a level line on the house.
■ Align the top of the 2×6-inch ledger with this line and fasten the ledger through the siding into the framing with ½×6-inch lag screws.
■ Install Z-flashing or use washers or other spacers to create a ½-inch gap between the ledger board and the house siding. This gap will prevent moisture from becoming trapped behind the ledger, which would cause the siding to rot.

POSTS: Set the posts in the post anchors, and tack them in place.
■ Plumb them with a level, and brace the posts securely.
■ Mark all the posts at the same height as the bottom of the ledger using a water level or a line level and mason's line.
■ Take the posts down, cut them; and then set them in place again.
■ Plumb the posts, temporarily brace them, and then fasten them to the post anchors. See pages 160–161 for more information on setting posts.

BEAMS: Attach the 2×6 beams to the posts with ½×6-inch carriage bolts, positioning them so the tops of the beams are flush with the tops of the posts.
■ Stabilize the structure with 2×6 knee braces connecting each post to the beams as shown at right.

RAFTERS: Starting at one end of the ledger, lay out rafters every 12 inches. Nail joist hangers to the ledger at these marks.
■ Cut half of the rafters to extend 12 inches beyond the beam; cut the remaining rafters 6 inches beyond the beam. If you wish, you can shape the outside ends of the rafters with an angle or a decorative curve.
■ Set the rafters in the hangers and nail them in place with hanger nails driven through the hardware.
■ Attach the rafters to the beam with hurricane/seismic anchors, which make simple work of the job and strengthen the joints.

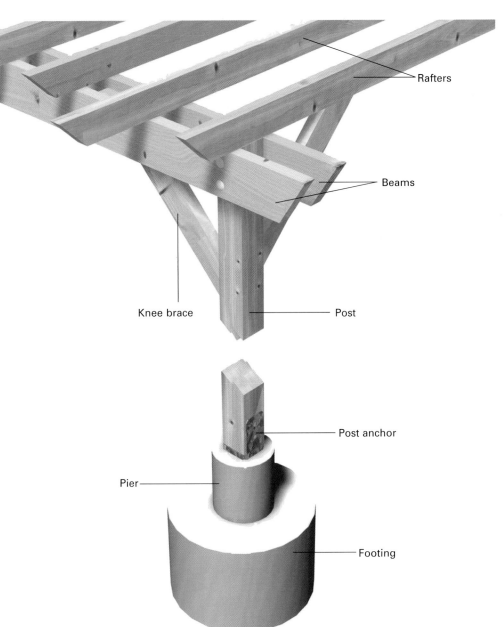

Rafters

Beams

Knee brace

Post

Post anchor

Pier

Footing

COURTYARD PATIO WITH ARBOR

Once you've completed this project, your guests will probably notice the sturdy arbor before they notice the patio surface itself. Without a doubt, the arbor dominates and complements the design.

An arbor like this works well on almost any patio, and can be added to any of the other patio plans in this chapter. It's an excellent way to provide relief from the bright sun. You can increase the shade by placing the rafters closer together. Planting vines to cover the top provides even more shade (see the illustration on page 166).

CONSTRUCTION HIGHLIGHTS

Because the arbor is freestanding, there's no complicated connection between the house (or roof) and the arbor. The arbor posts stand on concrete footings that are independent of the rest of the patio. If the footings shift, they can do so without cracking the patio.

Taken one step at a time, building the arbor is a manageable job. Footings come first, and are poured before the rest of the patio.

Once the footings cure, attach the posts, plumbing and bracing them carefully. The rest of the job is a matter of nailing beams to the posts, joists to the beams, and rafters to the joists.

The patio surface is a poured concrete slab with permanent wood forms as decorative wood edging. Dividers run across the surface to add visual interest and to keep the job of pouring the slab more manageable.

Make the arbor and the forms from the same kind of lumber to tie the two together visually. Concrete will stain the wood, so protect the wood by applying finish to the forms before you pour.

Each square is only 36 square feet, so you can mix your own concrete and pour each square separately. That way you can break the work into sections, floating and finishing one at a time, instead of having 540 square feet of concrete facing you all at once. Premix bags are an option, but mixing your own from dry ingredients will be more efficient (see page 129).

OVERHEAD VIEW

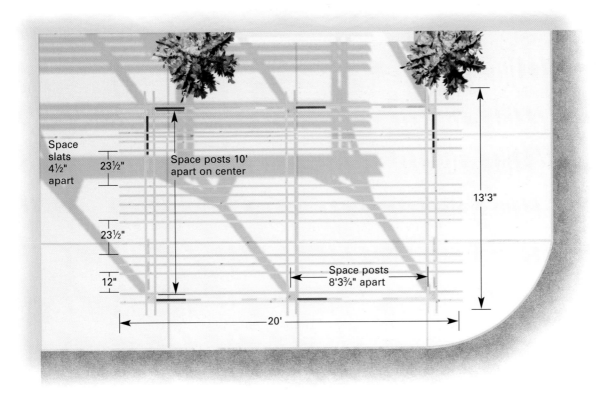

You can, of course, do the job in one pour with ready-mix. It all depends on how much time, stamina, and help you have.

LAY OUT THE SITE

■ Set the corner stakes for an 18×30-foot rectangular patio. Lay out the site with batter boards and square the corners, ignoring the curve for now (see page 107).
■ Lay out the interior dividers, creating 6×6-foot squares. (You can also set 6×10-foot squares or the 6×7½-foot squares, but it will make layout of the curve more difficult.)
■ To lay out the curve, drive a stake at the point nearest the curve where two dividers meet. (If you're using squares larger than 6×6, lay out a 6×6-foot square in the curved corner, and drive a stake at the corner opposite the curve.) Tie one end of a rope to the stake. Tie a bottle of powdered chalk to the rope so that it's 6 feet away from the stake. To draw the curve, pull the rope tight, and move it in an arc around the stake while squeezing the chalk bottle.

MATERIALS LIST

Element	Quantity*	Material	Length
18×30 PATIO			
	10 cu. yd.	crushed rock or class-5 gravel	
	540 sq. ft.	reinforcing wire mesh 6-6-10-10	
	30 ft.	expansion joint	
	2 lbs.	16d hot-dipped galvanized common nails	
	7 cu. yd. (varies)	ready-mix concrete	
14×20 ARBOR			
Framing**			
Posts	6	6×6s	10'
Built-up beams	4	2×8s	20'
Rafters	6	2×6s	14'
Slats	11	2×4s	20'
Fasteners			
	6	galvanized post anchors	
	24	½×10" carriage bolts, nuts, washers	
	10 lbs.	16d hot-dipped galvanized common nails	

*All quantities may vary with site conditions.

**Use rot-/insect-resistant lumber.

COURTYARD PATIO WITH ARBOR
continued

PATIO AND FORMS

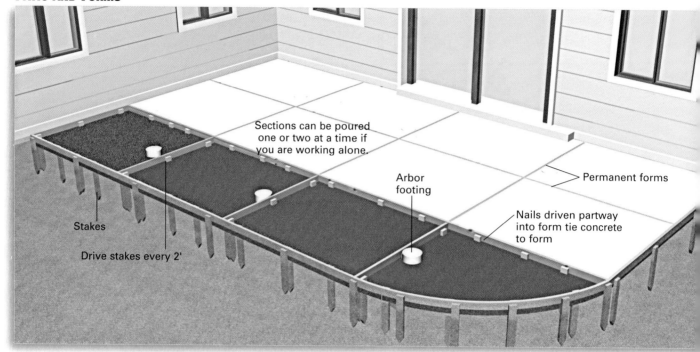

Sections can be poured one or two at a time if you are working alone.

Arbor footing

Permanent forms

Stakes

Drive stakes every 2'

Nails driven partway into form tie concrete to form

EXCAVATE

■ You can build this patio on compacted earth, if local codes allow. For added stability, you should include a gravel base for improved drainage. If the base is subsoil, it should be undisturbed subsoil, so don't fill in any irregularities with loose soil.
■ Dig out the area to the depth that will accommodate a 4- to 6-inch gravel base and the slab.
■ Slope for surface drainage—1 inch per 4 linear feet. Use a slope gauge or slope the layout lines and put up grid lines if necessary. Measure down from the lines to keep the slope consistent. (See pages 106–110 for more information on excavation techniques.)

ARBOR FOOTINGS

After excavating, and before putting down the patio base, pour concrete piers and footings for the arbor posts.
■ Start by marking the exact locations of the posts on the ground. Make the footings at least 18 inches in diameter and 6 inches deep, or the depth recommended by local codes.
■ Place and brace 8- to 10-inch diameter fiber form tubes in the holes for the piers.
■ Pour each footing and pier at the same time, placing post anchors in the wet concrete of the piers. Make sure the anchors are level, plumb, and correctly aligned.

■ When the concrete has hardened, wrap flexible expansion joint material around the base of the piers.

MAKE THE FORMS

Lay out the forms as you would for any concrete patio. Because these forms are permanent, be sure to choose an appropriate wood—pressure-treated lumber rated for ground contact or heartwood of redwood, cedar, or cypress. Tape the top of the forms or apply a finish to keep the concrete from staining the wood.
■ Build 2×4 forms and stake them as illustrated on page 110. Drive the stakes below the tops of the forms.
■ Set and stake the dividers on the layout lines strung earlier. Toenail (driving a nail in diagonally) the dividers at their intersections and to the perimeter forms.
■ Partially drive 16d hot-dipped galvanized nails through the sides of the dividers at 16-inch intervals. These will tie the concrete and the dividers together, keeping the concrete on the same plane with the forms as it settles.
■ Pour in 4 inches of gravel and compact it thoroughly. Hand tampers, available at most home-improvement centers and hardware stores, are fine for small jobs, but given the size of the patio, it's a good idea to rent a power tamper.

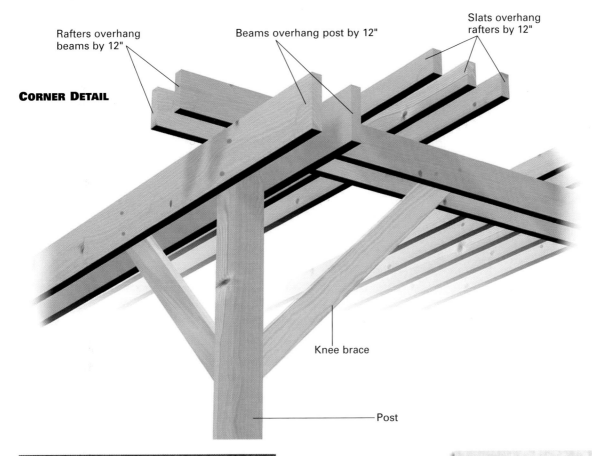

Rafters overhang
beams by 12"

Beams overhang post by 12"

Slats overhang
rafters by 12"

CORNER DETAIL

Knee brace

Post

POUR THE PATIO

■ Install reinforcing wire mesh cut to fit the forms, then pour the site using the techniques shown on pages 128–131. Order the ready-mix and have a crew on hand to help.
■ Take care to protect the forms, whether you mix and pour the concrete in small sections or have the ready-mix truck deliver it. A wheelbarrow full of concrete can knock them out of alignment, so use a 2×12 runway to support the load.
■ Let the slab cure for three to five days.

BUILD THE ARBOR

Center the arbor over the patio and build it with 6×6 posts. If desired, face the posts on two sides with 1× lumber. Use 2×8 beams, 2×6 rafters, and 2×4 slats of rot-/insect-resistant lumber.

POSTS: Set the posts in the post anchors, but do not fasten them yet.
■ Plumb the posts and hold them in place with temporary bracing (see page 161).
■ Using a water level or a line level and mason's line, mark all the posts at the same height—8 feet, 6 inches above the patio.
■ Take the posts down, cut them, and then set them in place again.
■ Plumb the posts, fasten them to the post anchors, and temporarily brace them.

BEAMS AND RAFTERS:
■ Cut the beams to extend 12 inches beyond the posts on each side.
■ Align the tops of the beams 5 inches below the tops of the posts, and attach them to both sides of the posts with ½×10-inch carriage bolts, nuts, and washers.
■ Cut rafters to extend 12 inches beyond beams.
■ Set the rafters atop the beams so that they sandwich the posts; then bolt them to the posts with ½×10-inch carriage bolts.
■ To stabilize the framework, attach 2×6 knee braces between the posts and beams at a 45-degree angle to the posts.
■ Fasten the braces to the beams with ⅜-inch carriage bolts and to the posts with ⅜-inch lag screws.

SLATS: Cut the 2×4 slats to extend 12 inches beyond the rafters. Attach them to the rafters with hurricane/seismic anchors.

FINISH: Finish the arbor with a clear sealer, a wood stain followed by a clear sealer, or a semitransparent stain, as desired. Or, if you prefer, finish it with a coat of primer and one or two coats of latex or alkyd exterior paint.

SETTLING

Settling is a concern wherever a patio meets an existing structure such as a house or driveway. The patio is likely to settle at a different rate than an established structure, which may have already settled. Isolate the patio from existing structures with an expansion joint.

BRICK PATIO

Although many existing patio designs are conceived as space for single uses, most households will profit by installing a patio divided into separate areas. A low, flat expanse of even the finest paving material can look formless and feel uncomfortable if there aren't any visual clues as to how to use the space.

Simple features help organize this brick patio. The raised dining platform visually divides the surface. The location of the platform near the doors makes it convenient to the kitchen and creates a corridor between the two spaces. The areas on either side of the corridor become their own outdoor "rooms." The smaller area has the yard as its focal point. The larger area focuses on a tree that provides shade and a sense of shelter at the far end of the patio. You can either plant a tree before you build the project or build the patio around an existing tree.

540 square feet of space, plenty of room for outdoor comfort. The length of this design is ideal for certain situations: for small backyards, for backyards with large gardens, or for integrating long houses with their yards. With adaptation, this patio would also work well in a narrow side yard.

The entire patio, including the platform, relies on sand-set installation techniques. A gravel drainage base supports a sand bed and the brick paving. For more information about sand-set techniques, see pages 114–117.

The herringbone brick pattern featured here requires a lot of cutting and if it's more than you want to do, you can set the paving in any pattern of your choice. Other options appear on page 77. For any pattern, such as the herringbone, that calls for a lot of cutting. Renting a water-cooled masonry saw will prove worth the extra expense.

CONSTRUCTION HIGHLIGHTS

The patio measures 12×45 feet—a long expanse that, though narrow, still provides

LAYING OUT THE SITE

■ Set the corner stakes for a 12×45-foot rectangular patio. Lay out the site with batter boards and square the corners (see page 107).

OVERHEAD VIEW

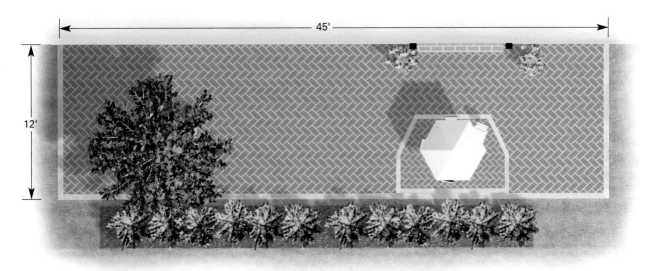

Laying out the perimeter of a brick patio requires careful planning to align the forms as precisely as you can.

EXCAVATING

■ Excavate the patio area deep enough for a 4-inch to 6-inch gravel subbase, a 2-inch-thick sand bed, plus the thickness of the bricks or pavers.

If you're excavating around an existing tree, be careful around the roots.
■ Stake a rectangular or square area around the tree that is well back from the roots, and do not excavate inside that zone. When planning a patio that will surround a mature tree, a consultation with your local garden center will probably prove useful. If you plan to plant a new tree, make sure the enclosure will be large enough to allow proper planting and fill in the tree pocket with appropriate soil. Ask your nursery supplier for the components of a soil mix compatible with the tree species.
■ Slope for surface drainage—1 inch per 4 linear feet. Use a slope gauge or slope the layout lines and put up grid lines, if necessary. Measure down from the lines to keep the slope consistent. See pages 106–110 for more information on excavation techniques.

BUILDING THE PLATFORM

Construction of this patio begins with the raised dining platform.
■ Build a frame around the edges with 6×6 pressure-treated timbers rated for ground contact. Cut joints half-lap as shown on page 193.

MATERIALS LIST

Element	Quantity*	Material	Length
12×45 PATIO			
	12 cu. yd.	crushed rock or pea gravel	
	5 cu. yd.	sand	
Paving Brick	2,700	4×8×2¼" bricks	
Edging			
Tree well	1	6×6	12'
	2	6×6s	10'
	4	6×6s	8'
Patio	2	6×6s	12'
	9	6×6s	10'

All quantities may vary with site conditions.

■ Cut and install the lower layer of timers.
■ Cut and position the top level so the timbers at the 90-degree corners overlap the joints below.
■ Bore holes through the timbers and stake them with No. 6 (¾-inch) rebar long enough to reach at least 2 feet into the soil below.
■ In the corners with overlapping joints, put one stake through the center of the overlap. Stake the other corners on each side.
■ Fill the center of the dining platform with gravel a little at a time, tamping it as you go and stopping when it's 4 inches below the top of the timbers.

BRICK PATIO
continued

DINING PLATFORM

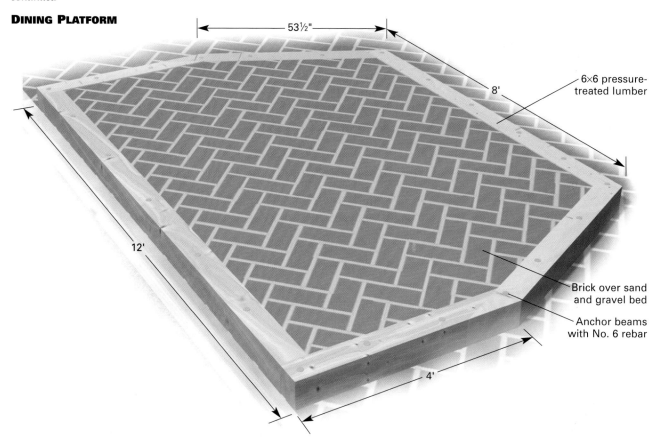

53½"

8'

6×6 pressure-
treated lumber

12'

Brick over sand
and gravel bed

Anchor beams
with No. 6 rebar

4'

INSTALLING THE EDGING, SUBBASE, AND SAND BED

With the dining platform in place, stake 6×6 timbers around the edge of the patio.
■ Place a temporary 2× edging around the tree opening.
■ In the main section of the patio, place and tamp a 4-inch gravel subbase.
■ Pour in and level a 2-inch sand bed on top of the gravel—both in the main part of the patio and the dining area. (See pages 114–117 for more information.)

PAVING THE SURFACE

■ Using the techniques illustrated, set the brick paving in a herringbone pattern.
■ When a course of bricks gets within about a brick length of the temporary forms around the tree, replace the forms with permanent 6×6 timber edging. Position the timbers so that the final course will fit snugly against them. That way, you'll save the time spent cutting bricks. Stake the timbers to the ground with rebar.
■ Set and level each brick, then sweep sand into the joints as illustrated on page 117.

PATIO CROSS SECTION

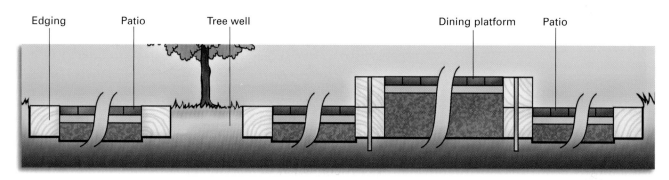

Edging   Patio   Tree well   Dining platform   Patio

LAYING A HERRINGBONE BRICK PATTERN

1. The key to laying a herringbone pattern lies in the first four bricks. Starting in one corner, set the long side of the first brick across the corner at a 45-degree angle to the edging, and set a second against the first, its top corner touching the lumber form.

Set a third brick at 90 degrees to the first and flush with the second brick's narrow end, and a fourth brick between it and the edging of the other lumber pieces.

2. The next row of bricks wraps around these four bricks, running diagonally between the anchor timbers.

3. Continue wrapping one row of bricks around the next, as shown. The rows will get progressively longer. Check periodically that each end of the row is equidistant from the corner.

4. When you've laid all the full bricks, cut partial bricks to fit in the spaces around the edge.

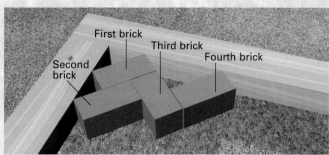
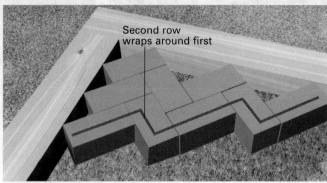

First brick
Second brick
Third brick
Fourth brick

FIRST ROW

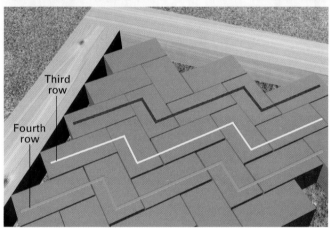

Second row wraps around first

SECOND ROW

Third row

Fourth row

PATTERN CONTINUED

Cut bricks to fill in spaces

COMPLETED PATTERN

POCKET-GARDEN PATIO

For those who love to garden, a walk-out patio located just beyond the kitchen door can be the perfect place to grow flowers, herbs, and small vegetables. Pockets, or openings in the paving, make convenient garden beds that you can fill with good, rich garden soil as you're building the patio.

MATERIALS LIST

Element	Quantity*	Material	Length
Base			
	1.5 cu. yd.	topsoil	
	9 cu. yd.	crushed rock or class 5 gravel	
	465 sq. ft.	weed-blocking fabric	
	3 cu. yd.	washed sand, concrete grade	
Edging	20	6×6s	10'
Brick pavers	2,250	4×8×2¼" bricks	

*All quantities may vary with site conditions.

CONSTRUCTION HIGHLIGHTS

This 18×30 foot walk-out patio contains six garden beds, each measuring about 3×5 feet, but there's nothing dictating their proportions. Modify their size to suit your site and your needs and alter the placement of the planting beds to what works best for you and your family.

Constructing the patio with brick pavers makes it easy to incorporate the planting pockets into the overall plan. Each pocket is lined with 6×6 pressure-treated timbers rated for ground contact. So is the edging.

When you plant your gardens, keep in mind that annuals and herbs will fare well in the pocket gardens, while deep-rooted vegetables and perennials are best grown in deeper soil. If you plan to put in the latter, you can always reexcavate the beds after you finish the patio, filling the excavation with suitable soil.

OVERHEAD VIEW

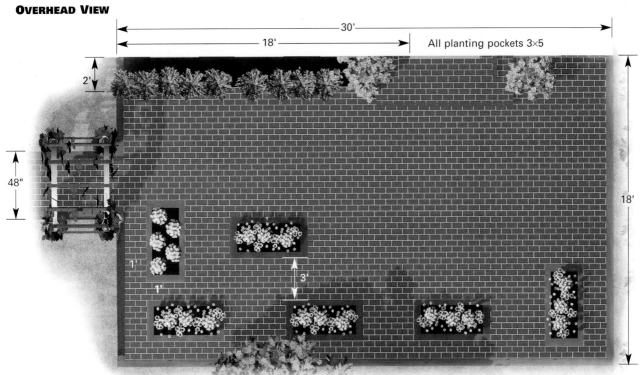

All planting pockets 3×5

SITE PREPARATION

LAYOUT: Set the corner stakes for an 18×30-foot rectangular patio. Lay out the site with batter boards and square the corners. (see page 107).

EXCAVATING: Excavate the patio area deep enough for a 4-inch to 6-inch gravel subbase, a 2-inch sand bed plus the thickness of 4×8-inch brick pavers.
■ Slope for surface drainage—1 inch per 4 linear feet. Use a slope gauge or slope the layout lines and put up grid lines if necessary. Measure down from the lines to keep the slope consistent. See pages 106–110 for more information on excavation techniques.

SETTING THE FORMS

Most plants don't grow well in sand or gravel, so before you build the base, stake and edge the garden pockets so they don't fill up with base material.

GARDEN POCKETS: Lay out the corners of each 3×5-foot planting pocket with stakes and mason's line.
■ Edge the pockets with 6×6 pressure-treated timbers rated for ground contact. You can make the corners of the planting pockets by butting the ends of the timbers together, but the corners will look better and be stronger if you cut half-lap joints like the one shown in the illustration at right.

PLANTING POCKET

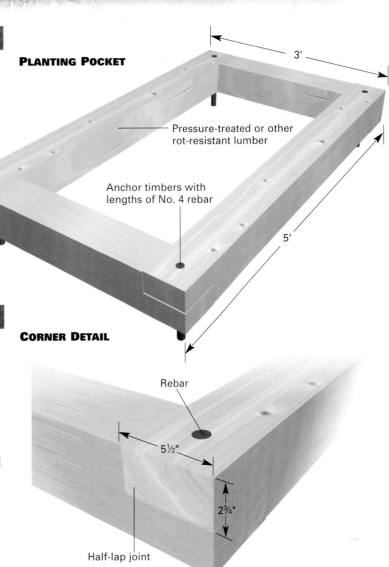

Pressure-treated or other rot-resistant lumber

Anchor timbers with lengths of No. 4 rebar

3'

5'

CORNER DETAIL

Rebar

5½"

2¾"

Half-lap joint

POCKET-GARDEN PATIO
continued

■ On the timbers, mark the joints with a heavy pencil, and cut the timbers with a reciprocating saw.
■ Anchor the timber edging with lengths of No. 4 rebar.
■ Tamp at least 2 inches of garden topsoil into the planting pockets to keep the gravel from slipping under the timbers.
■ Finish by filling the planting pockets with soil appropriate to the plants you intend to set. Consult with your garden supply center to select the best soil for your plantings.

PATIO BASE: Predrill the 6×6 pressure-treated timber edging for ½- or ¾-inch rebar every 2 feet.
■ Place the edging along the layout lines at the perimeter, but do not set it yet.
■ Shovel in the gravel subbase and tamp it.
■ Cover the gravel with weed-blocking landscape fabric and top it with a 2-inch layer of sand. A 2-inch layer of sand will put the bricks flush with the top of the edging.
■ Strike the sand smooth.

PAVING THE SURFACE

You can set the paving in any pattern, but a pattern that meets the edging at an angle will involve considerable cutting and fitting.

See page 77 for examples of optional paving patterns.
■ Set the first course of bricks in a line parallel to the house and along an edge of the outermost planting pockets, leaving a space of ⅛-inch or less space between them. Work from that line toward the house.
■ Complete the paving from that line out toward the perimeter of the patio.
■ Move the perimeter edging so that when you lay the last course of bricks, they will fit snugly against the edging.
■ Stake the edging in place.
■ When all the bricks are laid and the edges are set, sweep fine sand between the joints.
■ Wet the surface and repeat the process until the joints are packed full.
■ Fill the gap outside the perimeter edging with soil, and tamp it down. Top with sod or bedding plants.

PLANTING THE POCKETS

Growing flowers is one of gardening's joys, especially if you plan ahead to include flowers that bloom at different times of the growing season. Annuals are colorful bedding plants that may bloom through a season or two but will die before the year is over. Perennials come back year after year. Both add sparkle to your landscape. There are annuals and perennials that grow well in sun and plants that grow well in shade, so select plants that will thrive in the conditions in your yard.

To get the most impact for your money, consider a single flower color. Even one bed

PATIO CROSS SECTION

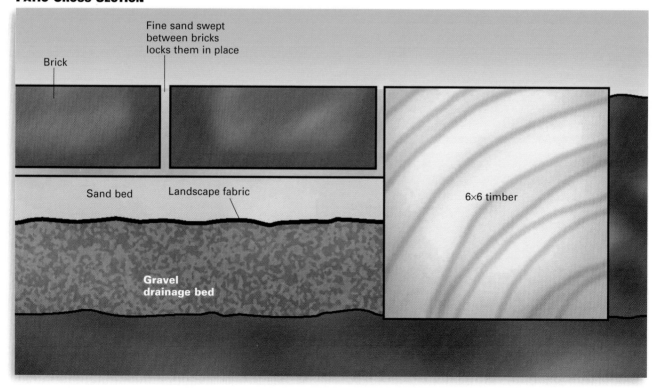

Brick

Fine sand swept between bricks locks them in place

Sand bed   Landscape fabric

Gravel drainage bed

6×6 timber

ANNUALS

Common and Botanical Name	Height	Color	Light	Comments
Ageratum (*Ageratum houstonianum*)	4–12"	blue	sun	appears as a blue haze
Alyssum (*Lobularia maritima*)	5"	white, blue, and pink	sun	compact
Annual phlox (*Phlox drummondii*)	12–18"	red, purple, white	sun	great bedding plant
Bachelor button (*Centaurea cyanus*)	18–36"	blue, pink, red, and white	sun	reseeds itself
Baby blue-eyes (*Nemophila menziesii*)	6–8"	blue with white centers	sun	well-suited to rock gardens
Begonia (*Begonia semperflorens-cultorum*)	6–12"	mixed	sun	container and garden
Cosmos (*Cosmos bipinnatus*)	3'	red–yellow	sun	great show
Globe amaranth (*Gomphrena globosa*)	10–18"	red, white, other	sun	good for cutting
Impatiens (*Impatiens* hybrids)	5–14"	all except blue	partial shade	all-summer bloom
Joseph's coat (*Amaranthus tricolor*)	3'	red/orange	sun	dry areas
Marigold (*Tagetes*)	12–36"	yellow–orange	sun	beds, borders, containers
Petunia (*Petunia*)	12–18"	various colors	sun	bedding, containers

of solid-color annuals—yellow pansies, for example—can dress up your yard. Plant a thick patch in a highly visible place and save a handful of plants to grow in containers.

Think about adding flowers near the front door or at a garden entry. Surround a focal point or plant them at the end of a path. Mix different colors and textures in layered borders for a colorful, cottage-style appearance. Plant taller plants in the back where they won't overshadow their shorter companions. Consider sprinkling a unifying color throughout your composition.

Flowers show off best when planted in conjunction with a solid and neutral background. A bed of evergreen shrubs or groundcover, a wall, a fence, or a bench can provide an excellent background for flowers.

Incorporate flowers, especially perennials, into the landscape as a companion for shrubs and groundcovers. Perennials have a dormant season, so make sure your composition isn't barren looking until perennials reappear. Evergreen shrubs and groundcover planted near perennials provide bright blooms and foliage, a neutral background that shows colors to their best advantage. When the perennials go dormant, the evergreen plants keep the landscape from appearing empty.

PERENNIALS

Common/Botanical Name	Height	Color	Light	Zones
Aster (*Aster*)	1–4'	blue	sun	4–8
Blanket flower (*Gaillardia*)	2–4'	red, yellow, and others	sun	5–9
Blazing star (*Liatris*)	4'	purple	sun	5–9
Coreopsis (*Coreopsis*)	6–24"	yellow with brown centers	sun	6–10
Crocus (*Crocus*)	2–6"	purple, white, and others	sun	2–8
Daylily (*Hemerocallis*)	6"–5'	yellow, orange, and combos	sun	3–9
Lily of the Nile (*Agapanthus*)	4'	deep blue	sun	8–10
Mums (*Chrysanthemum*)	1–3'	yellow, bronze, and red	sun	4–8
Peruvian lily (*Alstroemeria*)	3'	red	partial shade	7–10
Pinks (*Dianthus*)	6"	blue and rose	sun	2–10
Plantain lily (*Hosta*)	6–18"	blue and white, but grown for foliage	shade	4–8
Red hot poker (*Kniphofia*)	6'	red and yellow	sun	6–9
Rose mallow (*Hibiscus moscheutos*)	6'	pink, purple, and white	sun	5–9
Yarrow (*Achillea*)	18"	yellow, red, and others	full sun	3–8

GARDEN COURTYARD

Open your patio to designs beyond boxes. Modern materials make curved and rounded patios relatively easy to build, including this circular patio inspired by the classic Celtic cross.

CONSTRUCTION HIGHLIGHTS

The patio is set on a sand bed, eliminating the need for curved concrete forms. Although the surface looks like cobblestone, it's actually set with pavers designed for circular designs, such as this one. Cast to look like keystones, they allow circular layouts without having to cut the curves and angles.

To shape the garden beds that give this patio its character, use flexible plastic edging, shown on page 93. It bends easily to the desired radius and holds the pavers in place.

Set in the center of a flower and herb garden, the patio consists of a nearly 30-foot-diameter core surrounded by circular planting rings. Four pathways, clearly marked by a change in the paver pattern, cut across the circle, leading to an inner circle with comfortable benches and a birdbath.

Either make the benches yourself or purchase manufactured furnishings. Although you can purchase any of several well-made commercial trellises for the main entrance, the patio instructions include directions for building the one shown here. It's designed with the moderately experienced do-it-yourselfer in mind.

OVERHEAD VIEW

14½'
8½'
10½'
12½'
6'

LAYING OUT THE SITE

Laying out the patio is essentially a task that involves marking a series of circles that designate the different parts of the patio design.

■ Begin by driving a stake in what will be the center of the patio.

■ Tie one end of a rope to the stake and the other end to a squeeze bottle filled with colored chalk or lime.

■ Pull the rope taut and walk around the stake, squeezing the bottle to mark the ground as you go.

■ Lay out the outside edge of the patio with the bottle tied 14½ feet from the stake; then mark circles with radii of 12½, 10½, and 8½ feet to lay out the remaining sections.

■ Lay out the ends of the beds by stretching two lines at right angles across the patio. Measure 3 feet on each side of the lines to mark the ends of the beds.

GARDEN COURTYARD
continued

PLASTIC EDGING

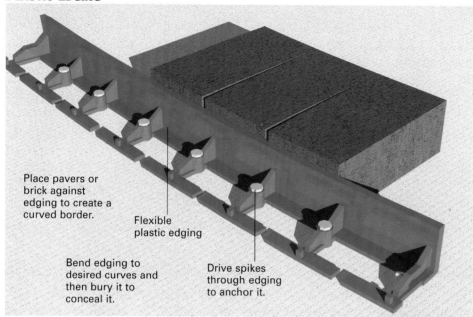

Place pavers or brick against edging to create a curved border.

Flexible plastic edging

Bend edging to desired curves and then bury it to conceal it.

Drive spikes through edging to anchor it.

EXCAVATING

Dig along the chalk lines with a spade, excavating the patio and walkways.
- Excavate a bed deep enough to hold 4 inches of gravel, 2 inches of sand, plus the thickness of the pavers.
- Slope for surface drainage—1 inch per 4 linear feet. Use a slope gauge or slope the layout lines and put up grid lines if necessary. Measure down from the lines to keep the slope consistent (see pages 106–110 for more information on excavation techniques).

MATERIALS LIST

Element	Quantity*	Material	Length
Base			
	15 cu. yd.	crushed rock or class-5 gravel	
	4 cu. yd.	washed sand, concrete grade	
	2 cu. yd.	topsoil	
	227 sq. ft.	weed-blocking fabric	
Edging	343 ft.	plastic patio edging	
Brick edging	1,200	4×8×2 bricks	
	varies with style	cobblestone pavers	
Purchased birdbath	1		
3×6×8 TRELLIS			
Footings		gravel and concrete to build four	
		8"-diameter footings to code	
Framing			
Posts	4	4×4s	12'
Arches	2	1×12s	12'
Side and top rails	6	1×4s	8'
Finials	4	Size as desired	
Fasteners		1½" deck screws	
		2" deck screws	

All quantities may vary with site conditions.

INSTALLING THE PATIO

Before you set the main body of pavers, install the circumference edging—bricks set on end (called soldiers)—supported by buried structural plastic edging. (See pages 114–117 for more information about installing a brick-in-sand patio.)
- Set the flexible plastic forms against the edge of the excavation and drive the anchors in the ground.
- Set the forms that outline the planting beds.
- Place gravel in the bed, tamp, then cover with landscape fabric and 2 inches of sand.
- Set the pavers on the sand in the pattern shown. When all the pavers are in place, sweep sand between them and tamp the surface with a rented power tamper.
- Reexcavate the planting beds, if necessary, to accommodate your plants and fill them with rich topsoil.

BUILDING THE TRELLIS

A trellis is among the simplest garden structures to build. For this design, use 4×4 pressure-treated posts rated for ground contact. Set the posts 4 feet apart on center from one side of the arch to the other, and 3 feet apart front to back. Cut the sides and top rails from 1×4s and the arched beams from 1×12s.

TRELLIS CONSTRUCTION

■ Place 12-foot 4×4 posts in postholes, leaving 8 feet exposed.

■ Plumb and square the posts.

■ Make an arch pattern as shown. Cut four arches from a 1×12 board, following the pattern. Cut four more pieces from ¼-inch plywood, and screw the plywood to the solid stock for reinforcement.

■ Attach the arched beams flush with the tops of the posts.

■ Then cut 1×3 rafters long enough to rest on top of the inner beams and meet flush with the outer beams.

■ Set the rafters on edge and drill pilot holes through the rafters into the arches, and screw the rafters in place with 1½-inch deck screws.

■ Nail the side strips in place and attach a finial to the top of each post. Stain or paint the trellis to match or complement your overall landscape design.

Top rail

Arched beams

Post

Side rail

8'

3'

4'

ARCH TEMPLATE

Cut arch from 1×12

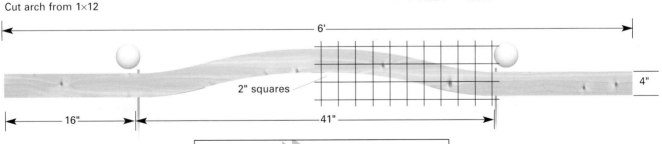

6'

2" squares

4"

16"

41"

TRELLIS DETAIL

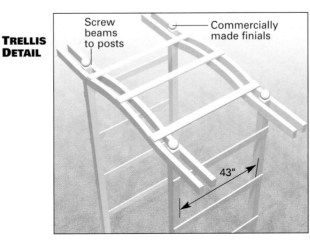

Screw beams to posts

Commercially made finials

43"

HILLSIDE PATIO WITH RETAINING WALL

Hillsides can present problems when building patios, often lying in the way of the perfect spot for your project. This design offers a solution for a hilly site. It requires some grading, but it results in a patio that can look as if it were carved right into its natural surroundings.

CONSTRUCTION HIGHLIGHTS

Erecting a retaining wall is an enterprise well within the ability of the average homeowner because it's made of interlocking landscape blocks. You simply stack one course on top of the previous course, and the precast tabs help hold the blocks in place—no mortar required.

Many communities have codes that govern the construction of retaining walls, especially those more than 3 feet high. Most codes require permits and inspections, so be sure to consult your local building authority before you begin your project.

INTERLOCKING BLOCKS

Interlocking blocks come in different sizes and styles. Some have fiberglass pin connectors; others have overlapping flanges (see illustration on page 202). All are designed to slope back into the hill to resist the natural pressure of the hillside. Different manufacturers recommend different footings. Some require only a well-compacted gravel base; others call for a concrete footing. Follow the manufacturer's specifications and local building codes.

If you're building a patio against an existing retaining wall, install an isolation joint before pouring the concrete base.

LAYING OUT THE SITE

■ If local codes require a footing for your wall, extend the dimensions of the sides that abut the slope by the amount required by code. Allow a 1½-foot to 2-foot clearance for the retaining wall in addition to the patio dimensions.
■ Lay out the site with batter boards and square the corners. (See page 107 for more information about layout techniques.)

EXCAVATING

Excavate for the patio, the walk, and the wall at the same time.
■ Excavate to a depth that will accommodate a gravel base, a 4-inch concrete slab, mortar bed, and a ½-inch- to 1-inch-thick cut and dressed flagstone. See pages 106–110 for more information on excavation techniques.
■ Use a slope gauge or slope the layout lines and put up grid lines if necessary. Measure down from the lines to keep the slope consistent (see page 110).
■ Orient the slope toward the open corner opposite the walled corner.
■ You can increase the slope of this patio surface to 1 inch per 4 linear feet if required by local codes to accommodate the potential increase in runoff from behind the wall.

OVERHEAD VIEW

Landscape-block retaining wall

30'

18'

EXCAVATING FOR A RETAINING WALL

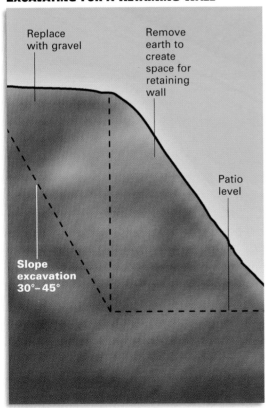

Replace with gravel

Remove earth to create space for retaining wall

Patio level

Slope excavation 30°–45°

MATERIALS LIST

Element	Quantity*	Material	Length
18×30 Patio			
Base			
	10 cu. yd.	crushed rock or class-5 gravel	
	540 sq. ft.	reinforcing wire mesh 6×6-10/10	
Slab	7 cu. yd. (varies)	ready-mix concrete, 4" thick	
Paving			
	540 sq. ft.	flagstone, cut irregular shapes, 2" thick	
	81 bags	mortar, type M mortar mix, 60-lb. bags	
Landscape-Block Retaining Wall			
	3 cu. yd.	crushed rock or class-5 gravel	
Stepping-Stone Path, Each 3 Ft.-Sq. Section			
Base			
	28	12–24" layout stakes	
	12 ft.	mason's line	
	0.25 cu. yd.	crushed rock or class-5 gravel	
	9 sq ft	reinforcing wire mesh 6×6-10/10	
Forms			
Temporary forms	4	2×6s	3'
	8	12–24" stakes for temporary forms	
Slab	0.15 cu. yd. (varies)	ready-mix concrete	
Paving	9 sq. ft.	flagstone, cut irregular shapes	
Mortar	2	60-lb. bags type M mortar mix	

All quantities may vary with site conditions.

HILLSIDE PATIO WITH RETAINING WALL
continued

In any case, the highest point of the surface should be the rear corner where the retaining walls meet.

POUR THE STEPS

■ Build the forms from 2x6s ripped to 4 inches and stake as illustrated on page 110.
■ Place and tamp the gravel base.
■ Install reinforcing wire mesh cut to fit the forms and pour the site using the techniques shown on pages 122–123.

FLANGED-BLOCK WALL

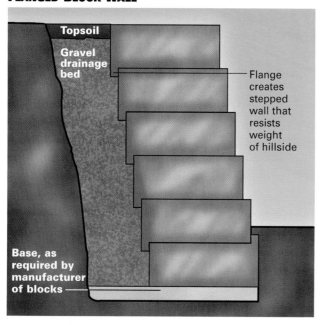

Topsoil

Gravel drainage bed

Flange creates stepped wall that resists weight of hillside

Base, as required by manufacturer of blocks

PINNED-BLOCK WALL

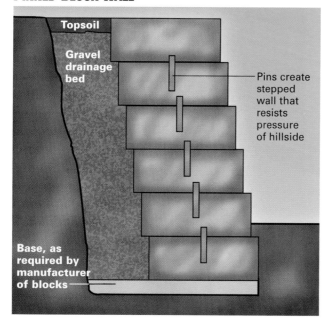

Topsoil

Gravel drainage bed

Pins create stepped wall that resists pressure of hillside

Base, as required by manufacturer of blocks

■ Order the ready-mix and have a crew on hand to help with the pour.
■ Once the concrete has set up (but not cured), scarify the surface—scratch it with a board into which you've driven nails about an inch apart. Mortar bonds more firmly with the rough surface this creates.
■ Make individual 3×3-foot concrete bases for the walk.
■ Cut control joints in the slab after an initial floating.
■ Let the slab and footings cure for three to five days.

BUILDING THE WALL

■ Lay landscape fabric in the wall excavation as shown on pages 155–157.
■ Place the faces of the blocks as snugly as possible against the slab and level them side to side and front to back.
■ After you've laid a few feet, check the tops of the blocks with a 4-foot carpenter's level.
■ If you're setting the wall on a gravel base, put extra gravel under blocks that are too low and remove gravel from under ones that are too high.
■ When the first row is done, shovel gravel into the void between the blocks and the soil.
■ Set the second course of blocks on top of the first in a running bond pattern, with the upper block centered over the seam below.
■ If you're using flanged blocks, hook the flanges over the back of the block below it to give the wall its required slope (see at left).
■ Align the holes in a pin-system block (see at left) to create the proper slope.
■ Shovel gravel behind the second course.
■ Continue laying blocks and shoveling gravel. Fill in behind the last row of blocks with soil.
■ Cap the retaining wall either with solid units sold by the manufacturer or mortar the same dressed stone you used for the paving.
■ Backfill behind the caps with topsoil, then plant a groundcover.
■ Sweep mason's sand into the joint between the retaining wall and the slab. Moisten with a garden hose and repeat until the joint is packed full.

PAVING THE PATIO

Finish by paving the patio with flagstones set in a mortar bed.
■ No matter which type of stone you choose, begin by piecing the stones together on the

BACKFILLING BEHIND WALL

patio, arranging them to fit together with joints no more than ½ inch wide.
■ When you're happy with the paving pattern, number the stones with chalk, so you can put them in order again later. Remove the stones and set them aside.

The mortar bed for a patio stone should be about an inch thick, level, and uniform.
■ Using the techniques outlined on pages 124–125, spread the mortar with a trowel and screed it level.
■ Spread a section at a time and lay the stone in that section. Don't spread too large an area or the mortar will set up and become useless.

■ Depending on your skill and how quickly the mortar sets up, start with some mortar mix and a small section to be paved. Gradually increase your work size and mortar amount as your skill develops, to avoid mortar setting up.
■ If necessary, raise a low stone by buttering its underside with mortar, as described on pages 124–125.
■ When the mortar bed has set up (overnight will usually do), apply mortar between the joints with a mortar bag, wiping off excess with a burlap rag.

PATIO WITH A FORMAL POND

A large shallow pond adds sparkle and an architectural focus to this attractive patio. The 8×16-foot pond is flanked on each side by a tiled patio section, measuring 15×18 feet. The total patio area is 540 square feet, not including the pond.

CONSTRUCTION HIGHLIGHTS

This patio features ceramic tile borders and matching tile strips that visually divide each section of the patio into four areas. Any color will do, of course, but be sure to choose one that complements your overall landscape design and color scheme.

Tiles border the pond also, outlining its shape and unifying the total setting. In areas with heavy winters, tile may be a poor choice of material; use milled flagstone instead.

Because tiles must be supported by a concrete base, pour the base first, leaving an opening in the middle for the pond. Once the concrete is in place, begin making the pond by lining the opening with a flexible waterproof liner. After the pond is lined, set the tile.

A fountain in the pond adds sparkle and life while aerating the water. Add perimeter plantings to screen and shelter the patio and soften its contour. Make sure you install GFCI outlets in the garden to run the fountain pumps.

Pond maintenance will vary by climate and seasons; consult a local pond supplier to determine whether plumbing or sewer utilities are required or desirable for a pond in your area.

If needed, have the lines roughed-in by professionals during layout and excavation. Then complete the work after you've finished the patio.

LAYING OUT THE SITE

Grade and stake the pond and the patio at the same time, following the instructions outlined on pages 106–110 and 171. Set the corner stakes for an 18×38-foot rectangular patio. Lay out the site with batter boards and square the corners.

EXCAVATING

The surface of the patio should be no more than ½ to 1 inch above grade.

■ Excavate to a depth that will accommodate all the layers of the finished patio: a 4- to 6-inch gravel subbase, a 4-inch-thick concrete slab, a ½- to 1-inch mortar bed, and the thickness of the tile. See pages 106–110 for more information about excavation techniques.

■ Slope for surface drainage. Each patio

OVERHEAD VIEW

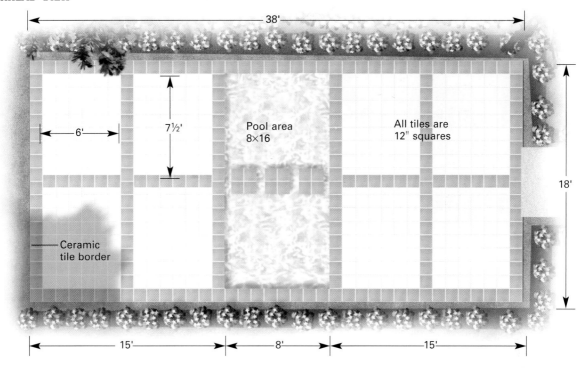

38'

7½'

6'

Pool area
8×16

All tiles are
12" squares

18'

Ceramic
tile border

15'   8'   15'

section must slope from the pond at the rate of 1 inch for every 4 linear feet of surface so that rain and garden runoff don't drain into the pond. If you're building the patio near a house, position the patio so water doesn't drain toward the house.

■ Slope the layout lines and put up grid lines, if necessary. Measure down from the lines to keep the slope consistent (see page 110).

BUILDING THE PATIO

■ After the general excavation, lay out the 8×18-foot pond with batter boards and line.
■ Dig a space for the pond 3 inches deeper than the surrounding patio and 4 inches wider on each side than the finished pond dimension.

EXCAVATING FOR THE PATIO

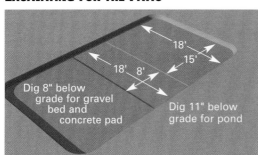

18'

15'

18'   8'

Dig 8" below grade for gravel bed and concrete pad

Dig 11" below grade for pond

MATERIALS LIST

Element	Quantity*	Material	Length
Base			
	15 cu. yd.	crushed rock or class-5 gravel	
	540 sq. ft.	reinforcing wire mesh, 6×6-6/6	
Slab	7 cu. yd. thick (varies)	ready-mix concrete	4"
Tiles			
	375	ceramic tiles, 12" squares	
	260	ceramic tile trim, 12" squares	
	8	60-lb. bags type-M mortar mix	
8×16 POOL			
	1	flexible pond liner, 14×24'	
	2	pond liner protection fabric, 8×36"	
	12	concrete blocks, 8×16×8"	
	1	60-lb. bag type-M mortar mix	
	12	concrete pavers, 12×12"	
	1	GFCI exterior outlet	
	2	submersible pump with fountain	
	As needed	concrete blocks to hold pump and fountain apparatus	

All quantities may vary with site conditions.

PATIO WITH A FORMAL POND
continued

■ Set 2×12 forms into the pond excavation about 4 inches from the sides of the patio. The forms will keep the gravel out of the pond during the next step and create the edges of the pond when you pour the concrete.

■ Stake and brace the boards on the inside of the pond, but don't nail them together.

■ Place and tamp a 4-inch gravel bed inside the patio excavation but not inside the pond opening. Keep the gravel about 10 inches away from the pond forms.

■ Stake and brace the forms around the patio perimeter.

■ Caulk any gaps between the forms at the corners.

■ Follow the basic instructions for building a concrete base on pages 126–135, reinforcing the slab with wire mesh and reinforcing the edge of the pond with ½-inch rebar.

BUILDING THE POND

■ After the concrete slab has cured, remove the forms inside the pool and smooth the soil at the bottom of the pond recess as much as possible. If necessary, fill depressions in the soil with dry sand tamped into place.

■ Install a strip of plastic pond liner in the pond recess, positioned under where the stepping-stones will go.

■ Next, let the flexible pond liner warm in the sun to soften it. Get a group of helpers together and billow the liner over the pond like a parachute.

■ After it starts to settle into the pond, loosely weight the edges of the liner with stones to keep the liner in place. Allow plenty of slack so the liner can settle all the way into the corners.

■ Normally you would fill a pond with water to help push the liner into place in the corners, but this pond has to stay dry while you build the stepping-stones. Instead of filling the pond with water, step into it with soft, clean shoes and carefully sweep the dry liner into place from the center of the pond toward the edges.

PATIO FORMS

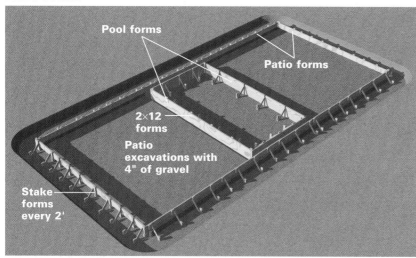

Pool forms
Patio forms
2×12 forms
Patio excavations with 4" of gravel
Stake forms every 2'

PATIO CONSTRUCTION

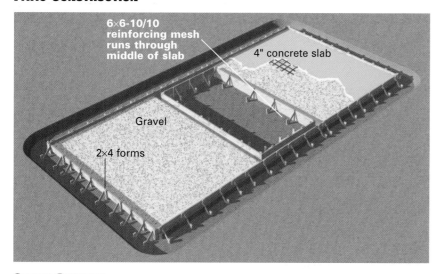

6×6-10/10 reinforcing mesh runs through middle of slab
4" concrete slab
Gravel
2×4 forms

CROSS SECTION

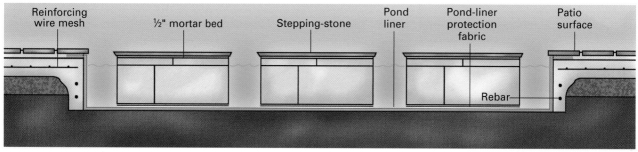

Reinforcing wire mesh ½" mortar bed Stepping-stone Pond liner Pond-liner protection fabric Patio surface

Rebar

■ Fit the liner up over the edges, pleating it in the corners.

■ Weight the edges temporarily.

INSTALLING STEPPING-STONES

Work carefully to prevent damage to the pond liner.

■ Lay a strip of liner protection fabric 26 inches wide by 8 feet long across the center of the pond bottom. (To protect the liner while working, lay down a wider piece to walk on and trim it after the stones are completed.)

■ Make a base for each stepping-stone by mortaring four concrete blocks together, as shown at right.

■ Fill the center with concrete and screed it to create a flat surface.

■ Cover each base with four 12-inch-square concrete patio pavers set in mortar. Work carefully to avoid getting mortar on the flexible pool liner.

FINISHING UP

■ Set bricks or concrete blocks, if required, on pieces of liner protection fabric on the bottom of the pond to hold submersible fountain pumps. Pumps are available at pond, pool, and aquarium suppliers and at home centers.

■ After the stepping-stone mortar has set, fill the pond with water to just below the surface of the stepping-stones. The weight of the water will push the liner into place.

■ Smooth and trim the liner so it lays over the edge of the pool by about 5 inches.

■ Starting ½ inch from the edge of the pond, spread a ½-inch layer of mortar for the 12-inch-square accent tiles that border the pool. Work in small sections at a time, setting the tiles so they are flush with each other and with the edge of the pool.

■ Bed the tiles with a scrap board and a rubber mallet.

■ Working in small sections, tile the remaining surface of the patio in a ½-inch mortar bed, with the accent tiles arranged according to the plans.

■ After a day, fill the joints between the tiles with mortar. Immediately wipe off the tiles with a clean piece of burlap.

STEPPING-STONE BASE

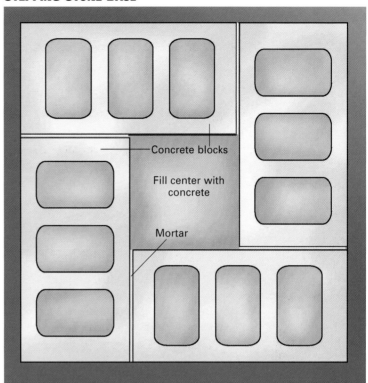

Concrete blocks

Fill center with concrete

Mortar

STEPPING-STONE CONSTRUCTION

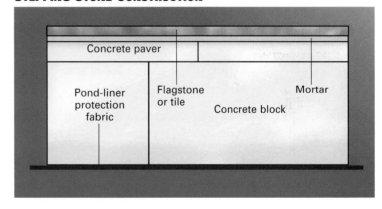

Concrete paver

Pond-liner protection fabric

Flagstone or tile

Mortar

Concrete block

PUMP INSTALLATION

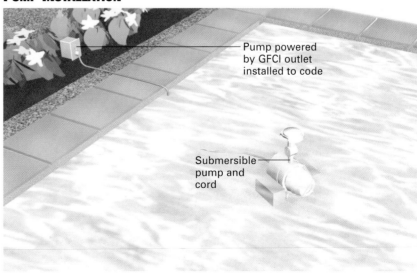

Pump powered by GFCI outlet installed to code

Submersible pump and cord

WRAPAROUND PATIO

This patio wraps around a corner of the house and steps down to a lower patio in the side yard, creating a smaller private outdoor area adjacent to the house.

The smaller space is protected from view, and its isolation makes it perfect for a quiet dining area, children's play space, or private morning space if adjacent to a bedroom.

This arrangement creates a side patio readily accessible to the upper tier and the house—a configuration that is ideal if the upper level adjoins the kitchen. The structure is sheltered on one side by a tall fence with open slats, which provides plenty of privacy without making the space seem confined.

CONSTRUCTION HIGHLIGHTS

Wrapping a patio around the corner of a house makes it possible to take advantage of the light, sun, and breezes from several directions. The corner of the house also divides the patio into distinct functional areas.

The patio is built to accommodate a slight slope in the terrain, one that you can easily level with hand tools. Varying the number of steps would make this plan equally suitable for a side yard that falls more steeply away from the house. Such an installation would likely require professional grading.

This patio is built of concrete pavers set in a sand bed. Pavers need an edging to hold them in place. In this case, the edging is made of 6×6 beams.

CAREFUL PLANNING

It's unlikely that this patio plan (or any plan for that matter) will match the specific requirements of your terrain and other landscape features perfectly. Like all potential landscaping obstacles, you can turn this problem into an asset with careful planning.

Begin by carefully drawing the patio plan on graph paper to fit the specifics of your site. Draw everything to scale—the placement of the pavers, the size and location of the edging boards, and the width and placement of the fence panels—so they fit together on your site exactly as you want them.

LAYING OUT THE SITE

Follow the basic instructions for building a sand-set paver patio and install permanent wood edging (see pages 142–145 and 111).

■ Set the corner stakes for the two sections—an 18×20-foot section and a 10×18 section. Lay out the site with batter boards and square the corners (see page 107).

■ Slope for surface drainage—1 inch every 4 feet. Slope the layout lines and put up grid lines if necessary. Measure down from the lines to keep the slope consistent (see page 110 for more information on excavation techniques and pages 106–110 for more information on layout techniques).

EXCAVATING

■ Excavate a bed deep enough to hold 4 inches of gravel, 2 inches of sand, plus the thickness of the pavers.

■ Make sure the entire excavation follows the correct slope.

FINISHING THE PATIO

■ Edge the upper patio with two courses of pressure-treated 6×6 beams rated for ground contact.

■ Stake them in place with No. 4 rebar, driven 2 feet into the ground at the corners and every 4 feet in between.

■ Edge the lower patio with a single course of 6×6s set level with the grade.

■ Lay gravel and sand beds until the pavers are even with the top of the edging; then set the pavers in place.

OVERHEAD VIEW

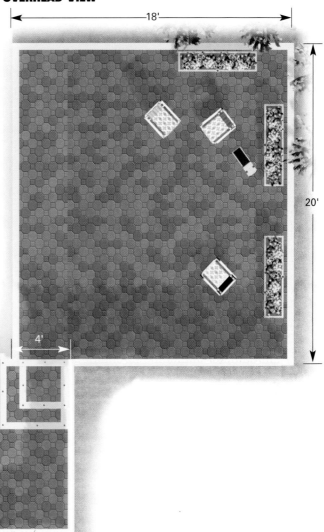

PATIO CROSS SECTION

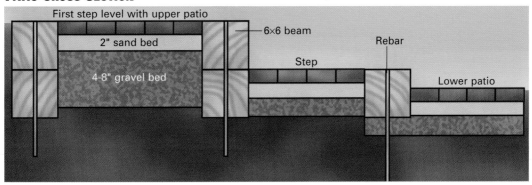

WRAPAROUND PATIO
continued

MATERIALS LIST

Element	Quantity*	Material	Length
Base			
gravel	7 cu. yd.	crushed rock or class-5 pea	
	540 sq. ft.	weed-blocking fabric	
	4 cu. yd.	washed sand, concrete grade	
Edging			
Upper patio	16	6×6s	10'
	8	6×6s	8'
Lower patio	2	6×6s	12'
	2	6×6s	10'
	2	6×6s	8'
Steps	4	6×6s	8'
	4	6×6s	10'
Rebar	28	No. 4	48"
	19	No. 4	30"
Paving	340	18×18×2" pavers	
PRIVACY FENCE			
Footings		gravel and concrete to build 8"- to 12"-dia. postholes	
Lumber, per panel**			
Posts	1	4×4	8'
Rails	2	2×4s	8'
Wide fence boards	3	1×6s	8'
Medium fence boards	4	1×3s	8'
Narrow fence boards	10	1×2s	8'
End post**	1	4×4	8'
Gate**			
Rails	1	2×4	8'
Brace	1	2×4	8'
Wide board	1	1×6	8'
Medium boards	1	1×3	8'
Narrow boards	1	1×2	8'
End boards	2	1×4s	8'
Fasteners	4 per panel 6d HDG nails	galvanized fence brackets as needed	
	48 per panel	2" galvanized deck screws	
	1	gate latch	
	2	gate hinges	

All quantities may vary with site conditions.

**Use rot-/insect-resistant lumber.*

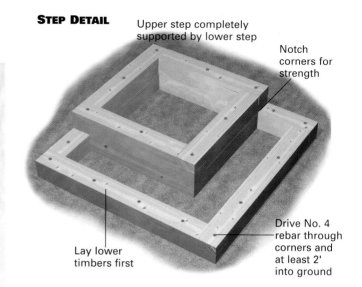

STEP DETAIL

Upper step completely supported by lower step

Notch corners for strength

Lay lower timbers first

Drive No. 4 rebar through corners and at least 2' into ground

BUILDING THE STEPS

■ Construct the frames for the steps for this project from 6×6 pressure-treated lumber rated for ground contact. The exact dimensions will depend on the style and size of the paver you choose. Pick a size that will minimize the number of pavers you need to cut.
■ Make the frame for the lower step first.
■ Set a second, smaller frame on top of the first.
■ Support the floating edge with additional sections of timbers.
■ Stake the timbers with ½-inch rebar long enough to reach at least 2 feet into the ground.
■ Fill the step centers with gravel, leaving room for a 2-inch sand bed.

OVERHEAD VIEW OF STEPS

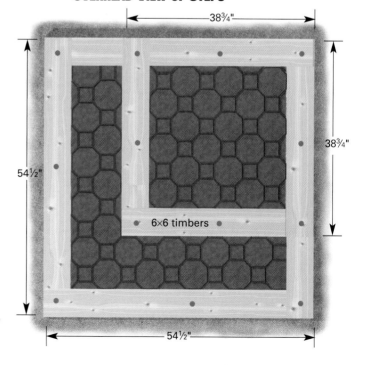

38¾"

38¾"

54½"

54½"

6×6 timbers

■ Compact the gravel, line it with landscape fabric, add sand, and lay the pavers.

Repeat the process for the patio sections and set the pavers throughout the entire surface area.

BUILDING THE FENCE

■ Lay out the fence with batter boards and mason's line.

■ Stake the positions of the posts along the line, setting them 6 feet on center, and dig holes for setting the posts. (The fence panels are designed to be 6 feet wide but can be adjusted to fit the available space.)

■ Set the 4×4 posts so they are 6 feet high. For more information, see page 161.

PANELS: Stretch a chalk line about 6 inches above the ground between the two end posts. Then level the chalk line with a line level, and snap the line to mark the posts.

■ Set the bottom edges of galvanized fence brackets on these lines, and nail the brackets to the posts.

■ Lay out and install mounting brackets for the top rail, positioning them 12 inches below the top of the post.

■ Working one section at a time, measure the exact distance between the two posts and cut rails to fit the brackets.

■ Slip the rails into their brackets and nail in place.

■ Cut all of the vertical boards to length.

■ Screw the first slat to the rails with 2-inch deck screws, plumbing it carefully.

■ Cut and then use a spacer to help you position the next slat.

■ Continue attaching slats until the fence is complete, checking occasionally to make sure the slat is plumb.

GATE: Screw the boards to the rails, as shown below, with 2-inch deck screws.

■ Add a diagonal brace cut to fit between the bottom and top rails.

■ Attach the hinges to the gate, mount the gate on the gate post, and install the latch.

FENCE CONSTRUCTION

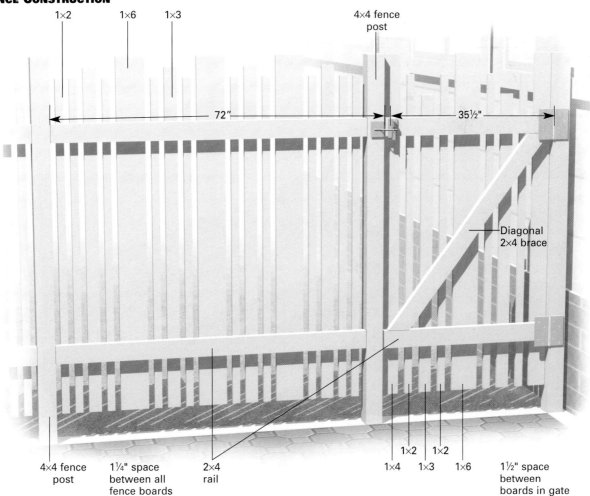

1×2 1×6 1×3

4×4 fence post

72"   35½"

Diagonal 2×4 brace

4×4 fence post

1¼" space between all fence boards

2×4 rail

1×2 1×2

1×4 1×3 1×6

1½" space between boards in gate

MULTILEVEL PATIO WITH SPA

A spa and a patio are a great combination, but making the spa look like part of the patio can be tricky. One solution is to set the spa above the surface of a flat patio. Unless there is a unifying structure, such as an overhead, both the spa and the steps leading to it can look like afterthoughts.

This split-level patio offers another solution. The spa is located on the lower level and placed against the upper level. Half the spa is reached from the upper level of the patio, so people can easily walk up to the spa, sit on its edge, swing their legs around, and slip into the water.

Putting the spa in this location provides easy access to the house for changing and getting towels. The mortared brick paving unites and emphasizes the solid construction of the entire complex.

CONSTRUCTION HIGHLIGHTS

Note that the elevated spa and lower patio level sit on the same grade. Depending on your site's terrain, you will probably need to move large quantities of dirt or build up the upper level with a concrete base. As such, the construction of this patio can be achieved with one of two methods.

■ One requires grading both surfaces out of a slope in the yard, leaving the upper level soil intact and building forms in three sections— one for the upper level, one for the steps, and one for the lower level. This method requires three separate pours on different days.

■ The other requires constructing forms for the upper level and steps as a single element and pouring them as a unit when the spa base is poured. The lower patio base will be poured later.

OVERHEAD VIEW

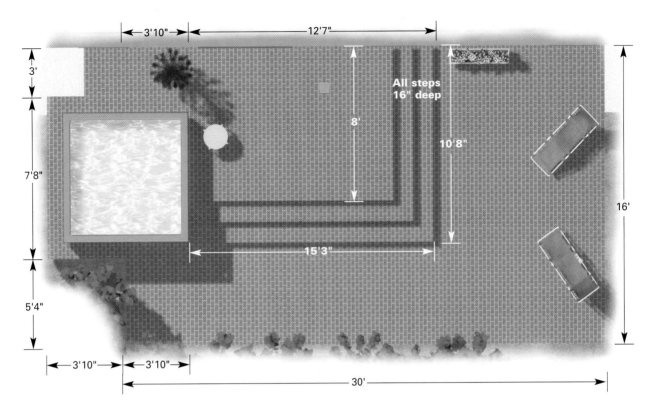

The latter method works better for a site with fairly level soil because it allows the upper level to be adequately supported by a concrete-and-rubble-fill base (see pages 152–153, "Building Concrete Steps").

It is not wise to build a raised patio on a surface that requires the addition of soil. Even well-tamped soil will settle, causing the patio to crack and break up.

Both methods require the installation of underground circuits before pouring concrete. Hiring a licensed electrician for this purpose may not only save you time in the long run, it also may be required by local codes.

BUILDING ON A SLOPE

Build a patio on a slope requires careful grading. You may want to enlist the assistance of a professional for the job.

Once the grading is complete, you can construct forms deep enough to support the concrete footing and slab. Strengthen the concrete with wire-mesh steps designed especially for such installations. Leave sufficient room between the soil and the footing forms so the footing is as wide as specified by local codes.

■ Build the forms for both the upper level and the spa surround, stake them securely, add and tamp gravel, and then pour the slab and footing and the spa surround, screeding the surface as illustrated on page 127.

■ Remove the forms when the concrete has

set up; then let the concrete cure.

The steps must sit on the same base as the patio, so build them before pouring the lower level.

■ Insert an isolation joint at the bottom of the spa surround and upper-level footing and build forms for the two steps. Then pour the steps and let the concrete cure.

■ If you have not already done so, lay out the lower level of the patio with batter boards and construct it as you would any other concrete slab.

MATERIALS LIST

Element	Quantity*	Material	Length
Base	10 cu. yd.	crushed rock or class-5 gravel	
	540 sq. ft.	reinforcing wire mesh 6×6-10/10	
	8 cu. yd.	ready-mix concrete (varies)	
	34 ft.	½×4" expansion joint	
	23 sq. ft.	8-mil polyethylene vapor barrier	
Paving	2,700	4×8×2¼" bricks	
	103	60-lb. bags type-M mortar mix	
		Purchased portable spa with cedar skirt (max. 7'8" sq. 36" deep)	
		underground 220-volt, 30-amp branch electrical circuit with GFCI	

All quantities may vary with site conditions.

MULTILEVEL PATIO WITH SPA
continued

CROSS SECTION FROM SIDE

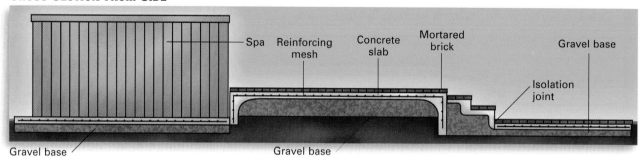

Spa — Reinforcing mesh — Concrete slab — Mortared brick — Gravel base — Isolation joint — Gravel base — Gravel base

CROSS SECTION FROM END

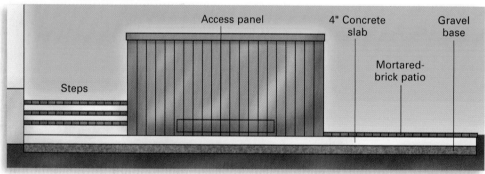

Access panel — 4" Concrete slab — Gravel base — Mortared-brick patio — Steps

CROSS SECTION THROUGH STAIRS

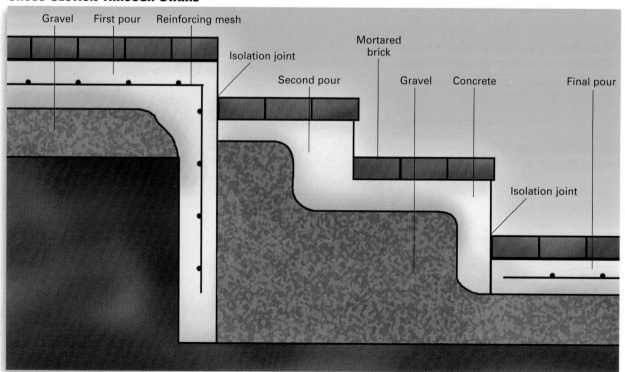

Gravel — First pour — Reinforcing mesh — Isolation joint — Mortared brick — Second pour — Gravel — Concrete — Final pour — Isolation joint

BRICKS ON STEPS

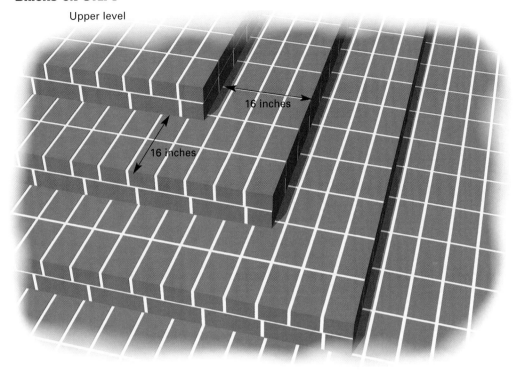

Upper level

16 inches

16 inches

Lower level

BUILDING ON LEVEL GROUND

Building this patio on level ground may also require grading to achieve a level grade throughout.

■ Once the site is graded, construct the forms for the upper level and the steps (treat them as a single unit).

■ Fill the recesses in the forms with rubble and gravel, leaving at least 4 inches of space so the thickness of the concrete will be ample.

■ Add wire mesh and complete the construction of the forms for the spa surround.

■ Pour both units on the same day, remove the forms when the concrete has set up, and let it cure.

■ Lay out the lower-level patio, install isolation-joint material around the base of the upper level, the stairs, and along the house foundation.

■ Build forms for the slab; then pour the slab, using the techniques illustrated on pages 126–135.

■ Cut a control joint in the concrete surface between the spa area and the rest of the lower level only.

PAVING THE SURFACE

■ Pave the surface of the patio and steps with mortar-set bricks. (See pages 118–119 for basic brick-laying instructions.)

■ Do not pave over the control joint; bricks placed here are likely to crack.

■ Lay bricks on either side of the control joint and fill the gap with flexible caulk instead of mortar. See page 77 for other brick patterns. The illustration above shows you how to set brick over the steps.

INSTALLING THE SPA

■ Install flexible isolation-joint material around the top edge of the concrete bay where the spa will be installed.

■ Set the spa snugly against it with its access panel on an exposed side.

■ Have a professional installer complete the installation and hookups according to the manufacturer's instructions and in compliance with local codes.

TWO-PART GARDEN PATIO

This two-part flagstone patio stretches out from the house and far into the yard. An attached 9×30-foot patio links the house with its surroundings. A path then extends the patio's reach dramatically to a 12×23½-foot section that the designer envisions as flanked by flower gardens. There, a combination garden seat and potting bench provides a place to relax as well as a base for garden chores.

LAYING OUT THE SITE

■ Set the corner stakes for two rectangular areas to the dimensions shown—or modify the measurements and materials list now to adapt this concept to your site. When you're satisfied with your refinements to the plan, including the distance between the two linked patios, lay out the site with batter boards and square the corners (see page 107).

EXCAVATE

■ Excavate deep enough for a 4- to 6-inch gravel subbase, a 4-inch-thick concrete slab, a mortar bed, and 1- to 2-inch thick flagstones. See pages 106–110 for more information on excavation techniques.
■ Slope for surface drainage—1 inch per 4 linear feet. Slope the layout lines and put up grid lines, if necessary. Measure down from the lines to keep the slope consistent (see page 110 for further instruction).
■ Then stake the locations for the six potting bench posts in the garden-area patio.
■ Build footings and piers with post anchors (see page 161 for techniques).
■ After the piers have set up, wrap expansion-joint material around them.
■ Lay out and stake forms for the slab that supports the flagstone. The slab is reinforced with mesh, as explained on page 123.

■ Set forms for the mortar bed, if necessary, and spread and level the mortar. Then set the stones, working a small section at a time.

BUILDING THE FENCE

■ Lay out the edges of the planting beds that surround the garden patio with batter boards and mason's lines.
■ Sink 4×4 pressure-treated fence posts rated for ground contact around the beds, spaced as shown in the illustration at right.
■ Nail 6-foot sections of prefab 3-foot-high cedar picket fence to the posts. Leave an opening for the walkway.

BUILDING THE BENCH AND SEAT

The frame for the combined potting bench and garden seat is built with 4×4 posts, 2×4s, and 2×6s. The louvers are 1×4s. The seat slats are 2×2s. All lumber used in its construction is pressure-treated stock, rated for ground contact. You can substitute other weather-resistant species, such as redwood, cypress, and cedar. Standard shelving is used for the potting bench.

FRAME: Pour the piers and footings and install the post anchors before you pour the base for the rest of the patio. Wrap them with expansion joint material the next day and pour the base for the patio. You can begin work on the potting bench when the concrete base has cured.

OVERHEAD VIEW

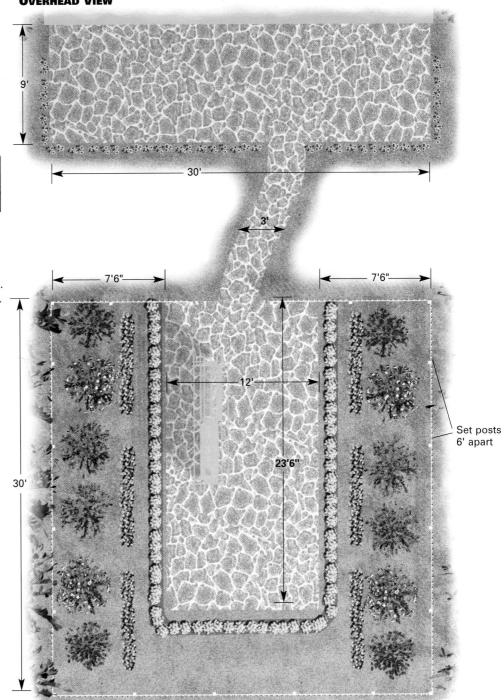

TWO-PART GARDEN PATIO
continued

POTTING BENCH AND GARDEN SEAT

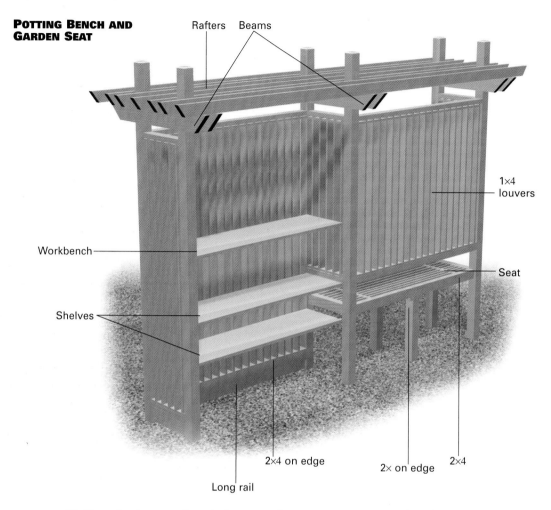

Rafters Beams

1×4 louvers

Workbench

Seat

Shelves

2×4 on edge

2× on edge

2×4

Long rail

■ Chamfer the top of six 4×4 posts and cut them to 9½ feet.

■ Install the posts in the post anchors, using temporary braces to keep them upright and plumb.

■ Cut six 2×6 beams 4 feet long and angle the ends. Fasten a beam on each side of the posts, with the bottom edges of the beams level and 8 feet above the patio surface. Fasten the beams with ½×4-inch lag screws.

■ Cut eight 2×4 rafters 14 feet long. (If you're unable to get straight 16-foot 2×4s, you can make each rafter from two 8-footers.)

■ Cut an angle on the ends that overhang the unit.

■ Set the rafters on the beams and fasten them with rafter ties.

LOUVERED PANELS:

■ Cut slats 5 feet long for the garden bench and center divider panels.

■ Cut slats 7 feet long for the potting bench back and end panels.

■ Position the slats with the help of 1×4 spacers 2¼ inches long. Begin by nailing a spacer to each rail so it is tight against the post.

■ Set a 1×4 louver against the spacer; nail through the rails to attach the louver.

■ Continue nailing spacers and louvers to the rails until you've completed the panel.

■ To keep the wide panels from sagging, support them with a long 2×4 installed on edge under the bottom rail and attached to the posts with brackets.

■ Screw the rails to the support approximately every 18 inches.

SEAT AND SHELVES

Make a 2×4 frame exactly wide enough and long enough to fit between the posts on the bench side of the unit. (The approximate measurements are 6 feet by 18 inches, but cut to fit the actual dimensions on your site.)

■ Fasten 2×2s to 1×2 spacers with deck screws to make a seat that fits inside the frame, as shown on the opposite page.

■ Fasten the seat flush with the top of the

SEAT DETAIL

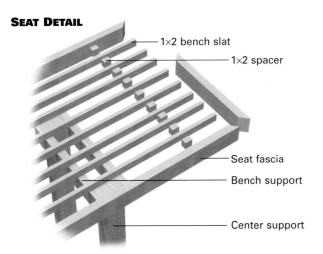

- 1×2 bench slat
- 1×2 spacer
- Seat fascia
- Bench support
- Center support

LOUVER DETAIL

2× on edge   2× flat

frame by driving ½×3-inch lag screws through the frame and into the spacers.

■ Slip the seat between the posts so that it's flush with the outside of the posts.

■ Build and attach the support as shown below. Level the seat.

■ Fasten the seat to the posts with ½×3-inch lag screws driven through the frame from under the seat.

■ Cut the shelves and worktable to fit; attach them with brackets to the front and back posts.

MATERIALS LIST

Element	Quantity*	Material	Length
Base	10 cu. yd.	crushed rock or class-5 gravel	
	10 cu. yd.	gravel	
	6 cu. yd.	concrete	
Paving	600 sq. ft.	Flagstone irregular shapes, 2" thick	
	90	60-lb. bags dry mortar mix	
	2	¼×4×8" expansion joint	
GARDEN SEAT AND POTTING BENCH			
Framing**			
Posts	6	4×4s	10'
Beams	6	2×6s	8'
Rafters	8	2×4s	14'
Long rails	4	2×4s	8'
Side rails	1	2×4	8'
Seat			
Fascia	2	2×4s	8'
Infill slats	10	2×2s	8'
Center supports	1	4×4	8'
Cleats	1	2×4	8'
Louvers	18	1×4s	8'
Spacers	1	1×4	8'
Bench rails	1	4×4	8'
Louvers	18	1×4s	8'
Bench spacers	1	1×4	8'
Bottom shelf	2	2×10s	8'
Worktable	2	2×10s	8'
Top shelf	1	2×12	8'
Fasteners	148	½×4" galvanized lag screws, washers	
	2 lbs.	8d HDG common nails	
	12	galvanized shelf brackets	
	6	post anchors	

*All quantities may vary with site conditions.

**Use rot/insect-resistant lumber.

SEAT CONSTRUCTION

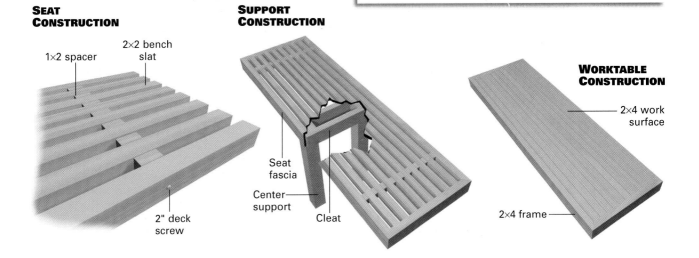

- 1×2 spacer
- 2×2 bench slat
- 2" deck screw

SUPPORT CONSTRUCTION

- Seat fascia
- Center support
- Cleat

WORKTABLE CONSTRUCTION

- 2×4 work surface
- 2×4 frame

GARDEN COLONNADE

Along, sheltered walkway—or colonnade—provides an inviting transition between a patio next to a house and an inviting outdoor spot nearby—in this instance, a detached patio in a quiet corner of the garden. There, benches with built-in planters provide a comfortable place to enjoy the scenery.

You can adjust the dimensions of the colonnade to conform to the available space on your site. Any adjustments to its length and width, of course, will require modifications in post spacing. Add interest to your design by setting the pavers in the colonnade in a random pattern. Plantings around the pavers turn the walkway into a garden as well.

OVERHEAD VIEW

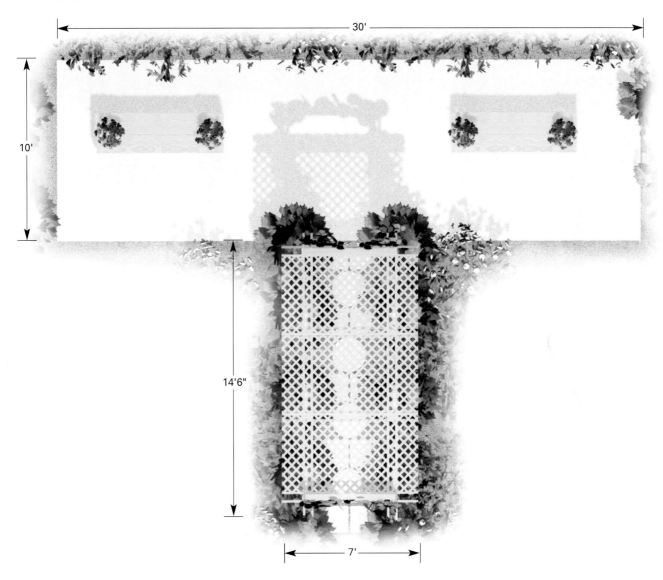

BUILDING THE PATIO

Follow the basic instructions for layout and excavation on pages 106–110 and for installing a sand-set patio on pages 116–117, working in sections. The patio can be any size that fits the profile and terrain of your landscape. The one shown is 9×18 feet, with a 14½-foot stepping-stone walkway. Pave both the patio and walk surfaces with large concrete pavers—12, 18, or 24 inches square—with an incised or textured surface.

Pavers are not designed to be set in mortar. See pages 144–145 for more information on setting pavers in sand.

GARDEN COLONNADE
continued

BENCH CONSTRUCTION

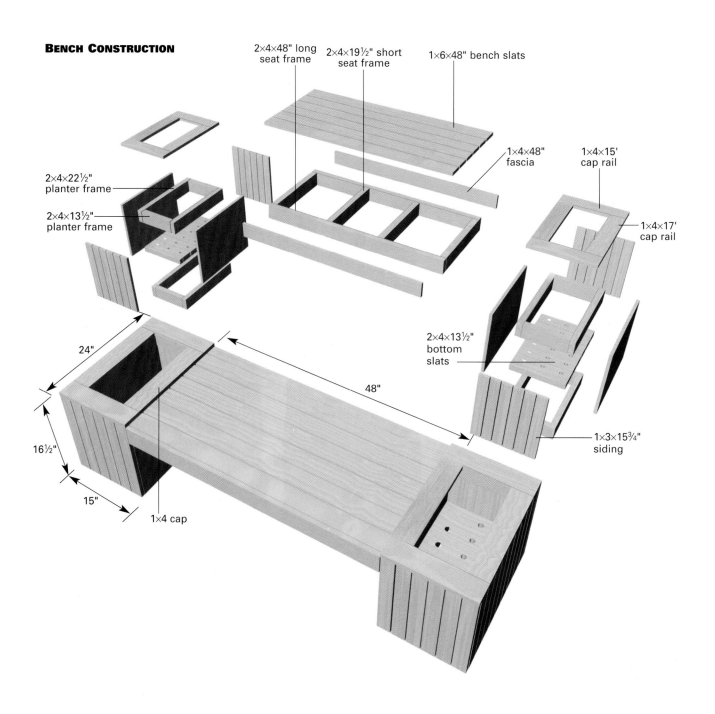

2×4×48" long
seat frame

2×4×19½" short
seat frame

1×6×48" bench slats

1×4×48"
fascia

1×4×15'
cap rail

2×4×22½"
planter frame

2×4×13½"
planter frame

1×4×17'
cap rail

2×4×13½"
bottom
slats

24"

48"

1×3×15¾"
siding

16½"

15"

1×4 cap

BUILDING THE BENCH

Build the benches for the detached patio area with redwood, cedar, cypress, or pressure-treated lumber. Construct the planters first; then build a bench seat and attach it to them.

PLANTERS: Assemble the four 2×4 frames, each 22½ inches long and 13½ inches wide. These function as the top and bottom frames of the two planters.

■ Cut and fasten the 2×4 floors to the bottom frame assemblies. Leave gaps between the 2×4s and drill ½-inch drainage holes in a scattered pattern across the floors.

■ Cut the siding into 15¾-inch lengths. Fasten one end of the siding to the corner of a bottom frame and the other end to the corner of a top frame.

■ Repeat at each corner, then fill in between the ends. If necessary, rip the fill to fit.

SEATING PLATFORM: Cut and assemble another 2×4 frame assembly, this one 48 inches long by 22½ inches wide.

■ Cut two 2×4s crosspieces to fit inside, as shown, and fasten them with 10d hot-dipped galvanized nails or decking screws.

■ Cut the fascia to length and nail it to the long sides of the box. Countersink the nail heads.

■ Cut six 1×4 slats to length. Space them as needed to fill the opening for the seat and nail them to the top of the frame with 6d hot-dipped galvanized nails.

■ Turn the planters upside down on a flat, level surface and center the seating platform between them.

■ Drill two ½-inch diameter pilot holes into the seating platform frame through each of the box frames. Fasten them together with ½×6-inch hex-head bolts.

■ Turn the assembly right side up.

■ Line the insides of the planter boxes from the tops down with plastic sheeting, poking holes through it into the drain holes made earlier.

■ Staple the edges of the sheeting to the tops of the siding and trim the excess.

■ Miter a 1×4 cap molding for each box opening and nail it over the plastic.

MATERIALS LIST

Element	Quantity*	Material	Length
Base			
	7 cu. yd.	gravel	
	4 cu. yd.	washed sand, concrete grade	
	156 ft.	plastic edging	
	540 sq. ft.	weed-blocking fabric	
Paving (size optional)			
	540	12×12" concrete pavers	
	240	18×18" concrete pavers	
	135	4×24" concrete pavers	
Colonnade framing			
Footings**		gravel and concrete to build 8 footings to code	
Posts	4	4×4s	12'
	4	4×4s	10'
Headers	8	2×6s	8'
Beams	4	2×6s	16'
Knee braces	6	2×6s	8'
Rafters	8	2×4s	8'
Lattice panels	3		4×8'
Bench (quantities for 1 bench)			
Planter frames	4	2×4s	8'
Planter bottom	2	2×4s	8'
Planter siding	10	1×3s	8'
Plastic sheeting***	as needed		
Planter trim	2	1×4s	8'
Seat			
Seat frames	2	2×4s	8'
Bench slats	4	1×4s	8'
Fascia	1	1×4	8'
Fasteners			
	1 lb.	6d hot-dipped galvanized nails	
	1 lb.	10d hot-dipped galvanized nails	
	4	½×6" galvanized hex-head bolts, washers	
	4	½×4½" galvanized carriage bolts, washers	
	64	⅜×4" galvanized carriage bolts, washers	
	8	galvanized post anchors	
	1 box	1" galvanized deck screws	

*All quantities may vary with site conditions.

**Use rot-/insect-resistant lumber.

***To line sides of boxes.

GARDEN COLONNADE
continued

COLONNADE

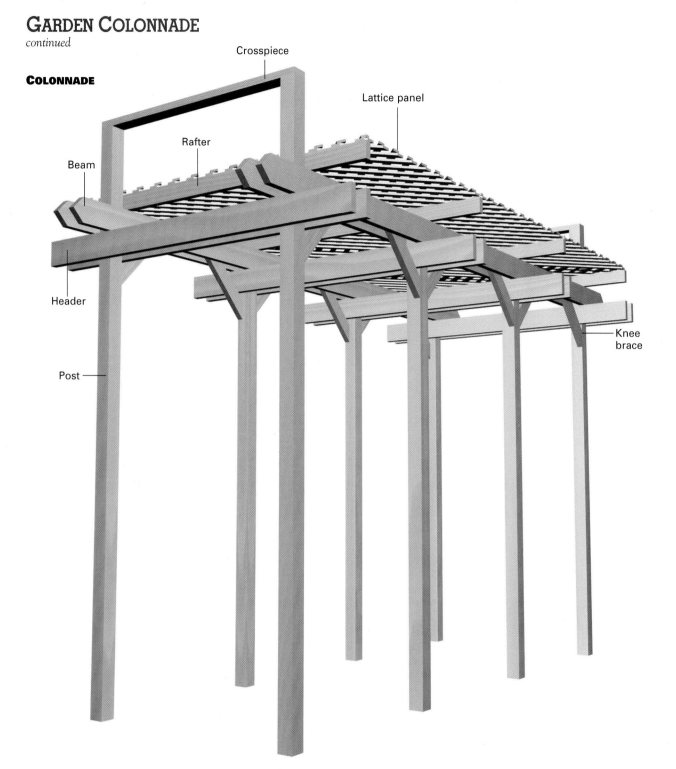

Crosspiece

Lattice panel

Rafter

Beam

Header

Post

Knee brace

BUILDING THE COLONNADE

Use the same wood for the colonnade that you used in making the planters and bench.

GROUNDWORK: Pour eight footings and piers to support the posts as shown in the Overhead View on opposite page. Make sure the piers are level and that the post anchors are aligned with each other. Refer to page 161 for general instructions on installing post footings.

■ Place large concrete-block pavers in a random or formal pattern to form a stepping-stone path through the colonnade. A sand bed is not absolutely necessary for a stepping-stone path, but it's wise to lay the pavers in sand for longevity. Here's how:

■ Set the pavers out in the pattern you want.
■ Outline the paver shape in the ground with a spade.

OVERHEAD VIEW

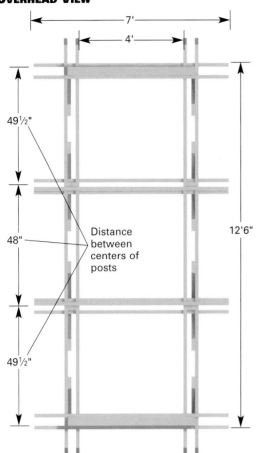

7'

4'

49½"

48"

Distance between centers of posts

12'6"

49½"

■ Dig out the ground 2 inches deeper than the thickness of the paver.
■ Level a 2-inch sand bed and set the pavers in place.

CONSTRUCTION: Cut four end posts 10½ feet long and four interior posts 9 feet long. Install the posts in post anchors, using temporary braces to keep them upright and plumb.
■ Cut the headers, beams, and rafters to length.
■ Drill pilot holes in each for the ½×4-inch lag screws that will fasten them to the posts. Bolt the headers to both sides of the posts 5½ inches below the tops of the interior posts and 23½ inches below the tops of the end posts.
■ Bolt 2×6 beams across the headers so they are flush with the tops of the interior posts and 18 inches below the tops of the end posts.
■ Bolt a beam to each side of the posts and attach 2×6 knee braces that run between the posts and beams at a 45-degree angle with ⅜-inch lag screws. The temporary post bracing can now safely be removed from the sides.
■ Drill pilot holes and nail 2×4 crosspieces to the top of the beams with 10d nails. Space the rafters 48 inches apart on center to support the edges of the lattice panels.
■ If necessary, trim lattice to fit; then screw the lattice panels to the rafters with 1-inch deck screws.

SIDE VIEW

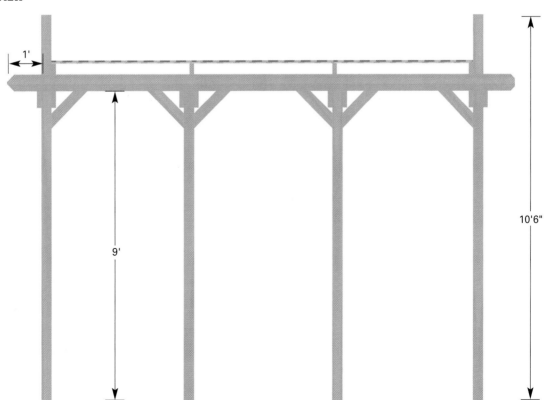

1'

9'

10'6"

Patio Care And Repair

Even the best-laid patio surfaces will, from time to time, need some tender loving care. As permanent as patios may seem, their surfaces can crack, chip, or break loose in spalls or pop-outs. In this chapter, you'll find techniques for repairing the most common problems.

One of the best solutions for avoiding large-scale repairs is to put yourself (and your patio) on a maintenance schedule. Proper maintenance, carried out regularly, will add years to your patio and to your enjoyment of it. Inspect the surface briefly every three months or so. Look for damage, stains, loose mortar, and weeds growing where they shouldn't be. Such an inspection will take five minutes or less and it will save you time and money in the long run—if you attend to any problems in a timely manner.

Remember to include your walls and fences in your routine maintenance inventory. Mortared stone walls fall victim to water and ice too. Pay special attention to the tops of mortared walls and repair any cracks or damage to the top course or cap.

In 20 or 30 years, any brick or block wall can show some signs of age. Mortar may develop cracks or it may simply wear away until it is unsightly and compromises the wall's strength. The solution is to remove the old mortar and refill the joints with new mortar. This time-consuming job is called pointing and, to avoid it, you should seal any mortared surfaces with a masonry sealer.

Seal or paint fences too, and replace damaged or rotted lumber. Any weakness in one area of a fence can affect the stability of the entire structure.

Weeds often take advantage of spaces between brick, or stones, or concrete slabs. To rid the joints of these intruders, apply a systemic weed killer on a sunny day. Dig out the dead weeds and fill cracks with topsoil.

CRACKS IN BRICK WALLS

Small cracks in an older brick wall can simply be repaired by pointing. Because an older wall may have completed its settling process, it will probably not develop additional cracks.

Cracks in a new wall are another matter, however. They may be caused by settling, and the crack may grow until the settling is complete. Test cracks in a new wall before pointing them. Place a piece of duct tape tightly over the crack. If it twists, tears, or pulls loose in the next month, the wall is still settling. Wait for settling to end before pointing.

When the mortar between the joints does begin to crumble or crack, point it as soon as possible. Untended cracks allow water to erode the supporting soil or sand. And ice in the cracks can lift and damage even the heaviest of surfaces.

Cracks in patio surfaces can be home to annoying weeds. When weeds and grass grow in the crack, their roots can lift the paving. When you pull the weeds, the roots will hang on to some of the mortar, soil, or sand, leaving voids that can ultimately settle. Spraying with a systemic weed killer will kill the plants without hastening the damage to the surface.

Pointing masonry extends the life of brick patios and walks. When mortar becomes crumbly and loose, scrape it out and apply fresh mortar. Although time-consuming, pointing costs less than replacing masonry.

EVALUATING YOUR OLD PATIO

Start your inventory of patio conditions by looking for large cracks and sagging sections. These are good indicators the base is not adequate.

Dig along the perimeter; you're looking for a 4-inch gravel base and 4 inches of concrete for a slab or mortared patio or a 4-inch gravel base and 2 inches of sand for dry-set surfaces.

If an adequate subbase is present, check the surface. It should be sloped for drainage—at least 1 inch for every 4 feet, and if you're going to mortar brick, tile, or stone on top, it should not contain any high spots more than $\frac{1}{8}$ inch in 10 feet.

If the surface is crowned in the center for drainage, that's okay for mortaring, as long as the crowning is gradual. Minor holes or flaking can be repaired. So can loose or damaged dry-set brick and tile. But if the patio's base is inadequate, it's time to start over.

GENERAL CARE AND MAINTENANCE

Sand-set flagstone lets you be selective about your patio repairs—you don't have to remove the entire surface. Pry up the cracked stone with a crowbar and replace it with one of similar shape and size.

Algae can grow quickly on outdoor surfaces. In addition to its unsightly appearance, algae is slippery and dangerous underfoot. Scrubbing with a solution of household bleach, laundry soap, water, and trisodium phosphate will return the patio to its original condition.

Don't rip out an old patio just because it shows some wear. If it's solid and its surface is in relatively good shape—and you like its location—it may be worth saving.

A few broken bricks or concrete chips aren't fatal flaws in the lives of patios—unless you're just itching to build a new one. Bear in mind that tearing out an old patio is hard work, so take a close look before you get out the sledgehammer. Those first few swings might be rollicking good fun, but it's amazing how quickly a sledge gains weight.

KEEPING PUDDLES AWAY

The best way to save your patio from the damaging effects of standing water is to keep it from collecting in the first place. Water between or soaked into bricks or stones can cause serious cracking when it freezes.

Take a look at your patio after a rain. If you have puddles on the bricks, or the puddles at the edges don't dry up after a day, you can do something to prevent damage.

The solution may be as simple as redirecting a gutter downspout away from the patio. If the puddles are at the perimeter of the patio, dig a drainage trench and fill it with gravel or wood chips.

If perimeter puddles stay for days, you need a serious drainage system. Dig a trench sloping away from the house and ending in a large gravel-filled dry well. Line the trench with gravel and perforated drainpipe leading to the well (see pages 66–67).

Puddles may occur because of an inadequate slope. Remove bricks or pavers that are causing a small dip, add sand, and reinstall the bricks or pavers so that water runs off.

DRY-SET MAINTENANCE

Dry-set brick and flagstone generally wear well and don't require much attention. If the edging and base have been properly installed, you need do no more than keep it well swept. Perhaps pull an occasional weed and refill the joints with sand every year or two years. (To refill the joints, follow the instructions on pages 145.) Beyond that, you may have to periodically remove moss or algae, replace a heaved or damaged brick, or apply sealer.

REMOVING MOSS AND ALGAE: Make a cleaning solution of 1 ounce laundry soap, 3 ounces trisodium phosphate (or a nonphosphate TSP substitute), 1 quart chlorine bleach, and 3 quarts water. Brush it on, leave it for five minutes, and then rinse.

REPLACING BRICK OR STONE: Pry up a heaved brick or flagstone with a sturdy crowbar. Some bricks will come out if you use two putty knives, one on each end.

Moisten the sand and reset the unit, tapping it with a rubber mallet. If it's still high, scrape a little sand out and reset it.

If you can't get a damaged piece out with a crowbar, break it up with a cold chisel (drive it with a baby sledge—pavers are hard). Then moisten and tamp the sand (use a 2×4) and set in new brick or stone. Sand-fill the joints as you would for a new patio.

APPLYING SEALER:

Concrete pavers and flagstones are strong and not very absorbent, so they usually do not need a sealer. Unglazed bricks may be sponge-like, so an application of clear masonry sealer can help. Apply the sealer with a brush, roller, or a pump sprayer.

Chip out a brick using a baby sledge and a cold chisel.

Removing a concrete slab may call for the power of a rental jackhammer. Wear protective clothing and safeguard your eyes whenever you tear into mortared surfaces.

CONCRETE MAINTENANCE

A few simple steps can greatly lengthen the life of concrete surfaces.

PREVENTION: Keep moisture damage to a minimum. Painting or sealing concrete protects surfaces from moisture damage and improves its appearances. To make patios and walks water-resistant, apply clear acrylic concrete sealer with a paint roller. To test whether the concrete needs a new coat, sprinkle water on the surface; if it soaks right in, reapply sealer. On aggregate-concrete surfaces, use an aggregate sealer. It prevents freeze-thaw cycles from popping the stones.

CLEANING: The next step is keeping surfaces clean. To remove grease or oil, use concrete cleaner and a stiff brush. Or soak sawdust in mineral spirits, rub it onto the spot, and then sweep.

Use muriatic acid to etch away stains that won't come out with standard cleaners. Mix 1 part acid to 9 parts water. Wear rubber gloves, old clothes, and eye protection—muriatic acid is highly caustic. Scrub the mixture into the area with a stiff brush and let it stand 5 to 10 minutes. Rinse thoroughly.

DEMOLITION

Sometimes you have to get tough. If you have some masonry that just isn't making the cut, it won't leave gracefully.

CONCRETE SLAB: With or without a mortared surface, breaking up concrete is heavy work. You will need at least a 10-pound sledge—heavier is better, if you can handle it—and crowbars.

■ Start at a corner and crack small sections. Pry out the section with a crowbar and carry it away in a wheelbarrow.
■ Work your way across the surface, cracking and prying. The crowbar should do most of the work—concrete pries up more easily than you can pound it down.

If the slab is thicker than 4 inches, or you have a large area to remove, rent a masonry saw or jackhammer to make the job easier. Save your strength for toting away the broken concrete instead.

■ Keep yourself safe—heavy gloves, steel toed-boots, and safety goggles are a must.

DRY-SET SURFACES: These surrender more readily. To remove dry-set brick or flagstone, pry up a corner and remove each piece. Set the pieces aside if they're not damaged and use them on your new surface.

CLEANING STAINS

Most grease and oil stains will come out of paving materials with a little scrubbing with laundry detergent and warm water.

Stains that have penetrated need a more thorough treatment. Saturate the stain with mineral spirits and cover it with dry portland cement or cat litter. Let it stand overnight and sweep it away.

For more stubborn stains, try a paste of benzol and cat litter or cement. Let it stand for an hour and repeat if necessary.

REPAIRING CONCRETE

Concrete is strong, but it is often subject to enormous pressures. Water is its chief enemy. Built-up water pressure and freeze-thaw cycles are the usual culprits when concrete cracks.

Not all concrete problems are major, however. Concrete surfaces suffer from small cracks and a few other maladies that are more routine:
- **Dusting**: the surface wears away easily.
- **Scaling**: the surface flakes.
- **Spalling**: deeper scaling.
- **Crazing**: a network of surface cracks.
- **Pop-outs**: small holes.

REPAIRING CRACKS

- Break out the surface along the crack with a small sledge and cold chisel or brickset to a depth of ½ to ¾ inch.
- Holding the chisel at an angle, "key" the outside edge of the area to be repaired (make it wider on the bottom than the top). Keying a repair helps lock the patch in place. (See top left illustration on opposite page.)
- Thoroughly clean away all loose material with a wire brush, and wash away dust using a scrub brush and water.

- If the crack is wider than an inch, fill it with sand to about ½ inch below its surface. Wet the sand; then, using a paintbrush, work latex concrete-bonding agent into the crack. (Coat the key; don't fill it.) Let the agent dry.
- Apply concrete-patching compound. Vinyl concrete-patching compound consists of two parts. Combine them; then fill the crack with a pointing trowel. Push the patching compound in with the flat side of the trowel and poke it with the tip to eliminate bubbles. Smooth the surface with a steel trowel and texture it to match the surrounding area.

POP-OUTS, SPALLS, DUSTING, AND SCALING

Repairing damage that affects even small areas of the surface requires some preparation.
- Use a circular saw equipped with a masonry blade to key-cut the surrounding area.
- Chip away the interior of the area so that the recess is at least ½ inch deep at all points.
- Remove dust and debris, and brush on a coating of acrylic bonding agent. Let the agent dry.
- For small holes, apply vinyl concrete-patching compound. For a larger area,

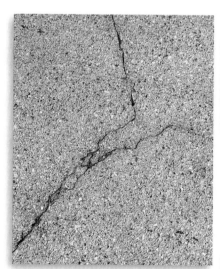

A maze of deep cracks, perhaps with some pieces actually coming loose, indicates that the entire section has failed, most probably because the slab is too thin, is not reinforced, or rests on an unstable base. Don't try to repair it. Break up the whole area, excavate, tamp down a bed of gravel, and pour a new slab.

Small holes, called pop-outs, occur because the surface was not properly floated. Fill larger pop-outs with patching concrete. Pop-outs on a wall should be stable, but those in a patio or walk may grow in areas with winter freezing.

Like crazing, spalling results from improper troweling. The pattern of pits will grow in time. Seal the surface, repour it, or resurface.

Improper troweling can result in crazing, a pattern of hairline cracks about ¼ inch deep. Clean it and apply concrete sealer to keep the problem from growing. Or resurface the concrete.

If one section is raised above another, the soil underneath has eroded. Remove the eroded section and repour it. Or hire a mud-jacking company to raise the slab, inject concrete beneath it, and then patch it.

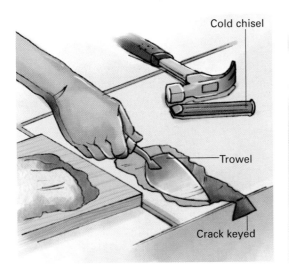

Chisel a "key" shape in a concrete crack, to keep your patch from popping out. Then press patching concrete into the opening. Finally, trowel the surface smooth.

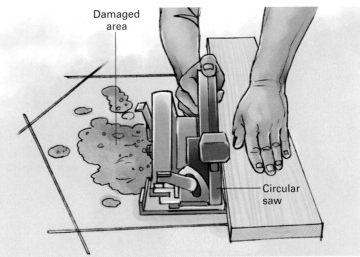

To patch a large area, create a keyed recess using a circular saw with a masonry blade. Set the blade at a 15-degree angle and cut around the damaged area. You may need to make several passes of the saw, with the blade set slightly lower each time. Chisel away the damaged concrete.

combine sand-mix concrete (which has no rocks in it) with extra portland cement (about two shovelfuls of cement per 60-pound bag of sand mix). Trowel the mixture in place, smooth and feather it with a magnesium float, then finish it to match the surrounding concrete.

REPAIR OR REPOUR?

You can repair most surface problems fairly easily and inexpensively. If cracking results from structural weakness, however, repairs will be a waste of time and money; the only real solution is to tear out the old concrete and start over.

When diagnosing problems in the concrete surface, check how deep the cracks are. If chunks of concrete are coming loose, don't bother to repair—it's time to repour.

Surface problems like crazing, pop-outs, and spalling do not indicate structural damage. If you leave them alone, however, they can grow worse. Often, applying concrete sealer is all it takes to keep a problem in check.

If the concrete has only a few cracks and its surface is generally solid, concrete caulk or patching compound can add many years to the slab's life. The patch may stand out because of its different color. If you don't like the appearance of the repair, you can resurface the area (see page 233).

If you have large areas that are buckling or sagging, consider hiring a mud-jacking contractor, who can raise and resupport slabs.

CONTROL JOINTS

Control joints prevent expansion and contraction from creating large cracks in the concrete. But they can actually cause smaller cracks, which can grow when water in the crack freezes. Treat wayward control joints with concrete-repair caulk.

CONCRETE-REPAIR CAULK FOR SMALL CRACKS

Here's a simple fix for small cracks in concrete. Clean out the crack thoroughly using a wire brush to remove all loose matter. Fill the crack with concrete-repair caulk, making sure that it penetrates deeply. Wipe the excess with a damp rag to feather the caulk and to keep water from entering the crack. You may need to recaulk or add more caulk twice a year or so.

REPAIRING CONCRETE STEPS

Even well-built and adequately reinforced concrete steps can suffer damage, especially at corners, edges, and where railings are attached.

REPLACE A CHIP: If a piece that has broken off a corner or edge is salvageable, gluing it back with epoxy cement may prove to be a permanent—and desirable—repair. The replaced chip will be less apparent than a patch because it is the same color.

Using a scrub brush and water, clean both the chip and the broken surface carefully so they do not crumble. Dry-fit the piece to make sure rough edges match. Mix the two parts of epoxy cement together; then apply it in a thin layer to both surfaces. Firmly press the chip into place. Wipe away excess epoxy with a rag soaked in mineral spirits.

FORM A CORNER: If you don't have a chip that fits, form the damaged area into a key that is at least ½ inch deep at all points. Use a hammer and chisel or a circular saw with a masonry blade. Brush away all loose material and clean the area with water. Paint the keyed surface with latex concrete-bonding agent and let it dry.

Make a plywood form and hold it in place with a cement block. Mix patching cement and fill the hole, pressing down to squeeze out bubbles. As soon as the patch hardens—which may take only minutes—remove the plywood and finish the edges.

FILL A HOLE: For a hole that is not at a corner, chisel out a key and clean off debris. Apply a stiff batch of patching concrete and use a trowel to stuff it into the hole and finish the surface.

RE-ANCHORING A RAILING BOLT

To reattach a loose anchor bolt for a railing, chip the area around it and remove the old bolt. Deepen and widen the hole with a drill equipped with a masonry bit. Make a cardboard template of the bolt pattern; use it to position the new bolt in the hole. Test to make sure the bolt will stick out enough to anchor the railing. Mix anchoring cement or epoxy putty and pack it firmly around the bolt so it is level with the surrounding area. Check that the bolt is plumb.

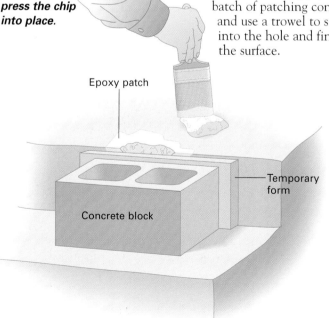

Paint both the chip and the hole with epoxy cement; then press the chip into place.

Epoxy patch

Temporary form

Concrete block

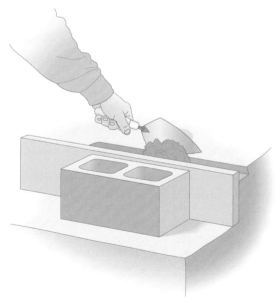

Patching concrete sets up quickly. Remove the plywood form as soon as possible to finish the patch and to smooth the edges to match the surrounding area.

RESURFACING CONCRETE

Resurfacing concrete is an intermediate repair, more substantial than patching but easier than tearing out the damaged concrete and repouring. Use this technique only if the damaged concrete is structurally sound. Resurfacing will not glue together chunks of broken concrete.

Along each side of the area to be resurfaced, remove a few inches of sod to make room for staked forms. Install 2×4 forms so they are at least an inch above the existing concrete surface and level with each other. Every few feet, drive 2×4 stakes slightly below the top of the forms. Attach them to the forms with 3-inch deck screws.

The new control joints should be directly above the old ones, so mark the top of the forms at their positions. Use a paint roller to apply a layer of latex concrete-bonding agent to the entire concrete surface.

Mix a batch of stiff and extra-strong concrete. Add two shovelfuls of portland cement to each 60-pound bag of sand-mix concrete. Or mix your own, using 1 shovelful of portland cement to four shovelfuls of sand. Add just enough water that the mix is completely wet but doesn't flow.

Shovel the concrete inside the forms, smacking it with the shovel to ensure a strong bond and to force out air bubbles. Then use a piece of 2×8 that spans the forms to pack the concrete mix, making sure the new surface is firmly pressed onto the existing concrete and eliminating air bubbles next to the forms.

Screed the area with a straight 2×4; then float it with a wood or magnesium float. Tool with an edger and a jointer, then with a steel trowel. (See pages 126–135 for more information.) Finish with a broom if you like.

Cover the new concrete with plastic or periodically spray it with water to keep it moist for a week or so.

STEPS TO RESURFACING CONCRETE

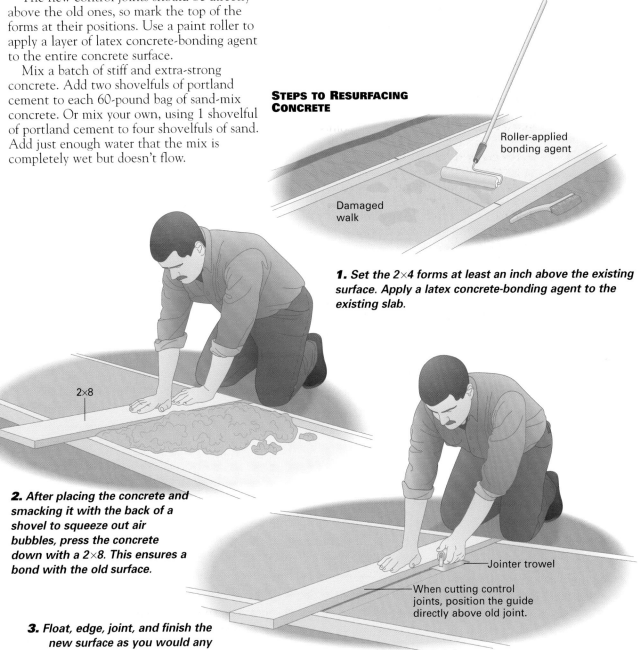

Roller-applied bonding agent

Damaged walk

1. Set the 2×4 forms at least an inch above the existing surface. Apply a latex concrete-bonding agent to the existing slab.

2×8

2. After placing the concrete and smacking it with the back of a shovel to squeeze out air bubbles, press the concrete down with a 2×8. This ensures a bond with the old surface.

Jointer trowel

When cutting control joints, position the guide directly above old joint.

3. Float, edge, joint, and finish the new surface as you would any concrete slab.

GLOSSARY

3-4-5 METHOD: A technique for checking whether a corner is square. Determined by marking a point 3 feet from the corner along one side and 4 feet from the corner along the other side. When the diagonal distance between the marks is exactly 5 feet, the corner is square.

ACTUAL DIMENSIONS: The actual physical dimension of a board or masonry unit as it is measured. See "Nominal Dimensions."

AGGREGATE: Gravel, sand, or crushed rock mixed with portland cement, and water to form concrete.

AIR-ENTRAINED: Concrete suffused with tiny air bubbles, making it more workable and better able to withstand frost. Air entrainment requires the addition of a special mixture during the mixing stage.

AWL: A sharp-pointed tool used for starting small holes for screws or for scribing lines.

BABY SLEDGE: A small sledge hammer, usually 2½ pounds, used for a variety of construction tasks and repairs when more weight is needed than can be supplied by a carpenter's hammer.

BACKFILLING: Replacing earth excavated during the construction process. A material other than the original earth may be used to improve the drainage or structure of the soil.

BASE: A prepared surface of gravel or sand designed to support bricks, pavers, or concrete.

BATTER BOARD: A 2×4 frame supported by stakes set back from the corners of a structure.

BEDDING SAND: Coarse sand used to make the bed for setting pavers or bricks.

BOND: A pattern in which masonry units, such as bricks, are arranged.

BRICK GRADE: The rating of a brick's durability, such as severe weather (SW) and moderate weather (MW).

BRICKSET: A wide-blade chisel used for cutting bricks and concrete blocks.

BROOM FINISH: A slip-resistant texture created by running a stiff or soft broom across fresh concrete.

BUILDING CODES: Local rules governing the way structures may be built or modified.

BULL FLOAT: A large, long-handled float used for reaching into the center and smoothing a large slab of wet concrete.

BUTT JOINT: A joint formed by two pieces of material fastened end to end, end to face, or end to edge.

BUTTER: To apply mortar on bricks or blocks with a trowel before laying them.

CARPENTER'S LEVEL: A tool for establishing level over short distances.

CATCH BASIN: A hole in the soil for collecting water; often connected to a drain pipe.

CEMENT: A powdered mix of gypsum and other materials that serves as the binding element in concrete and mortar.

CHAMFER: To bevel a piece of lumber.

COMMON BRICK: Brick intended for general-purpose building; can be used for patio paving in milder climates.

CONCRETE: A mixture of portland cement, fine aggregate (sand), course aggregate (gravel or crushed stone), and water. Concrete becomes harder and stronger with age.

CONCRETE PAVERS: Precast concrete units commonly used for driveways, patios, and sidewalks. Pavers are designed to be laid in a sand base. They come in many shapes and colors and may interlock in patterns.

CONTROL JOINTS: Grooves that are tooled or cut into the surface of wet concrete to make it crack in straight lines at planned locations, rather than cracking randomly.

COURSE: A row of masonry units, such as bricks or stones.

CRAZING: A pattern of hairline cracks about ¼ inch deep in the surface of a concrete slab, caused by improper troweling.

CRUSHED STONE: Quarried rock that has been mechanically crushed and then graded so that most of the stones are a similar size, with varying shapes and colors.

CUBES OR BANDS: Pregrouped and bound quantities of pavers that cover 16 linear feet.

CURING: The process of aging new concrete with proper moisture to reduce cracking and shrinkage and to develop strength.

CUT STONE: Any of several kinds of natural rock quarried and cut into regular shapes with straight edges.

DARBY: A hand tool with a long sole made of smooth wood or metal, used for smoothing a concrete slab after initial leveling.

DIMENSION LUMBER: A piece of lumber that has been dried and cut to modular dimensions. Refers to boards at least 2 inches wide and 2 inches thick.

DRAINAGE TRENCH: A shallow excavation for carrying water away from higher ground.

DRY-STACKED WALL: A wall of masonry units (stones) laid without mortar.

DRY WELL: A hole in the soil dug at a level below the patio site and connected to the site by a drainpipe.

EDGER: A tool for rounding and smoothing concrete edges to finish and strengthen them.

EDGING: A border used to contain and define a surface; common materials are brick, concrete, plastic, and wood. Also, the rounded edges of a concrete slab that are resistant to cracking.

EFFLORESCENCE: A white powdery substance that appears on masonry surfaces, caused by the leeching of chemical in the material.

EXCAVATION: Digging out earth to a level that is hard and uniformly graded.

EXPANSION JOINT: See "Isolation Joint."

EXPOSED AGGREGATE: A decorative concrete treatment that exposes a layer of stones embedded in the surface of concrete.

FINISH: A coating applied to a surface to protect it against weathering, or a treatment such as texturing applied to concrete.

FLAGSTONE: Irregular shapes of flat natural stone, such as granite, bluestone, redstone, sandstone, limestone, and slate.

FLOAT: A rectangular wood or metal hand tool used to smooth and compress wet concrete.

FLOATING: Smoothing the surface of soft concrete after it has been leveled. This action fills in divots and low spots and drives large aggregate below the surface. Floats may be made of steel, aluminum, magnesium, or wood.

FLUSH: On the same plane as, or level with, the surrounding surface.

FOOTING: The bottom portion of any foundation or pier. The footing distributes the weight of the structure into the ground. For decks, it often refers to the concrete structure consisting of the pier as well as its footing.

FORMWORK: The wooden forms that shape wet concrete.

FROST HEAVE: Movement or upheaval of the ground when there is alternate freezing and thawing of water in the soil. This is one of the reasons concrete slabs crack, making control joints necessary.

FROST LINE: The lowest depth at which the ground will freeze. It determines the code-required depth for footings.

GROUT: A thin mortar mixture used to fill the joints between tiles.

HARDSCAPE: Those elements in a landscape that are made of wood, stone, or other hard, permanent materials.

ISOLATION JOINT: Strips of material installed in formwork to completely separate new concrete from existing construction or from other new construction. Allows sections to move independently of one another if the ground shifts because of factors like frost heave. Sometimes called expansion joints.

JOINTER: A tool used for making control joints, or grooves, in concrete surfaces to control cracking.

JOINTING SAND: Fine sand that is spread over brick pavers and swept into the spaces between them—often sold as mason's sand.

LAG SCREW OR BOLT: Heavy-duty screw with a bolt head for attaching structural members to a wall or to material too thick for a machine bolt to go through.

LANDSCAPE FABRIC: Tightly woven fabric that allows water to flow through but prevents weeds from growing.

LAP JOINT: The joint formed when one member overlaps another.

LEVEL: The condition that exists when any type of surface is at true horizontal. Also a hand tool for determining this condition.

MASONRY CEMENT: A mix of portland cement and hydrated lime for preparing mortar.

MASON'S HAMMER: A tempered-steel hammer with a square face and a chisel-shaped claw. Used for cutting brick, stone, and other masonry material.

MASON'S LINE: Twine used to make sure posts, patios, footings, and structures are laid level. Preferred because it will not stretch and sag, as regular string does.

MITER JOINT: The joint formed when two members meet that have been cut at the same angle, usually 45 degrees.

MODULAR: A term describing a unit of material that has dimensions proportional to one another.

MORTAR: A mixture of cement, fine aggregate, and water used to bond bricks, blocks, or stones.

MUD-JACKING: The process by which fallen sections of a concrete slab can be raised to level by injecting a mixture of mud and concrete under them.

NOMINAL DIMENSIONS: The stated dimensions of a masonry unit or board, representing the proportion of one measurement to the other. Often refers to the actual dimension such material occupies, including its mortar or grout. For masonry, it includes the thickness of the mortar joints on one end and at the top or bottom. See "Actual Dimensions."

PAVERS/PAVING: Any tile or thin masonry material for use on driveways, patios, floors, and sidewalks.

PAVING BRICK: Brick of very dense clay, fired to high temperatures to be hard and durable.

PIER: A small concrete or masonry structure that holds a post off the ground. It has its own footing and can be precast or cast in place.

PLAN DRAWING: An overhead view of a structure, which shows locations of footings and framing.

GLOSSARY
continued

PLASTIC CONCRETE: Concrete that has not hardened.

PLUMB: The condition that exists when a surface is at true vertical.

PLUMB BOB: A tool used to align points vertically.

POP-OUTS: Small holes in a concrete surface. Caused by improper floating.

PORTLAND CEMENT: A type (not a brand name) of cement that is a basic ingredient of concrete and mortar.

POST: A vertical framing piece, usually 4×4 or 6×6, used to support a beam or a joist.

PREMIX: Any packaged mixture of ingredients for preparing concrete or mortar.

PRESSURE-TREATED WOOD: Lumber or plywood soaked in a solution to make the wood resistant to water. One commonly used pressure treatment is waterborne chromated copper arsenate (CCA). CCA specified for aboveground use is labeled LP-2 or .25. CCA rated for ground contact is labeled LP-22 or .40.

READY-MIX CONCRETE: Wet concrete that is ready to pour. Transported in a truck from a concrete supplier.

REBAR (REINFORCING ROD): Steel rod used to reinforce concrete and masonry structures.

REINFORCING WIRE MESH: Steel wires welded into a grid of 6- or 10-inch squares and embedded in concrete. Ties a concrete pad together to minimize cracking.

RETAINING WALL: A wall constructed to hold soil in place.

RIVER ROCK: Medium-size stones that have been smoothed by river or lake water.

RUBBLE: Uncut stone, often used for dry-stacked walls.

SCRATCH COAT: The first coat of mortar or plaster, roughened (scratched) so the next coat will stick to it.

SCREED: A straight edge used to level concrete as it is poured into a form or to level the sand base in a form.

SEGREGATION: Separation of the elements of concrete, such as water rising to the top or aggregate sinking to the bottom due to overworking or bouncing (as in the motion of a wheelbarrow).

SET: The process during which mortar or concrete hardens.

SETBACK: The minimum distance between a property line and any structure, as defined by local building codes.

SITE PLAN: A map showing the location of a new building project on a piece of property.

SMALL SLEDGE: See "Baby Sledge."

SOLDIERS: Bricks standing on end with the narrow faces exposed. Often set this way as an edging.

SPACER BLOCKS: Small blocks, also called dobie blocks, used to support reinforcing wire mesh for pouring concrete.

SPALLING: Areas of pitting in the surface of a concrete slab. Caused by improper troweling.

SQUARE: The relationship that exists when one surface is at a 90-degree angle to another. Also, the tool used to test this orientation.

STRIKING: The process of finishing a mortar joint.

SUBBASE: Soil or gravel compacted to hold a base surface of gravel or sand.

SWALE: A shallow depression made in a landscape used to collect runoff. See "Drainage Trench."

TAMPER: A tool for compacting soil, sand, or other loose materials.

TROWEL: A flat and oblong or flat and pointed metal tool used for handling or finishing concrete and mortar.

TROWELING: Giving the concrete a smooth final finish with a steel trowel. This step is for interior applications since it creates an extremely smooth and possibly slippery surface.

WATER LEVEL: A tool composed of two clear plastic tubes that attach to a hose, used for establishing level over long distances or irregular surfaces.

WEEP HOLE: An opening made in a mortar joint to allow water to drain through.

YARD: A unit of volume by which ready-mix concrete is sold; equal to a square yard (27 cubic feet).

INDEX

METRIC CONVERSIONS

U.S. Units to Metric Equivalents			Metric Units to U.S. Equivalents		
To Convert From	Multiply By	To Get	To Convert From	Multiply By	To Get
Inches	25.4	Millimeters	Millimeters	0.0394	Inches
Inches	2.54	Centimeters	Centimeters	0.3937	Inches
Feet	30.48	Centimeters	Centimeters	0.0328	Feet
Feet	0.3048	Meters	Meters	3.2808	Feet
Yards	0.9144	Meters	Meters	1.0936	Yards
Square inches	6.4516	Square centimeters	Square centimeters	0.1550	Square inches
Square feet	0.0929	Square meters	Square meters	10.764	Square feet
Square yards	0.8361	Square meters	Square meters	1.1960	Square yards
Acres	0.4047	Hectares	Hectares	2.4711	Acres
Cubic inches	16.387	Cubic centimeters	Cubic centimeters	0.0610	Cubic inches
Cubic feet	0.0283	Cubic meters	Cubic meters	35.315	Cubic feet
Cubic feet	28.316	Liters	Liters	0.0353	Cubic feet
Cubic yards	0.7646	Cubic meters	Cubic meters	1.308	Cubic yards
Cubic yards	764.55	Liters	Liters	0.0013	Cubic yards

To convert from degrees Fahrenheit (F) to degrees Celsius (C), first subtract 32, then multiply by $\frac{5}{9}$.

To convert from degrees Celsius to degrees Fahrenheit, multiply by $\frac{9}{5}$, then add 32.